This old map of the Neversink watershed before the building of the Neversink Reservoir is excerpted from *The Angler's Guide to Sullivan's Big Five* by Clayton B. Seagers, ©1935 by Clayton B. Seagers. Used by permission of Joan E. Lawrence, from whom copies of the full map are available at Outdoor Publications, P.O. Box 355, Ithaca, NY 14851.

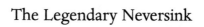

The Legendary Neversink

The Legendary Neversink

A Treasury of the Best Writing
About One of America's Great Trout Rivers

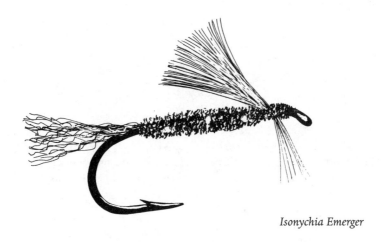

Isonychia Emerger

EDITED AND WITH AN INTRODUCTION BY
JUSTIN ASKINS

Skyhorse Publishing

www.skyhorsepublishing.com

10   9   8   7   6   5   4   3   2   1

Library of Congress Cataloging-in-Publication Data
    The legendary Neversink : a treasury of the best writing about one of America's
great trout rivers / edited and with an Introduction by Justin Askins.
        p.   cm.
    Includes bibliographical references.
    ISBN-13: 978-1-60239-114-7 (alk. paper)
    ISBN-10: 1-60239-114-9 (alk. paper)
    1. Trout fishing—New York (State)—Neversink River.   2. Fly fishing—
New York (State)—Neversink River.   3. Neversink River (N.Y.)   I. Askins, Justin.

SH688.U6L45   2007
799.17'570974738—dc22

                                                                2007018007

Printed in the United States of America

This book is dedicated to
Ben Wechsler,
a man of integrity and conviction

Contents

Acknowledgments xi

Introduction xiii

Speckled Trout 1
John Burroughs

Letters from a Recluse 13
Theodore Gordon

Little Talks about Fly-Fishing 23
Theodore Gordon

Conditions of the Life of Trout 37
Edward Ringwood Hewitt

The Point of View 53
George M. L. La Branche

Sunshine and Shadow 59
Ray Bergman

Some Big Fish on the Neversink 69
Larry Koller

With Hewitt on the Neversink 79
John Atherton

The Quest for Theodore Gordon 85
Sparse Grey Hackle

The Golden Age 113
Sparse Grey Hackle

Neversink Fishing 119
Ernest Schwiebert

The Woman Flyfishers Club 123
Austin M. Francis

Incident on the Bushkill 129
A. J. McClane

The Great Days 131
R. Palmer Baker

Salar Sebago 133
Leonard M. Wright, Jr.

The Endless Belt 145
Leonard M. Wright, Jr.

Last Days Are for Dreamers 153
Nick Lyons

A River's Tale 159
Justin Askins

The 100-Year Fly 167
Phil Chase

Intimations at Denniston's Flats 173
John Miller

A Camp on the Neversink 181
Jay Cassell

Brief Selected Bibliography 185

Appendixes: Eyes on the River 187
• The Gorge Controversy   Justin Askins
• Catskill Victory Nears   Phil Chase
• On the Road in the Catskills: The Lost River of Xanadu   Peter Borelli
• Fishing Prohibited in New State Park   Harold Faber
• State Owns Prime Fishing Spot but Can't Use It   Sam Verhovek
• Two Neversink Tributaries to Be Named   Nelson Bryant
• New York Plans Action on Neversink Land   Nelson Bryant
• Debate Over a Proposed Park   Jack Hope
• Historic Neversink River: A Legal Dispute Runs Through It   Pete Bodo
• The Neversink War   Jerry Kenney
• Neversink Gorge Controversy: One View   Rod Cochran

Some Effective Flies on the Neversink 211

Credits 215

Catskill Clipper

Acknowledgments

There are many people who assisted with this project. Jay Cassell was instrumental in making the connections that led to its acceptance by Skyhorse Publishing, and has helped throughout the publication process. Mike Larison, Director of Natural Resources for the Frost Valley YMCA, was a great help, as was Phil Chase, with his knowledge of the river and the people who worked to protect it, as well as with his tying a number of flies to be used for the illustrations. Sylvia Stevenson Adelman assisted with the Hewitt section, and Jim Krul, Director of the Catskill Flyfishing Museum, offered his expertise on a number of queries. Bill Burns of the Sullivan County Historical Society also assisted on several questions.

Marina Weiner, Tom Joy, and Nora Sokolowski read the manuscript and offered much useful feedback.

Mike Bailey provided computer scanning help and Lisa Clark and Laurel Sutton corrected the sprawling and disheveled manuscript. Claire Vincent proved an admirable research assistant.

Rosemary Guruswamy, chair of the English Department at Radford, was constantly supportive.

My partner Tracy Neyhart deserves the most appreciation for all her timely suggestions and continual involvement.

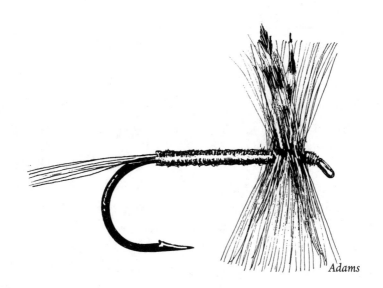

Adams

Introduction

I have explored many of the Catskill rivers, including sections of the Beaverkill, the Willowemoc, the Esopus, both branches of the Delaware, and the main stem. Each of these rivers has been celebrated by numerous writers, and every visit has given me great pleasure. But the Neversink Gorge, with its rich fly-fishing history and seven miles of cascading water and long pools, is closest to my heart.

Initially, I thought the river was a marvelous find, an isolated place where wild fish could be stalked and the tensions of graduate school could be abandoned. That first spring I walked in the two miles from the end of Katrina Falls road to the Campground Pool almost every day, savoring the hemlocks and pines, the rhododendron and laurel, and started fishing when the caddis flies began to hatch.

Soon after, as locals began to tell me about New York State's controversial attempts to purchase land for a new park from major landowner Ben Wechsler, I began to explore the situation. After speaking to many individuals including Wechsler, I found myself questioning my heretofore unwavering belief in public acquisition. I began to write about the politics of the Gorge and what should be done to protect it, each word increasing my connection.

I also started reading about the fly-fishing history of the river, and my attachment to the Gorge grew further. I now saw the Neversink as much more than just a place to catch a few trout. It had become the place John Burroughs describes: "One's own landscape comes in time to be a sort of outlying part of himself; he had sowed himself broadcast upon it, and it reflects his own mood and feelings."

Like a twin-headed naiad, the Neversink begins as two tumbling, brook-trout-laden creeks on the flanks of 4,204-foot Slide Mountain. As they leave the environs of Slide, the branches, though still rocky and rapid, begin to display some longer and deeper pools where larger trout might hide. After twelve miles or so, and having dropped over 500 feet, the two branches meet at the Forks. There the mainstream Neversink flows for five miles before being interrupted by the Neversink Reservoir (my boundary between the upper and lower rivers), and then continues on its generally more gradual path to the Delaware, some forty miles distant.

Since its present incarnation after the last Ice Age, the upper Neversink has never been an especially productive fishery. The underlying rock formation lacked the major fertilizing minerals of potash, nitrates, carbonates, and sulfates. Then thousands of years ago glaciers scoured the region, leaving thin deposits of more infertile soil, thus further limiting the trout-supporting insect life in the river. The geology also lent itself to slightly acidic water, another factor not conducive to larger trout.

Such conditions, however, favored the growth of hemlock and at one time the entire area was covered with enormous groves of that evergreen. Naturalists John and William Bartram noted the dominance of the species even while praising the rich mixture of other trees. The first fishermen found the heavily canopied river full of small brookies.

This idyllic situation started to end with the discovery that hemlock bark produced the perfect tanning agent, and soon four-foot-diameter hemlocks were being cut down across the Catskills. Alf Evers in *The Catskills* writes of "the struggle between men and hemlock trees that was begun in earnest by Colonel [William] Edwards about 1816 and did not end until the hemlocks were completely routed during the 1870s." A tannery was established in Claryville in 1847, and the river below quickly suffered from siltation and pollution, the volatility of the water flows increasing dramatically as the clear-cut land couldn't act as a buffer to devastating spates. Such conditions reduced the brook trout population but fortunately, as John Burroughs recalled in his "Speckled Trout," fishing remained outstanding on the waters above the reach of the loggers. The introduction of the more tolerant brown trout in 1886 helped maintain and perhaps improve the fishery, as the browns grew larger and were longer lived.

A later threat, logging to supply the acid factories with charcoal to produce wood alcohol and acetone, was avoided, possibly because of the remoteness of the upper river. But the valley had changed dramatically, the massive hemlocks replaced by oak, maple, beech, and other hardwoods, growing on land that had lost even more of its scanty humus and topsoil.

It is during this time that Theodore Gordon began fishing the Neversink. He represents the major figure in the transition from wet to dry-fly fishing in the United States. Although fishing with the dry fly had been mentioned by Thaddeus Norris in his *The American Angler's Book* (1865) and in several articles by other authors, Gordon became the great practitioner of the technique after he had received a number of dry flies from the Englishman Frederic Halford in 1890. Based on British insects, Halford's flies poorly imitated American hatches, but Gordon embraced the innovative technique and began an arduous study of native entomology that resulted in many indigenous patterns, including his most famous, the Quill Gordon.

Gordon never published a book, but in his many "Little Talks on Fly Fishing," first in the *Fishing Gazette* (from 1890) and then in *Forest and Stream* (from 1903), he emerged as a consummate fisherman who was also one of the most creative and prolific flytiers in the country. Gordon's attention to the art of fly tying is at the center of his writing, especially his collected letters. He was always searching for better materials and better methods—American materials and techniques often seemed second-rate—and later in life he made much of his income from tying professionally.

This same attentiveness comes through in his evaluation of rods. He experimented with many rods, with an especial fondness for the Leonard brand, and wrote often about various flaws in almost all of the rods he tried.

Gordon's own fishing practices show a rare devotion to refining his casting methods and an almost obsessive quest to "match the hatch": "I rarely fish other than flies I have dressed myself; I like to make them from day to day to suit the occasion."

By the time Gordon began writing, Burroughs and John Muir had well established a conservationist ethic, and the battle over damming the Tuloume River had already been fought. Gordon saw the dangers to his beloved Neversink, Beaverkill, and Willowemoc from deteriorating stream conditions due to a number of sawmills and continual logging. The former dumped tons of sawdust into the river and the logging itself contributed to spring flooding and silt accumulation. Gordon also pointed out the dangers of overfishing, particularly from bait fishermen, noting that "Worm fishing kills many small fish which, if taken with fly, could be returned unimpaired." He suggested a number of stream improvements and became very active in helping New York State stock the public streams.

Gordon did not seem particularly disturbed by the building of the Ashokan Reservoir on the Esopus, feeling, if it were correctly managed, it would provide habitat for many large trout. Perhaps his reaction would have been different had he known that the Pepacton and Cannonsville reservoirs were not far in the future, and that his own residence along with miles of his favored haunts would be lost with the building of the Neversink Reservoir.

Edward Ringwood Hewitt and George M. L. La Branche had a permanent impact on the Catskill tradition. Close friends, and fishing companions, they often tested the Neversink waters along with Ambrose Monell, the first American to fish the dry fly for salmon and the owner of 10,000 acres in the Neversink Gorge.

Hewitt was the first fly fisherman to study trout and their habitat scientifically, and his ingenious experiments about how trout see are still worth reading. His *A Trout and Salmon Fisherman for Seventy-Five Years* (1948) shows him as an eclectic master at technique: "I have never been one of those dry-fly purists who hold up their hands in horror at anything but dry-fly fishing. I think I have mastered this art as well as most of its devotees, but I have also known the pleasures of wet-fly and nymph fishing, as well as many forms of bait fishing in which I used to excel." Hewitt owned five miles of the upper river (now mostly covered by the reservoir) and had his own hatchery where he tested his numerous theories about what conditions trout favored. He also published the first book on stream improvements, *Better Trout Streams*.

Prior to George La Branche, almost all dry-fly fishing was done on relatively slow water, where the fly could be clearly seen and the line easily mended. La Branche, however, began to fish the dry in quicker and more turbulent water, and his classic, *The Dry Fly and Fast Water* (1914), offered great insight into his new techniques, including his curved cast. Disdaining anything but the dry fly, La Branche represents the purist approach to fly-fishing, and his defense of the technique, written with elegance and intensity, is a formidable document.

The slightly more fertile lower river saw the same destruction of the hemlock forest to feed the insatiable tanneries, with the exception of the canyon area of the Neversink Gorge. The Palen tannery at Fallsburg was established in 1832 and used more than 4,000 cords of hemlock bark a year. After the tanning industry began to decline, the area also suffered secondary logging to supply a paper mill at Fallsburg and numerous sawmills. Slowly, however, many of the mills fell silent and the clear-cuts began to grow back. It was during this transition that Ray Bergman and Larry Koller began to fish and later to write about the lower river.

Ray Bergman's encyclopedic *Trout* has been a classic since it was first published in 1938. His focused, no-nonsense approach is refreshing, as this comment on fly selection illustrates: "In fact I believe we'd do better with only a few, because then we'd concentrate on using skill and knowledge to catch fish, instead of wasting valuable time searching through a confusingly large number of flies for the one pattern that the fish couldn't refuse."

Larry Koller began fishing on smaller streams, but, as he recalled in his *Taking Larger Trout* (1950), "my thoughts were ever straying to the Neversink, only a few miles from home, but the great flow and majesty of this stream held me off. I felt that I was not ready either with casting skill or background of experience to seek the heavy trout I knew were there." *Taking Larger Trout* remains a compelling volume: the book is filled with strategies for capturing the two- and three-pounders that still inhabit the Gorge.

During this time, the river above the town of Neversink also continued to attract the attention of writers. In 1951 John Atherton published his *The Fly and the Fish,* in which he recounted fishing the river with an aging Hewitt. By this time the Neversink Dam was under construction, and Sparse Grey Hackle, in *Fishless Days, Angling Nights,* recalled a visit just before the reservoir drowned both the residence where Gordon died and Hewitt's fishing camp.

The completion of the reservoir flattened five miles of the upper river and had immediate consequences below. At first, releases were remarkable, often 133 million gallons per day (5 MGD would be the full flow from a 55-gallon drum lying on its side, so 133 MGD would be approximately 26 drums). The thermal plume reached the main stem of the Delaware at Port Jervis, thus allowing another twenty miles of trout water.

However, there were problems. Since the releases were made quickly and unpredictably, the river level changed rapidly and dangerously to anyone fishing it. Such extreme fluctuations also affected the trout population and the insect life. Nevertheless, the river maintained a substantial trout fishery, and as Harry Darbee said at the time, "Enjoy it while you can."

Darbee's advice proved correct: in the early 60s flows were reduced to 10 MGD in summer and a little over 3 MGD in winter. Previously deep and clear, the river was now ankle high and polluted at Bridgeville. The Gorge, though helped by its many feeder streams, suffered also.

To compound the problem, as the towns of Woodbourne, Falls-burg, and South Fallsburg expanded, pollution from untreated sewage became a substantial concern, especially from a number of hotels (there were nine between Fallsburg and South Fallsburg alone) with anti-quated and ill-maintained treatment facilities that were pumping raw sewage into the water, giving the river a whitish tinge.

Fortunately, a group of individuals, led by Dr. Bernard Cinberg, Phil Chase, Sam Levine, Ben Wechsler, and Frank Mele, began to fight for more releases and strict enforcement of pollution regulations. By the early 1970s, they had stopped the major polluters—including quarries at Fallsburg and Bridgeville—and in 1976 had an agreement with the state for tripling the summer releases to 30 MGD, which later was increased to 37 MGD, then 45 MGD, and currently 73.4 MGD.

Nick Lyons visited the Gorge after the new flows started, and in "Last Days Are for Dreamers," he wrote of fishing the central part when the other Catskill rivers were too warm for decent fishing.

The upper river never faced such struggles, the primary reason being that a number of large sections were preserved, mainly through private ownership. The Winnisook Club and the Connell property on the West Branch, the Frost Valley YMCA lands on both branches, and the state-owned headwaters of the East Branch have been instrumental in keeping the upper river in a natural condition. One of those owners, Leonard M. Wright, Jr., produced two of the best books about the river.

Wright's *The Ways of Trout* (1985) and *Neversink* (1991) are superb volumes, the first detailing his curiosity about rivers and trout, the second an intimate portrayal of his relationship to his home water. *The Ways of Trout* explores a number of hypotheses concerning trout behavior, including Wright's innovative belief that trout feed most heavily in response to rapidly changing water temperature. However, the most engaging section is "The Endless Belt," a celebration of freshwater that includes the author's exploration of a favorite pool with mask and snorkel.

Perhaps the finest volume written on the river is *Neversink*. Wright's engaging style, his self-deprecating humor, and his competent research all merge into the most readable work on the river: "For over two decades I have drunk from it, fished it, studied it, and struggled to improve it. I have examined it every month of the year, charting changes in its streambed and looking into the numbers, types, and habits of the life forms it produces. I have also scoured libraries and questioned biologists and hydrologists to learn more about running waters in general and this one in particular. It is an exercise that never ends: I am still learning and discovering." Every page in *Neversink* is worth reading, but in order to cover the reservoir, the chapter *"Salar Sebago"* has been included. This section details New York State's attempt to introduce landlocked salmon into the reservoir.

The above-mentioned writers are the core of this anthology, but I have included other authors who visited the Neversink. The decline of the fishing below the dam is noted by Ernest Schwiebert in "Neversink Fishing," from *Remembrances of Rivers Past*. Al McClane's contribution is an amusing anecdote about fishing a posted stretch of the Bushkill, a major tributary of the Neversink, with Walter "Beedle" Smith, Assistant Secretary of State and later head of the CIA. A chapter on the Lady Flyfishers, who gathered at their cottage on the West Branch, is worth reading, as is an excerpt from R. Palmer Baker, the author of *The Sweet of the Year*. Later writers include Phil Chase's tale of recreating one of Gordon's lost flies, Jay Cassell's tribute to the Gorge, and John Miller's experience in fishing the middle part of the river below South Fallsburg.

The future of the Neversink is reasonably secure. The surrounding forest has recovered for the most part, thus stabilizing the flow of the upper river. Below the reservoir, present releases are maintaining a decent fishery, and sewage concerns have been largely addressed. The

DEC has also added some access areas. However, there is some development on the upper river, and present flows on the lower river should be
maintained since they have little effect on New York City's daily usage
of almost a billion gallons per day.

After all the challenges it has faced and continues to face, the
Neversink remains a varied, fecund, and major Catskill river.

—JUSTIN ASKINS

The Legendary Neversink

Woodchuck

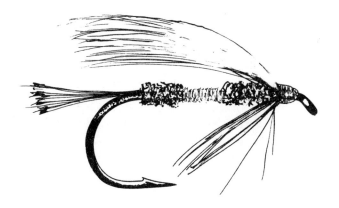

Royal Coachman Wet

Speckled Trout

JOHN BURROUGHS

The trout is dark and obscure above, but behind this foil there are won-
drous tints that reward the believing eye. Those who seek him in his
wild remote haunts are quite sure to get the full force of the sombre and
uninviting aspects,—the wet, the cold, the toil, the broken rest, and the
huge, savage, uncompromising nature,—but the true angler sees farther
than these, and is never thwarted of his legitimate reward by them.

   I have been a seeker of trout from my boyhood, and on all the expe-
ditions in which this fish has been the ostensible purpose I have brought
home more game than my creel showed. In fact, in my mature years I
find I got more of nature into me, more of the woods, the wild, nearer
to bird and beast, while threading my native streams for trout, than in

almost any other way. It furnished a good excuse to go forth; it pitched one in the right key; it sent one through the fat and marrowy places of field and wood. Then the fisherman has a harmless, preoccupied look; he is a kind of vagrant that nothing fears. He blends himself with the trees and the shadows. All his approaches are gentle and indirect. He times himself to the meandering, soliloquizing stream; its impulse bears him along. At the foot of the waterfall he sits sequestered and hidden in its volume of sound. The birds know he has no designs upon them, and the animals see that his mind is in the creek. His enthusiasm anneals him, and makes him pliable to the scenes and influences he moves among.

Then what acquaintance he makes with the stream! He addresses himself to it as a lover to his mistress; he woos it and stays with it till he knows its most hidden secrets. It runs through his thoughts not less than through its banks there; he feels the fret and thrust of every bar and boulder. Where it deepens, his purpose deepens; where it is shallow, he is indifferent. He knows how to interpret its every glance and dimple; its beauty haunts him for days.

I am sure I run no risk of overpraising the charm and attractiveness of a well-fed trout stream, every drop of water in it as bright and pure as if the nymphs had brought it all the way from its source in crystal goblets, and as cool as if it had been hatched beneath a glacier. When the heated and soiled and jaded refugee from the city first sees one, he feels as if he would like to turn it into his bosom and let it flow through him a few hours, it suggests such healing freshness and newness. How his roily thoughts would run clear; how the sediment would go downstream! Could he ever have an impure or an unwholesome wish afterward? The next best thing he can do is to tramp along its banks and surrender himself to its influence. If he reads it intently enough, he will, in a measure, be taking it into his mind and heart, and experiencing its salutary ministrations.

Trout streams coursed through every valley my boyhood knew. I crossed them, and was often lured and detained by them, on my way to and from school. We bathed in them during the long summer noons, and felt for the trout under their banks. A holiday was a holiday indeed that brought permission to go fishing over on Rose's Brook, or up

Hardscrabble, or in Meeker's Hollow; all-day trips, from morning till night, through meadows and pastures and beechen woods, wherever the shy, limpid stream led. What an appetite it developed! a hunger that was fierce and aboriginal, and that the wild strawberries we plucked as we crossed the hill teased rather than allayed. When but a few hours could be had, gained perhaps by doing some piece of work about the farm or garden in half the allotted time, the little creek that headed in the paternal domain was handy; when half a day was at one's disposal, there were the hemlocks, less than a mile distant, with their loitering, meditative, log-impeded stream and their dusky, fragrant depths. Alert and wide-eyed, one picked his way along, startled now and then by the sudden bursting-up of the partridge, or by the whistling wings of the "dropping snip," pressing through the brush and the briers, or finding an easy passage over the trunk of a prostrate tree, carefully letting his hook down through some tangle into a still pool, or standing in some high, sombre avenue and watching his line float in and out amid the moss-covered boulders. In my first essayings I used to go to the edge of these hemlocks, seldom dipping into them beyond the first pool where the stream swept under the roots of two large trees. From this point I could look back into the sunlit fields where the cattle were grazing; beyond, all was gloom and mystery; the trout were black, and to my young imagination the silence and the shadows were blacker. But gradually I yielded to the fascination and penetrated the woods farther and farther on each expedition, till the heart of the mystery was fairly plucked out. During the second or third year of my piscatorial experience I went through them, and through the pasture and meadow beyond, and through another strip of hemlocks, to where the little stream joined the main creek of the valley.

In June, when my trout fever ran pretty high, and an auspicious day arrived, I would make a trip to a stream a couple of miles distant, that came down out of a comparatively new settlement. It was a rapid mountain brook presenting many difficult problems to the young angler, but a very enticing stream for all that, with its two saw-mill dams, its pretty cascades, its high, shelving rocks sheltering the mossy nests of the phoebe-bird, and its general wild and forbidding aspects.

But a meadow brook was always a favorite. The trout like meadows; doubtless their food is more abundant there, and, usually, the good hiding-places are more numerous. As soon as you strike a meadow the character of the creek changes: it goes slower and lies deeper; it tarries to enjoy the high, cool banks and to half hide beneath them; it loves the willows, or rather the willows love it and shelter it from the sun; its spring runs are kept cool by the overhanging grass, and the heavy turf that faces its open banks is not cut away by the sharp hoofs of the grazing cattle. Then there are the bobolinks and the starlings and the meadowlarks, always interested spectators of the angler; there are also the marsh marigolds, the buttercups, or the spotted lilies, and the good angler is always an interested spectator of them. In fact, the patches of meadow land that lie in the angler's course are like the happy experiences in his own life, or like the fine passages in the poem he is reading; the pasture oftener contains the shallow and monotonous places. In the small streams the cattle scare the fish, and soil their element and break down their retreats under the banks. Woodland alternates the best with meadow: the creek loves to burrow under the roots of a great tree, to scoop out a pool after leaping over the prostrate trunk of one, and to pause at the foot of a ledge of moss-covered rocks, with ice-cold water dripping down. How straight the current goes for the rock! Note its corrugated, muscular appearance; it strikes and glances off, but accumulates, deepens with well-defined eddies above and to one side; on the edge of these the trout lurk and spring upon their prey. The angler learns that it is generally some obstacles or hindrances that makes a deep place in the creek, as in a brave life; and his ideal brook is one that lies in deep, well-defined banks, yet makes many a shift from right to left, meets with many rebuffs and adventures, hurled back upon itself by rocks, waylaid by snags and trees, tripped up by precipices, but sooner or later reposing under meadow banks, deepening and eddying beneath bridges, or prosperous and strong in some level stretch of cultivated land with great elms shading it here and there.

But I early learned that from almost any stream in a trout country the true angler could take trout, and that the great secret was this, that, whatever bait you used, worm, grasshopper, grub, or fly, there was one thing you must always put upon your hook, namely, your heart: when you bait your hook with your heart the fish always bite; they will jump clear from the water after it; they will dispute with each other over it; it is a morsel they love above everything else. With such bait I have seen the born angler (my grandfather was one) take a noble string of trout from the most unpromising waters, and on the most unpromising day. He used his hook so coyly and tenderly, he approached the fish with such address and insinuation, he divined the exact spot where they lay: if they were not eager, he humored them and seemed to steal by them; if they were playful and coquettish, he would suit his mood to theirs; if they were frank and sincere, he met them halfway; he was so patient and considerate, so entirely devoted to pleasing the critical trout, and so successful in his efforts,—surely his heart was upon his hook, and it was a tender, unctuous heart, too, as that of every angler is. How nicely he would measure the distance! how dexterously he would avoid an over-hanging limb or bush and drop the line exactly in the right spot! Of course there was a pulse of feeling and sympathy to the extremity of that line. If your heart is a stone, however, or an empty husk, there is no use to put it upon your hook; it will not tempt the fish; the bait must be quick and fresh. Indeed, a certain quality of youth is indispensable to the successful angler, a certain unworldliness and readiness to invest your-self in an enterprise that doesn't pay in the current coin. Not only is the angler, like the poet, born and not made, as Walton says, but there is a deal of the poet in him, and he is to be judged no more harshly; he is the victim of his genius: those wild streams, how they haunt him! he will play truant to dull care, and flee to them; their waters impart some-what of their own perpetual youth to him. My grandfather when he was eighty years old would take down his pole as eagerly as any boy, and step off with wonderful elasticity toward the beloved streams; it used to try my young legs a good deal to follow him, specially on the return trip. And no poet was ever more innocent of worldly success or ambition. For, to paraphrase Tennyson:

> Lusty trout to him were scrip and share,
> And babbling waters more than cent for cent.

He laid up treasures, but they were not in this world. In fact, though the kindest of husbands, I fear he was not what the country people call a "good provider," except in providing trout in their season, though it is doubtful if there was always fat in the house to fry them in. But he could tell you they were worse off than that at Valley Forge, and that trout, or any other fish, were good roasted in the ashes under the coals. He had the Walton requisite of loving quietness and contemplation, and was devout withal. Indeed, in many ways he was akin to those Galilee fishermen who were called to be fishers of men. How he read the Book and pored over it, even at times, I suspect, nodding over it, and laying it down only to take up his rod, over which, unless the trout were very dilatory and the journey very fatiguing, he never nodded!

My first acquaintance with the Neversink was made in company with some friends in 1869. We passed up the valley of the Big Indian, marveling at its copious ice-cold springs, and its immense sweep of heavy-timbered mountain-sides. Crossing the range at its head, we struck the Neversink quite unexpectedly about the middle of the afternoon, at a point where it was a good-sized trout stream. It proved to be one of those black mountain brooks born of innumerable ice-cold springs, nourished in the shade, and shod, as it were, with thick-matted moss, that every camper-out remembers. The fish are as black as the stream and very wild. They dart from beneath the fringed rocks, or dive with the hook into the dusky depths,—an integral part of the silence and the shadows. The spell of the moss is over all. The fisherman's tread is noiseless, as he leaps from stone to stone and from ledge to ledge along the bed of the stream. How cool it is! He looks up the dark, silent defile, hears the solitary voice of the water, sees the decayed trunks of fallen trees bridging the stream, and all he has dreamed, when a boy, of the haunts of beasts of prey—the crouching feline tribes, especially if it be near nightfall and the gloom already deepening in the woods— comes freshly to mind, and he presses on, wary and alert, and speaking to his companions in low tones.

After an hour or so the trout became less abundant, and with nearly a hundred of the black sprites in our baskets we turned back. Here and there I saw the abandoned nests of the pigeons, sometimes half a dozen in one tree. In a yellow birch which the floods had uprooted, a number of nests were still in place, little shelves or platforms of twigs loosely arranged, and affording little or no protection to the eggs or the young birds against inclement weather.

Before we had reached our companions the rain set in again and forced us to take shelter under a balsam. When it slackened we moved on and soon came up with Aaron, who had caught his first trout, and, considerably drenched, was making his way toward camp, which one of the party had gone forward to build. After traveling less than a mile, we saw a smoke struggling up through the dripping tress, and in a few moments were all standing round a blazing fire. But the rain now commenced again, and fairly poured down through the trees, rendering the prospect of cooking and eating our supper there in the woods, and of passing the night on the ground without tent or cover of any kind, rather disheartening. We had been told of a bark shanty a couple of miles farther down the creek, and thitherward we speedily took up our line of march. When we were on the point of discontinuing the search, thinking we had been misinformed or had passed it by, we came in sight of a bark-peeling, in the midst of which a small log house lifted its naked rafters toward the now breaking sky. It had neither floor nor roof, and was less inviting on first sight than the open woods. But a board partition was still standing, out of which we built a rude porch on the east side of the house, large enough for us all to sleep under if well packed, and eat under if we stood up. There was plenty of well-seasoned timber lying about, and a fire was soon burning in front of our quarters that made the scene social and picturesque, especially when the frying-pans were brought into requisition, and the coffee, in charge of Aaron, who was an artist in this line, mingled its aroma with the wild-wood air. At dusk a balsam was felled, and the tips of the branches used to make a bed, which was more fragrant than soft; hemlock is better, because its needles are finer and its branches more elastic.

There was a spirt or two of rain during the night, but not enough to find out the leaks in our roof. It took the shower or series of showers of the next day to do that. They commenced about two o'clock in the afternoon. The forenoon had been fine, and we had brought into camp nearly three hundred trout; but before they were half dressed, or the first panfuls fried, the rain set in. First came short, sharp dashes, then a gleam of treacherous sunshine, followed by more and heavier dashes. The wind was in the southwest, and to rain seemed the easiest thing in the world. From fitful dashes to a steady pour, the transition was natural. We stood huddled together, stark and grim, under our cover, like hens under a cart. The fire fought bravely for a time, and retaliated with sparks and spiteful tongues of flame; but gradually its spirit was broken, only a heavy body of coal and half-consumed logs in the centre holding out against all odds. The simmering fish were soon floating about in a yellow liquid that did not look in the least appetizing. Point after point gave way in our cover, till standing between the drops was no longer possible. The water coursed down the underside of the boards, and dripped in our necks and formed puddles on our hat-brims. We shifted our guns and traps and viands, till there was no longer any choice of position, when the loaves and the fishes, the salt and the sugar, the pork and the butter, shared the same watery fate. The fire was gasping its last. Little rivulets coursed about it, and bore away the quenched but steaming coals on their bosoms. The spring run in the rear of our camp swelled so rapidly that part of the trout that had been hastily left lying on its banks again found themselves quite at home. For over two hours the floods came down. About four o'clock Orville, who had not yet come from the day's sport, appeared. To say Orville was wet is not much; he was better than that,—he had been washed and rinsed in at least half a dozen waters, and the trout that he bore dangling at the end of a string hardly knew that they had been out of their proper element.

But he brought welcome news. He had been two or three miles down the creek, and had seen a log building,—whether house or stable he did not know, but it had the appearance of having a good roof, which was inducement enough for us instantly to leave our present quarters. Our course lay along an old wood-road, and much of the time we were to our knees in water. The woods were literally flooded everywhere. Every little rill and springlet ran like a mill-tail, while the main stream rushed and roared, foaming, leaping, lashing, its volume increased fiftyfold. The water was not roily, but of a rich coffee-color, from the leach-ings of the woods. No more trout for the next three days! we thought, as we looked upon the rampant stream.

After we had labored and floundered along for about an hour, the road turned to the left, and in a little stumpy clearing near the creek a gable uprose on our view. It did not prove to be just such a place as poets love to contemplate. It required a greater effort for the imagination than any of us were then capable of to believe it had ever been a favorite resort of wood-nymphs or sylvan deities. It savored rather of the equine and the bovine. The bark-men had kept their teams there, horses on the one side and oxen on the other, and no Hercules had ever done duty in cleansing the stables. But there was a dry loft overhead with some straw, where we might get some sleep, in spite of the rain and the midges; a double layer of boards, standing at a very acute angle, would keep off the former, while the mingled refuse hay and muck beneath would nurse a smoke that would prove a thorough protection against the latter. And then, when Jim, the two-handed, mounting the trunk of a prostrate maple near by, had severed it thrice with easy and familiar stroke, and, rolling the logs in front of the shanty, had kindled a fire, which, getting better of the dampness, soon cast a bright glow over all, shedding warmth and light even into the dingy stable, I consented to unsling my knapsack and accept the situation. The rain had ceased, and the sun shone out behind the woods. We had trout sufficient for present needs; and after my first meal in an ox-stall, I strolled out on the rude log bridge to watch the angry Neversink rush by. Its waters fell quite as rapidly as they rose, and before sundown it looked as if we might have fishing again on the morrow. We had better sleep that night than either night before, though there were two disturbing causes,—the smoke in the early part of it, and the cold in the latter. The "no-see-ems" left in disgust; and, though disgusted myself, I swallowed the smoke as best I could, and hugged my pallet of straw the closer. But the day dawned bright, and a plunge in the Neversink set me all right again. The creek, to our surprise and gratification, was only a little higher than before the rain, and some of the finest trout we had yet seen we caught that morning near camp.

We tarried yet another day and night at the old stable, but taking our meals outside squatted on the ground, which had now become quite dry. Part of the day I spent strolling about the woods, looking up old acquaintances among the birds, and, as always, half expectant of making some new ones. Curiously enough, the most abundant species were among those I had found rare in most other localities, namely, the small water-wagtail, the mourning ground warbler, and the yellow-bellied woodpecker. The latter seems to be the prevailing woodpecker through the woods of this region.

That night the midges, those motes that sting, held high carnival. We learned afterward, in the settlement below and from the barkpeelers, that it was the worst night ever experienced in that valley. We had done no fishing during the day, but had anticipated some fine sport about sundown. Accordingly Aaron and I started off between six and seven o'clock, one going upstream and the other down. The scene was charming. The sun shot up great spokes of light from behind the woods, and beauty, like a presence, pervaded the atmosphere. But torment, multiplied as the sands of the seashore, lurked in every tangle and thicket. In a thoughtless moment I removed my shoes and socks, and waded in the water to secure a fine trout that had accidentally slipped from my string and was helplessly floating with the current. This caused some delay and gave the gnats time to accumulate. Before I had got one foot half dressed I was enveloped in a black mist that settled upon my hands and neck and face, filling my ears with infinitesimal pipings and covering my flesh with infinitesimal bitings. I thought I should have to flee to the friendly fumes of the old stable, with "one stocking off and one stocking on;" but I got my shoe on at last, though not without many amusing interruptions and digressions.

In a few moments after this adventure I was in rapid retreat toward camp. Just as I reached the path leading from the shanty to the creek, my companion in the same ignoble flight reached it also, his hat broken and rumpled, and his sanguine countenance looking more sanguinary than I had ever before seen it, and his speech, also, in the highest degree inflammatory. His face and forehead were as blotched and swollen as if he had just run his head into a hornets' nest, and his manner as precipitate as if the whole swarm was still at his back.

No smoke or smudge which we ourselves could endure was suffi-cient in the earlier part of that evening to prevent serious annoyance from the same cause; but later a respite was granted us.

About ten o'clock, as we stood round our campfire, we were star-tled by a brief but striking display of the aurora borealis. My imagina-tion had already been excited by talk of legends and of weird shapes and appearances, and when, on looking up toward the sky, I saw those pale, phantasmal waves of magnetic light chasing each other across the little opening above our heads, and at first sight seeming barely to clear the treetops, I was as vividly impressed as if I had caught a glimpse of a ver-itable spectre of the Neversink. The sky shook and trembled like a great white curtain.

The next morning boded rain; but we had become thoroughly sated with the delights of our present quarters, outside and in, and packed up our traps to leave. Before we had reached the clearing, three miles below, the rain set in, keeping up a lazy, monotonous drizzle till the afternoon.

The clearing was quite a recent one, made mostly by barkpeelers, who followed their calling in the mountains round about in summer, and worked in their shops making shingle in winter. The Biscuit Brook came in here from the west,—a fine, rapid trout stream six or eight miles in length, with plenty of deer in the mountains about its head. On its banks we found the house of an old woodman, to whom we had been directed for information about the section we proposed to traverse.

"Is the way very difficult," we inquired, "across from the Neversink into the head of the Beaverkill?"

"Not to me; I could go it the darkest night ever was. And I can direct you so you can find the way without any trouble. You go down the Neversink about a mile, when you come to Highfall Brook, the first stream that comes down on the right. Follow up it to Jim Reed's shanty, about three miles. Then cross the stream, and on the left bank, pretty well up on the side of the mountain, you will find a wood-road, which was made by a fellow below here who stole some ash logs off the top of the ridge last winter and drew them out on the snow. When the road first begins to tilt over the mountain, strike down to your left, and you can reach the Beaverkill before sundown."

As it was then after two o'clock, and the distance was six or eight of these terrible hunter's miles, we concluded to take a whole day to it, and wait till next morning. The Beaverkill flowed west, the Neversink south, and I had a mortal dread of getting entangled amid the mountains and valleys that lie in either angle.

Besides, I was glad of another and final opportunity to pay my respects to the finny tribes of the Neversink. At this point it was one of the finest trout streams I had ever beheld. It was so sparkling, its bed so free from sediment or impurities of any kind, that it had a new look, as if it had just come from the hand of its Creator. I tramped along its margin upward of a mile that afternoon, part of the time wading to my knees, and casting my hook, baited only with a trout's fin, to the opposite bank. Trout are real cannibals, and make no bones, and break none either, in lunching on each other. A friend of mine had several in his spring, when one day a large female trout gulped down one of her male friends, nearly one third her own size, and went around for two days with the tail of her liege lord protruding from her mouth! A fish's eye will do for bait, though the anal fin is better. One of the natives here told me that when he wished to catch large trout (and I judged he never fished for any other,—I never do), he used for bait the bullhead, or dart, a little fish an inch and a half or two inches long, that rests on the pebbles near shore and darts quickly, when disturbed from point to point. "Put that on your hook," said he, "and if there is a big fish in the creek, he is bound to have it." But the darts were not easily found; the big fish, I concluded, had cleaned them all out; and, then, it was easy enough to supply our wants with a fin.

The 100-Year Fly

Letters from a Recluse

THEODORE GORDON

It is a bitter cold winter's night and I am far away from the cheerful lights of town or city. The north wind is shrieking and tearing at this lonely house, like some evil demon wishful to carry it away bodily or shatter it completely. The icy breath of this demon penetrates through every chink and crevice, of which there appear to be many, and the wood-burning stove is my only companion. It is on nights such as these, after the turn of the year, that our thoughts stray away from the present to other scenes and very different seasons. We return in spirit to the time of leaf and blossom, when birds were singing merrily and trout were rising in the pools. We remember many days of glorious sport and keen enjoyment, and then somehow our thoughts take a turn and leap forward. Spring is near, quite near, and it will soon be time to go fishing. We want to talk about it dreadfully. O for a brother crank of the fly-fishing fraternity, one who would be ready to listen occasionally and not insist upon doing all the talking, telling all the stories himself. But if we cannot talk we can write, and it is just possible that some dear brother angler will read what we say upon paper. There is some comfort in that idea, so here goes.

Why is it that with all the improvements made in fishing tackle in recent years we have but few patterns of artificial flies copied direct from nature? From the hosts of flies to be found on many of the hard-fished waters of the Eastern and Middle States? The imitations sold in the shops were nearly all of them copied from English patterns origi-nally, and these, of course, were not taken from American flies. Our original pattems are largely fancies, combinations in colors pleasing to the eyes of man and are used as lures, not as imitations of any insect. Many of them are very killing in the waters for which they were cre-ated, but there is something extremely fascinating in the successful imitation of one of the smaller ephemera, when we can believe that our fine basket of trout was due to our care in getting the colors and size just right. Fancies and lures are very well and are absolutely essen-tial in Maine and the Dominion of Canada, but there are streams where at times and upon occasions our ability to match an insect on the water means a full basket, while all the fancies in creation will scarcely raise a fish. . . .

Probably all anglers of experience who fish the waters of New York and Pennsylvania can recall many instances when the trout were rising freely, yet would have little or nothing to do with any of the artificial flies presented for their acceptance. Usually no great effort is made to ascertain what the trout are taking. Frequently they are said to be midging or playing, when such is not the case. It is often difficult to see the natural flies upon the water, particularly in the evening, when the heaviest rise often takes place after the weather has become genial.

If the angler is in the habit of looking about for insects he will be apt to see a few specimens of the prevailing flies at odd times during the day, and these may serve as a guide when the rise comes on. Not only this, but if he can match the colors of the flies he finds he may take more and larger trout than he would with a purely fancy fly, even if he meets with but few rising fish during the entire day. A little attention paid to the entomology of our trout streams certainly adds considerably to the pleasure of fly-fishing. An illustrated work with which to identify them is very desirable; I do not know of any book of this kind published in America. It may be said that it is too much trouble to be always hunting about for insects, and that the occasions when an imitation of the natural fly is required are few and far between. This last is not true of some of our best streams, and no one who has ever hit off the right fly during a good rise of trout will be apt to consider his efforts or time wasted. Sometimes one may take fish almost as fast as he can cover the rises which may be seen on every hand. I have seen a large creel nearly filled in an hour or two. In one instance a skillful angler, familiar with the water, took over forty fair-sized native trout in less than one hour. He had but one fly that was of any service whatever; I had not even that one and could do nothing.

Fishing with a dear friend many years ago, I noticed that the trout were taking a small yellow fly, and found that I had two yellow hackles in my book. One of them was a very pale shade of yellow, the other a little darker. I gave the former to my friend and he began to kill trout at once. They would not take any other, so we arranged to fish turn about with his rod, each of us casting until we caught or lost a fish. Fishing with three flies in the old way, the whole catch has been made with the middle fly, the worst position on the cast. Queerer than this, a black hackle with a thin silk body was taken every time, while a precisely similar fly with black mohair body was entirely ignored. With the right fly you may have fine sport when better anglers on the same water are having little or none.

The body and legs of a fly are most important. If they are correct in coloring we can do without wings. There must be great numbers of American birds that have been ignored by the fly dresser. Who can tell me of a bird whose primary and secondary wing feathers are of a pale delicate dun color? It must not be a bird protected at all seasons by law, and the fibres of the feathers must be fine and cohesive. I never fancied dyed feathers for small flies, yet the art of dying is now comparatively easy to acquire, as a simpler process gives excellent results. As regards the imitation of natural flies, any man who does much of his fishing in one locality can get up an imitation or two that may add considerably to his success and pleasure. In doing this he will become familiar with the natural insect and acquire the habit of looking out for and studying them.

Fortunately, many of our flies are not mere atoms. I have some flies in a little tin box that are said to be the exact size of the natural insects which rise on the English streams, and the hooks are mere specks. All these flies are what we call midges, and only put up occasionally. Over there they are in daily use. We have many tiny insects, but the flies common to our waters certainly average much bigger than the little artificials I have mentioned. When used in these small sizes, hooks must be of first-rate quality or despair will be our portion. I remember fishing where small flies were the rule and quite necessary to success. I sent at once for a box of small hooks and dressed a lot of flies upon them. They proved to be brittle and I had a wretched time of it. It was all right as long as I hooked nothing over half a pound in weight, but at least three out of five fish above that weight were lost, many of them at the last moment, when they were done for and should have been mine.

There is great advantage in having confidence in the fly you are using. Much time is lost in making changes if one is in doubt as to the correct pattern. With a favorite fly one goes ahead, fishes his best and makes no alteration in his cast unless special conditions demand it. There are certain colors and combinations that can always be relied upon to kill a few fish. Other flies there are which are in good repute, yet sometimes are of no use whatever, except to catch baby trout. The fly we want is the one that will be accepted by the big fish. Two equally good anglers fishing together may take the same number of trout, but the fellow who has the right fly will have the heaviest creel. If a certain fly has been upon the water morning and evening for several days, even in small numbers, the larger fish will be apt to patronize an artificial of the same color.

We must put up the exact shade if possible. The backs of natural flies are usually much darker than the bellies, so they should be examined from below before making up an imitation. We sometimes find flies that greatly resemble insects common on the other side of the Atlantic. Last summer I saw a few corresponding to the beautiful little Jenny Spinner for the first time. They were larger and the red, instead of being at the head and tail of the fly, was under the wings in the middle of the body. The clear, glassy wings and milk-white body with this rosy tinge made up a very pretty fly. It would be impossible to match those wings in feathers, but a body of rose and white with a very pale creamy badger hackle might answer.

Usually I prefer to imitate the dun or subimago stage of existence, as the duns are more in evidence upon the water than spinners. In fact, a medium-sized dun is hard to beat as a standby on any stream. They are seen in many shades, as the temperature of the air affects the color, darker in cold, lighter in warm weather; and as all the ephemeridae pass through this stage of existence, several sizes are useful.

The question of size is a very important one, and it is often difficult to determine which is the best size of hook to use. To a certain extent only, one may be guided by the size of the stream he is fishing, as, in a general way, the larger the stream the more large flies one will see, and the bigger, in season, the hook may be. Hooks Nos. 8 to 14, old style of numbering, will answer most purposes in New York and Pennsylvania.

When we use the fly as a lure, representing something alive, not necessarily an insect, but appealing to the predatory savage nature of game fish, we are working upon a different basis of action and may try a very large pattern of unusual colors or make-up, more particularly if we are in pursuit of trout of unusual size which we have reason to believe are not often surface feeders. These big fish are not in the habit of feeding upon small flies, although they may accept one if they are in position in shallow water or near the surface, but they are seldom found in such positions. It is hard to raise trout over three pounds in weight, yet they will rise if one is fortunate enough to find them well on the feed. In fact, there are not many small things, seemingly possessed of life, that these Jumbos will not move at if they are hungry. They can do without food for some time. If the water is warm they feed little, but when they do go out to dine they want a regular gorge in many courses.

I cast over one three-pound trout that was feeding upon minnows near the edge of a gravel bar in a big pool for the best part of an hour. At last I went above, and getting out a long line almost hung the fly over the spot where the minnows were skipping. Then it was taken. This trout was simply crammed with fresh silvery minnows. They must all have been taken very recently, and there were lots more to be had near that bar, yet the old glutton grabbed my little dun, just by way of an olive or anchovy.

A combination of red and white may provoke a savage dash from a big fish, but speaking now of the Middle States, my experience is that they do not often take it in. If small flies fail I prefer something mothy-looking with good long hackles to give life to the fly. Occasionally they will take a floating fly, and I have had several very exciting experiences of this when big trout sprang out of the water in striking at the fly. They presented a splendid spectacle which I shall never forget. One cleared the surface and struck down with open mouth upon the fly, and kept it, as it was tied on cobweb gut. Another sailed into the air without touching the artificial, and I got him in the evening when the strong light was off the water. I did not dare to try him again immediately, as I thought he was suspicious, and the sun was still well up in the western sky.

The light has much to do with our success or non-success in fly-fishing. At times in strong sunshine and in certain states of the atmos-phere our artificial flies, even the very best of them, are the most transparent clumsy frauds imaginable. The finest gut shows up like an ocean cable, and we feel that we are miserable, low-down humbugs. With the light of day in our favor at the right angle, all things are vastly different. Our casting line is invisible and the flies appear on or in the water as dainty living insects, quite sufficient to deceive the wariest old three-pounder that ever wagged a fin.

Fortunately for the fly-fisher, all round-eyed creatures are deficient in visual impressions of form as compared with man and his almond eyes. Trout appear to be able to discriminate in the matter of color, as a slight difference in shade will sometimes affect the killing qualities of flies tied to the same pattern. They quickly detect any movement upon the part of the angler, and are often alarmed by shadows cast upon the water. A man standing perfectly still will not be noticed by fish, and this is true of many wild animals; deer, for instance. I was amused recently to note that the turkeys outside my window were greatly frightened by the shadows of sparrows which were flying from tree to tree.

Trout are wonderfully expert in concealing themselves in small brooks during long droughts in summer. One may be able to count every pebble on the bottoms of the pools and nothing may be seen except a few small trout, suckers and minnows, yet there may be trout of from one pound up in those very pools. The big fish know that they are in danger during the low water and become extremely shy. If they feed at all it will be at night. In a full stream, with an abundance of water above and around them, they feel safe. In dry seasons try the large pools after sunset. You may be rewarded. If you know the habitat of a big trout, go for him again and again. By persevering you will find him on the feed at last.

I fished for one fish for more than two weeks before I got him, and had cast over his lie at least fifty times on the successful evening before he rose. In this case a short line cast from a different direction turned the trick. One can never learn all that there is in fly-fishing. Only men of limited experience think that they know it all. A few patterns of flies will usually answer all purposes on any river or lake, but it is not wise to despise a large assortment. They can all be stowed away in small compass, and one never knows what strange combination of fur and feathers may be useful some day.

There are few things more interesting than a good collection of artificial flies. My fingers itch to open any old fly-book I see. All fishing cranks enjoy looking over a good angling kit, rods, flies, and tackles. A visit to a first-class fishing-tackle shop is more interesting than an afternoon at the circus. If one has leisure, fly-making is an absorbing occupation and there is considerable satisfaction in taking trout with the work of one's own hands. I was driven to it many years ago by the difficulty experienced at that time in getting just what I wanted at the stores. I wished to imitate certain insects, some of which were very small and required small hooks tied on fine-drawn gut. Nowadays I use eyed hooks as often as hooks tied on snells and find the Pennell very good for hooking and holding. It certainly is a nuisance trying to knot the eye to the cast when the light is bad. The sproat is excellent, if you can get it correctly made, and the sneck is also useful, but of late years there is a tendency among manufacturers to shorten the shanks of hooks unduly. This is bad, I think. I hate a dumpy hook for fly-fishing.

In many of our streams the European brown or yellow trout now outnumber the native fish, and one never knows when he may stir up a regular buster. Then, indeed, we are in need of the best possible hook and tackle. If we have been careless in regard to these things the result may be a most regrettable memory which may haunt our minds for years. Just imagine losing a trout above six pounds in weight through the use of an old fly with a worn gut link. I have had that bitter experience and others nearly as annoying. With an abundant supply of food there is almost no limit to the growth of these brown trout. They have been taken up to nine pounds at least, and I saw two specimens at large during low water in the Beaverkill that were very large. One of these could be seen any day from the public road, and was estimated at seven pounds. I thought he would weigh about six. The other I saw only twice, as he lived in a small hole in what was a big pool in a good stage of water, and was usually under a flat rock that barely covered his vast proportions.

The first time I saw the fish I was standing on the edge of this hole in shallow water watching a school of big suckers to see if any trout were among them. Suddenly this enormous fish appeared from under his stone, almost directly below me and not more than eight feet away. I did not move a muscle, and for some time he remained there, gently waving fins and tail and opening and shutting his great gills. Once or twice he opened his mouth and yawned; I suppose he was probably tired of low water and a slim diet. It was a male fish in grand condition, rather light in color and brilliantly spotted. In about ten minutes he swam quietly back to his house of stone, but had quite a time getting under cover. He went in head first and then worked around sideways until tail and body disappeared from view.

I found him taking the air only once, about two weeks after my first call, and this trout was absolutely unknown; no one had ever seen him. Not wishing to be considered a greater prevaricator than necessary, I have always reported this fish at eight pounds, but in my soul I believe that he weighed nearly or quite ten pounds. That trout has never been caught. He is there yet, and now weighs anything you please. Go and catch him, my brother; it will be a feather in your cap. What is more to the point, I will help you all I can by revealing, in strict confidence, the pool where he lived, and where he probably still remains. Those big fish dwell in the same place for many years. I had positive knowledge of two trout in the same pool for four or five years before they were snared, and had played one of them to the point of exhaustion when the hook broke at the bend.

To return to the fish. The pool is near the public road. You can slip in some evening and have him out in a jiffy. Be sure to carry a large grain sack with you to hide the fish in until you get to your quarters. I can tell you where to have him stuffed, and he will look bully on the wall of your sanctum. I would have caught him myself if the water had not been too low.

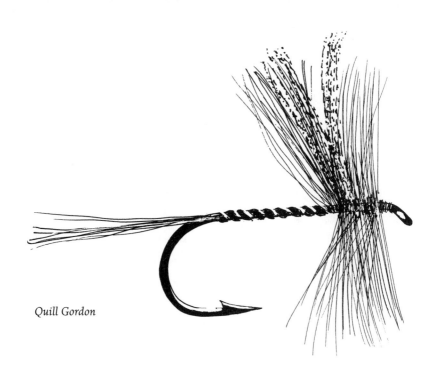

Quill Gordon

Little Talks about Fly-Fishing

THEODORE GORDON

(*Forest and Stream*, January 19, 1907)

Men who are not members of the great fraternity of anglers have no idea of the pleasure they have missed and are missing; of the savor and sweetness which a love of fishing, and particularly fly-fishing, adds to life on this old planet. Those who can say with Fishin' Jimmy, "I allers loved fishin' and knowed it was the best thing on the hull earth," are fortunate. It is not necessary, however, for a man to begin practicing the gentle art early in life; business, the practice of one of the professions, or location, may prevent many from going fishing until quite late in life. Sir Humphrey Davy was fifty years old before he took up his rod, yet he became a celebrated angler and wrote *Salmonia*.

One stores up many happy memories for all time. The incidents of past seasons rise before his mental sight on gloomy wintry days, and with the beginning of a new year he thinks of the joyful days to come, when he can snap the shackles which bind him and fly away to his favorite trout stream. Then there is so much pleasure to be had out of the accessories of the art, the rod, reel, and line, the beautiful artificial flies and filmy casting lines or leaders. If he is a moderately patient man and is gifted with a little mechanical ability, he may make most of these things himself. Many amateurs tie lovely flies, and some of the finest rods I have seen have been made by them. Where there was one fly-fisher fifty years ago, there are now a hundred, and we cannot fail to note the growing interest in the sport. Many books on angling have been written in recent years and none that I know of have failed to find readers.

Some people say that nothing can be learned from books, but I think this is quite a mistake. Practice is absolutely necessary, of course, but we gain many valuable hints in our reading as well as in conversation with anglers of experience. As an instance of this, many years ago I saw in a work on angling an illustration of a fly-fisher casting his fly, and this picture had great value for me. I had been, up to that time, rather a laborious wielder of the fly-rod. Frequently my arm ached so badly after a long day's work, or after several consecutive days on the stream, that my sleep was not sound or restful. I gained something from that illustration; I cannot say now just what it was, but I do know that from that time on fly-fishing has been more pleasurable and less fatiguing. The rod seems to do the work in ordinary stream fishing without conscious effort on my part and only the grasp of the hand is cramped or uncomfortable at the end of the day.

Again, I was fishing a large stream after a heavy freshet. The water had subsided considerably, yet the trout seemed to have remained in numbers in certain sheltered places. They were rising steadily under the bank of a long curving pool, but nothing I could offer them seemed to their taste. I could not see what they were taking until I went up stream and waded across. Then I found that a flight of ants was on, as it was in August. Why or how they got on the water I did not stop to consider, but went through my fly-book looking for an artificial ant. I found none and for a time was at a loose end. Suddenly I remembered having read somewhere that a small lead winged coachman would kill when ants were on the water, and soon found three of these insects on No. 12 hooks. To my notion they were not much like ants, but the trout welcomed them gladly and I killed in that long pool either twenty-two or twenty-eight good trout, I forget which. I found out afterward that I was indebted to that veteran angler, H. R. Francis (not F. F.) for this hint, and it was not intended for American anglers either.

I believe strongly in the purchase of a really first-class rod. If you are a beginner and think yourself clumsy or nervous, buy a cheap rod to begin with. Smash it in your early efforts to catch fish and then get the best rod you can afford to buy. A really first-rate weapon will do practically all the work in casting the length of line usually required, and is a source of constant pleasure to its possessor. There are some rods that one loves to cast with, even when there are no fish. It is best to have water to practice on, but a lawn or open field is good enough. You can get the idea of how to cast in a room, with a switch and a piece of string. Use the wrist in short casts and keep the elbow down near the side. In the back cast never allow the point of the rod to go much beyond the perpendicular. It is the spring of the rod and the wrist that does the trick. It is only in long casts that the whole arm comes into play. Make the rod spring with the wrist; don't just wave it to and fro. Begin with a short line, not much longer than the rod—the longer the line the more difficult it is to allow the correct time before coming forward.

One great advantage of the moderate split bamboo rod is its quick, snappy action. The old-fashioned rod was comparatively slow and soft. One had to allow more time behind. Some people call casting the fly-whipping, and there is some analogy between the fly-rod and a whip with a short stock and very long lash. I fancy that a good driver of oxen would use his wrist largely in neatly clipping a piece of hide out of one of the leaders, and we have all heard the story of the stage coachman who was so expert that he could twitch the pipe from between the lips of passing pedestrians with his whip lash as he drove by. It is not difficult to learn how to cast well enough to kill a few trout. After this your fate is sealed. You will never be able to drop angling, as you may some other sports, even if you have not time to become very expert. In the beginning try to acquire a good style. A high back cast is most important. Never allow the fly to touch ground or water behind you. A great many people throw the points of their rods too far back in casting and then wonder why so many hooks are broken and flies ruined. I have known men who could cast a long distance and who were quite successful in killing trout, who never got over this habit of smashing flies. It is ugly work and it is very expensive.

(*Forest and Stream*, March 2, 1907)
How we detest a sawmill on one of our favorite streams! The sappy, heavy sawdust not only floats on the surface, but sinks to the bottom and permeates the entire river. The trout will not rise; in fact, I do not believe that natural flies would be noticed, even if they would come up through the trash, and hatch out on the surface. Those sawmills are responsible for many muttered bad words, and for several melancholy days. There have been times when one had to wait until after 6 o'clock before he could hope to basket a trout. Country sawmills usually quit at 6. I wish they would quit at 6 A.M. and never start up again. What a lot of trees would be saved to glorify the forests. Wood has advanced so much in price that every little piece of pine or hemlock in the country is hunted out and doomed to swift destruction. Why not hold these remnants for a further advance? They cannot be replaced in a hundred years. We can only hope that deciduous trees will spring up in their place.

(*Forest and Stream,* July 27, 1907)
At times, in July, a smaller fly seems to be required than at any other time during the season. Yet again a larger mouthful may tempt the big fish. We can only try and try again. If we could reduce fly-fishing to an exact science, always follow one method and use the same flies, much of its charm would be lost. If there was no uncertainty, no disappointment, there would be no real success. These rivers are all very clear, but the Neversink is a "white" water stream. No lakes drain into it until it has danced for many miles down the valley and there is not a tinge of vegetable matter in its pellucid rifts or pools. Where in its rapid course it flows over golden sands between woods and meadows the effect is very beautiful. Unfortunately in many places great damage has been done by the floods of recent years and there seems to be no effectual way of checking these ravages.

(*Forest and Stream,* February 1, 1908)
A year ago at this time we began to think of spring, and how we would enjoy ourselves when that charming season arrived. Truly, we had long to wait, as in this region we knew not the fickle goddess called spring until about the middle of the first month of summer. Human nature is optimistic, and despite experience we are again making plans for a perfect vernal season. We are thinking of fresh yet balmy breezes, clear-rushing streams and deep, dark pools flecked with foam. The widening rings made by rising trout are easily seen if we shut our eyes for a moment. The duns are sailing down like tiny yachts with sails erect, and the little caddis flies are struggling and skittering on the water.

Let no man bury the pleasures of anticipation. When we cease to look forward we grow old rapidly. Not that we would forget the pleasures of past seasons. Every good angler's brain is a storehouse of happy memories. Without these how could we paint pictures of the good time to come? Not that we expect anything wonderful in the way of sport, but we may reasonably hope for a few days when we shall be in tune with nature, when soft airs are rippling the bright waters, and the stream is neither too high nor too low. A few flies should be hatching out, just enough to keep the fish interested in what is going on at the top and make them rise occasionally. We never forget the rare days when the big fish are feeding.

Last spring the weather was cold and the "time of the take" unusually short. The small insects did not appear until midday or later, and the rise was over by 3 o'clock. Odd fish were to be had by the strenuous angler all day long, but I did not see a good rise of flies and trout in the morning until the month of June. Sometimes when there are quantities of tiny flies on the water only the small trout will be feeding. Again, when not a rise is to be seen, good fish may be quite ready for business. However, the largest trout that I killed last year before the 1st of May were taken during a good rise of natural flies.

It is the constant—or inconstant—change, the infinite variety in fly-fishing that binds us fast. It is impossible to grow weary of a sport that is never the same on any two days in the year. I am fond of all sorts of fishing, in fresh or salt water, in the interior of the country, or on the coast, but trout angling takes a grip upon the imagination. It is more of a mental recreation than other methods. There is always something in question, something to discuss. In the mere matter of hooks alone there is much room for differences of opinion. Does anyone know the form of hook which is absolutely and always the best under all conditions for artificial flies? Sometimes I think I know, and then again I do not, and I have tried all of the forms known to manufacturers. Experience and skill will tell in the long run, but the element of chance plays a considerable part in angling. We can all remember instances when the tyro killed the best fish of the day. Many persons of limited experience think that all fishing is a matter of luck, and from this ancient belief arose the salutations, "Good luck" or "Good luck to you," and "What luck?" Good fortune is desirable in all our pursuits, and we have heard it said "that it is better to be born lucky than rich," but we have to attribute any marked success in fishing to skill and skill alone.

This is the reason why a few good trout killed under adverse conditions are fondly remembered after large baskets are forgotten. For instance, I often recollect the taking of three large fish one summer afternoon when the sun was bright and the water low. I please myself by fancying that not everyone could have caught those trout. The fly was one of my own patterns, dressed on a No. 14 hook, and this fact added to my pleasure, although it is quite possible that another fly tied by somebody else would have been quite as effective. The little ways that trout have are often quite puzzling and past finding out. An oval pool of fair depth in a small stream had been carefully fished on many occasions without stirring a fin until we happened along one day at about two of the clock. The first cast was rewarded by a rise and a large trout sprang into the air. This fish was extremely wild and thoroughly disturbed the pool, but we wished to investigate a little to see if it had companions. By crawling on hands and knees to the edge of a little bluff we were able to command the depths, as the light was just right, and were astonished by what we saw. My dear sir: there was a school of trout in that place—big fellows—at the upper end tapering away through various sizes down to little chaps on the shallows.

Two o'clock seemed to be their time for feeding. You might get one trout, possibly three, never more. I did not get a fish in the morning or late afternoon. A large tree stood upon the bank, and I fancied that there might be peculiar lights and shades over this bit of water.

One hundred yards lower down was a deep hole by a flat rock with quite a rush of water into it. The first time I saw the place my companion, who was in advance, declared that he had seen trout run up into it. He was right, but it was a long time before I was able to prove it. Then I killed two fish, one twelve inches, the other eighteen inches in length. We must not hasten to the conclusion that there are no trout simply because we cannot catch them. Big fish may haunt for years a large safe pool where there is good cover or hiding places for them.

Their presence may be known to many people who exert their best endeavors to catch them, but it is a long time before they are reduced to possession. I have heard that between dawn and sunrise was the best hours for a jumbo trout. I have always intended to try this recipe, but never did. It involves getting up in the middle of the night, and a long tramp on an empty stomach.

By the way, it will scarcely be believed, I saw a woodcock swim one day. There was no mistake about it. There was a long quiet reach of the stream with little current and I was standing in the water changing a fly. A big fat woodcock came out on the margin, and after walking about a little deliberately entered the water and oared itself across to the other side. I never saw a prettier sight, as the bird was not more than twenty feet away. I had stood like a statue from the moment it approached, and it paid no attention to me. Four woodcock were flushed during the day and a deer crashed away through the thick brush. We were very close, but were unable to catch a glimpse of the animal. The laurel was in bloom and the mountains exquisitely beautiful in the evening light, but O! the long drive in the darkness after we reached the valley. We were so overpowered by the slumber god that we almost fell out of the buggy. The man who drives is better off, as he has something to keep him at attention.

(*Forest and Stream,* August 8, 1908)
I wish there were more long, deep pools on these rivers. Trout soon become shy in quiet water and are harder to delude. Then the big pools hold fish through drouths and hot weather and serve as refuges for the large trout. The latter become wonderfully keen in the matter of self-protection. About ten years ago a wide, rather shallow pool on the Neversink held two enormous trout whose behavior was amusing and exasperating. They usually lay near the lower end, and by careful stalking might be approached within casting range. But drop a fly on the

water, be it ever so lightly, and they fled as if the devil was after them. They paid no attention to midges with finest drawn gut, but even these had to be very carefully manipulated. The slightest bungle in the cast and they were gone.

We fished for weeks that summer, trying to inveigle an old corker which was always at home and enjoying two bitter disappointments. The first time there was no barb on the hook and the second it lost its hold at the last moment, just when victory was about to perch upon our rod. The old sinner did not get scared and fatigue himself by wild rushes or leaps. He just kept away near the other shore, and at last allowed us to tow him slowly down stream. He looked fine sailing through the clear water, but it was not so agreeable to see him swimming slowly back to his hole, after he had recovered his liberty.

I always think of this trout as an "old he," but he may have been a she, and should have been described as an "it." The grammatical construction of fish stories is not always of the best.

(*Forest and Stream,* April 3, 1909)
Recently we have heard much talk of the dry fly and dry-fly fishing, and one would be inclined to fancy that this method of fly-fishing for trout was an art which had not been practiced to any extent in this country. As a matter of fact, it has been studied and utilized where the conditions favored that style of fishing by a great many American anglers. My attention was first seriously engaged soon after the publication of F. M. Halford's fine works in England. The first of these appeared, I think, in 1886, but the dry fly had been used successfully at least a quarter of a century earlier. In Thaddeus Norris' *American Angler,* published in Philadelphia about 1860, there is a description of dry-fly fishing on the Willowemoc, in Sullivan County. The water was low and quiet and Norris could do nothing with the flies commonly in use. His companion, however, tied two flies expressly for the occasion, and by using

a leader of the finest gut he was able to lay them so lightly upon the glassy surface of the stream that the trout rose and were hooked before the flies sank or were drawn away. The patterns used were the Grannon and Jenny Spinner.

Mr. Halford is a past master of his subject, but he writes more particularly for the benefit of English anglers whose field of action is found upon the placid chalk streams of the South of England. The practical lessons he teaches are most valuable, but require some adaptations when applied to the fishing of our mountain rivers.

The bacilli or microbe of the dry fly entered my system about the year 1889 or 1890 and the attack which followed was quite severe. I imported an English rod, dry flies, gossamer silkworm gut, and all other prescriptions which I presumed were necessary to effect a cure. From the first I caught trout, a few of them, but my success was not great. My rod and line were unnecessarily heavy and caused me great fatigue. I never fished "on spec," only for fish that were seen rising at natural flies. My first enthusiasm had waned considerably, when one afternoon I had a little experience that was of service. I was fishing down stream with two flies. The water was not very productive, but a long gliding run gave promise of sport. Casting over this in my best style from top to bottom I was favored with but one faint rise. Having an abundance of time, I sat down to meditate upon "the slings and arrows of outrageous fortune" and to watch the surface of the stream.

Presently two trout began rising within a yard of each other. I removed the stretcher fly and taking a little box of dry flies from my pocket I knotted one of these to the casting line in its place. As I expected to resume wet-fly fishing immediately, I allowed the dropper, a pet fly of my own make, to remain where it was. Now, this fly happened to be tied on a fine wired hook, while the dry fly was busked upon an eyed hook of heavier make. As I waded cautiously into position for those trout I kept the line in the air by a series of false casts and this process dried that old dropper fly thoroughly. The consequence was that it floated more cockily and attractively than the orthodox dry fly and was more attractive to the fish. In turn they passed by the tail fly and were hooked and killed by the dropper. Then a larger trout rose higher up the pool and that one also came to the basket. I could make my own dry flies, but decided not to make a habit of using two of them on the same casting line.

Since that experience I have tied my flies to suit the water and the season and have enjoyed excellent sport with dry fly, but have never abjured the wet fly and never expect to do so in the streams I usually fish nowadays. The wet fly often kills best; in fact, there are days when one may make a good basket fishing wet, yet would have little or no success with the dry fly. It is well to understand both methods and practice the one which pleases Master Speckles.

In dry-fly fishing it is usually advisable to fish upstream. There are exceptions, but this is the rule. Approach cautiously and get into position below your fish; or if you see no rise, the spot where you are confident a trout is lying in wait for your fly. Do not cast straight up, with the line over the trout's back, but from one side. Try to cast at an imaginary mark two feet above the surface of the water. Check the fly gently and allow it to fall of its own weight, from six inches to two feet above and in front of the fish. As the fly floats down with the current, recover line with the left hand. This takes in the slack and allows you to keep the rod in the best position for striking. If you get no rise this surplus line is shot through the rings on the next cast. If you hook a large trout this line will be taken out, probably on his first rush, and he can then be played from the reel. If too small for this the fish may be brought within reach with the left hand by taking in line. If a trout rises when you are casting a long line it will usually be necessary to raise the right hand and arm firmly in order to drive the hook into its mouth. With a short line, a gentle strike, the far-famed turn of the wrist is all that is required. For dry-fly fishing on our large mountain streams flies dressed on hooks numbered 16, 14, 12, 10 are satisfactory. The tiniest of midges may raise trout at times, but one will miss many fish when using such small hooks. Eyed hooks firmly knotted to the fine end of the leader by the Turle or outside figure-of-eight knot are very satisfactory, as one may use gut fine or stout.

If you find this process annoying, have your dry flies dressed on snelled hooks or take time on an off day when the light is good to tie short snells to your eyed flies. I confess that I find it exasperating to endeavor to tie on midges in a bad light. One great advantage which eyed flies possess is that a considerable number can be carried in a small box. Do not put wet flies in this box or allow water to drop into it. This spoils the set of the hackles for a time and also the appearance of the flies.

Begin your dry-fly fishing where the water flows steadily, but gently. Not on a rapid. A nice little ripple on the water from a light breeze will be in your favor. It is difficult to place your fly without a slight splash on absolutely still pools and even a fine leader is very conspicuous. You will be surprised to find that our trout soon become wise to the dry fly in quiet pools. Baffling currents, dragging flies, and many other difficulties will confront the angler, but he will conquer them all. A touch of oil, kerosene will do, will assist flotation and save fatigue. In all fly-fishing, the wet and the dry, we are constantly learning something, and this we fancy is the secret of the infinite charm which the sport possesses. If the trout will not take your dry fly, try a wet fly, or wet the dry one. If they fail to appreciate the wet dry fly, skim or bob your dropper fly. Try every known method, but always stick to the artificial fly.

(*Forest and Stream,* March 22, 1913)
A typical English dry-fly rod has been sent to me to try—not a rod made for America, but the sort that those English dry-fly men prefer who will not use an American rod. It is most interesting to compare its action with the actions of fine Leonard and Payne dry-fly rods, and it shall have the fairest possible trial. It certainly balances remarkably well, and most careful attention has evidently been paid to all details. It was built under the supervision of a master of the floating fly and was tried by half a dozen others who all approved of it, considering the action correct. Of course a line must be chosen to suit it, and I have on hand F, E and D. There is more cane in the top than in a fine American rod, and I fancy that only Tonquin cane will give the great stiffness and

resiliency attained by makers such as Leonard in joints of small diameter. The tournament rods have extraordinary power with least weight, and a good few Englishmen prefer them for chalk stream fishing. This occasioned a great controversy some years ago, which, without doubt, led to considerable alterations and improvements being made in English fly rods.

Lovers of the Neversink will be disgusted to learn that a sawmill has been moved up to the "Big Bend," one of the refuges for large trout during low water and drouths. Every stick of timber down to six inches in diameter will be cut, and it is reported that the sawdust will be disposed of in the stream. I can scarcely believe that this is true. No river in the country has such lovely "white" water as the Neversink, and in spite of damage by floods and wood chopping, it is still one of the most beautiful of our large streams. A good number of the best native anglers and landowners have put in applications for fingerling trout, and these will be distributed carefully, and to the greatest possible advantage.

Nowadays the best sportsmen think of putting trout in as well as taking them out, and endeavor to provide for the future and the younger generation of anglers. We do not wish to kill great numbers of trout, but to be able to find a few fish of size and quality, which will require a little skill and afford exciting sport—the kind that one is pleased to show and that present a handsome appearance when served upon the table.

The best anglers are apt to go where there is at least a chance of hooking a really big trout, and at present a good many fishermen are a bit uncertain where they will first wet their lines this season. I have fished the Ulster and Sullivan county streams so frequently of recent years that I feel some little inclination for the unknown or to return to streams that I have not seen for years. I found an old photograph of my first camp in the Maine wilderness recently and it recalled many delightful memories, but I shall probably put my trust in one of the hard-fished streams in New York or Pennsylvania, where there are no black flies or midges. One becomes attached to certain waters, and I notice that men come from all directions and from places far away to fish these old streams which have been celebrated for fifty years or more. They are associated with the names of nearly every well-known angler who flourished during the nineteenth century and have furnished sport for many thousand fishermen. One thinking of speculative changes usually remembers that he may go further and fare worse. Undoubtedly there is much first-rate dry-fly fishing within 200 miles of New York City, which is not well known or much exploited.

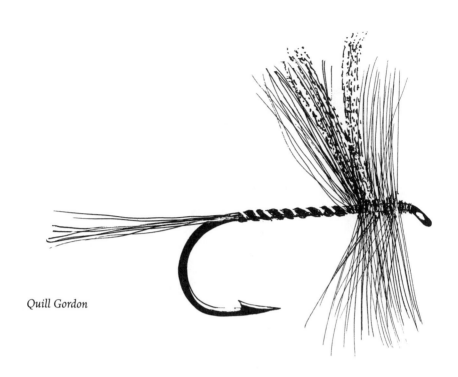

Quill Gordon

Conditions of the Life of Trout

EDWARD RINGWOOD HEWITT

The Ancients wrote of the three ages of man; I propose to write of the three ages of the fisherman.

When he wants to catch all the fish he can.

When he strives to catch the largest fish.

When he studies to catch the most difficult fish he can find, requiring the greatest skill and most refined tackle, caring more for the sport than the fish.

The first age is always true of the beginner, the second during the most vigorous part of life, while the third occurs in the more mature years. The pleasures derived at this later age may be even greater than during earlier life. Unfortunately few fish long enough to reach and enjoy this last age. I have known many of ripe years who have never passed the first two ages of the fisherman.

(From the "Preface" to *A Trout and Salmon Fisherman for Seventy-Five Years*)

The conditions under which trout exist are quite different from those of animals living in air, and they must be understood in order to get any clear idea of why they grow and thrive or fail and die. Few fishermen I have talked to have given this subject any serious study, as they are mostly interested in the fishing itself and not what makes it good or bad. It took me many years to gather enough information from all sources so that I felt that I had secured some understanding of the conditions of a trout's life. I will give the reader a short account of what I think are the most important points.

Trout, like all living animals, require oxygen, and they get this from that which is dissolved in the water they live in. They pass this water over their gills by the motion of the mouth and gill covers continually, so that the dissolved oxygen in the water can be allowed to diffuse through the thin membranes covering the gills within which the blood is circulating. The oxygen is taken up by the red corpuscles of the blood and carried to all parts of the body. The conditions under which this process can take place have very definite limits, beyond which it fails and the fish die. It is important to know these limits so that the fisherman can comprehend what goes on in the lives of the fish he fishes for.

Trout do best when the dissolved oxygen exceeds 6 parts per million. They die when it is 2.5 parts. Their death is more rapid at higher than at lower temperatures, because their metabolism is faster. The oxygen in water varies, if it is saturated, with the temperature and the pressure. Under natural conditions it rarely exceeds twelve parts per million and in most ordinary trout streams runs from eight to ten parts for most of the season. A very high oxygen content does not appear to be injurious to trout, but I have noticed in my hatchery that trout do not do so well when it is below 6 parts per million. Trout will avoid waters where the oxygen is 4 parts per million if they can find a better place to live. In operating a hatchery I would not want lower oxygen in the water than 6 parts at any time, if I expected to raise healthy fish, as the organic matter in the bottom of trout pools from the waste food and excrement consumes much oxygen. I noticed, in a pool twenty feet square having a water flow of sixty gallons a minute, that when the pool contained 500 pounds of trout, the oxygen was reduced from 8 parts per million to 6, while passing through. A fall of a foot over a board weir only added 1 part of oxygen to the water, but when the weir was made with a sharp saw tooth edge, the teeth of which were two inches across, I found that the oxygen was increased almost 2 parts by a single fall. With pools in series it is easily seen that the oxygen may become progressively reduced so that the water of the lower pools may be too low in oxygen. This matter must be carefully watched in any hatchery. With clean pools the oxygen consumption is much less, but the removal of the organic matter also greatly reduces the amount of insect life grown in the pool, and this is most necessary to supply adequate vitamins to the fish. I must say that I have had much better trout growth and healthier fish in pools which were left dirty than in those I kept clean.

Water temperatures have the greatest effect on trout life and the range they can stand is not very wide. Trout will live in water at 32 degrees F., but their metabolism is very much slowed up and they are not active, so they require very little food at this temperature. I have known them to live for five months with little loss of weight, although they had no food during this time. Digestion seems to be very much slowed up at these low temperatures. Observation of trout fed in this cold water on meat foods showed that some of the food was still in the stomach after two weeks, indicating that their digestion had almost stopped. In fact, I have known trout to be killed by a heavy feeding in cold water because the food would actually decay in the stomach before it could be digested. The law governing the digestion of food by the pepsin of the trout's stomach seems to be that the rapidity of digestion doubles for each increase of ten degrees F. At 42 degrees they seem to digest a meal in about five days, as my observation shows. At 52 degrees they seem to digest in about 24 hours and at 62 degrees in about 12 hours. The most rapid digestion appears to be at 66 degrees F. Above that they slack off and cease to eat at about 70 degrees F. This shows that the temperatures where trout digest well range from about 48 to 66 degrees F. and these are the temperatures where the fisherman can expect to have good fishing. On either side of this range his chances of having any sport are very much worse. Of course, it may depend on whether the trout have empty stomachs or not when he presents his lure.

Brook trout have been reported not to stand temperatures of over 72 degrees, but this depends somewhat on the amount of dissolved oxygen in the water. If the water is saturated, they may stand up to 78 degrees for half a day or even a day, but they would eventually die at this temperature, probably under any conditions. A few hours above 72 degrees in oxygen-saturated water will not hurt brook trout. Brown trout and rainbows can stand 78 degrees fairly well, and I have seen them alive at 80 degrees for a day or so, but they would die at this temperature if continued over a long time. This is one of the many reasons why the brown trout has supplanted the brook trout in so many of our streams where the water temperatures have increased over what they were some years ago, due to cutting down the shade trees over the streams and to some extent the reduction of the volume of spring waters feeding the streams.

It is perhaps fortunate that trout are not so likely to take a lure when they are full fed and that they take so long to digest a meal, otherwise the first fisherman to run across a trout would be almost sure to catch him and few would be left for others who follow. We must, of course, realize that trout take the lures offered to them for two reasons: first, because they are hungry and want food, and second, because they become excited at the motion or color of the lure and strike at it. This is what I call impressionistic fishing, where the fish is not hungry, but takes the lure due to some exciting brain impression. Trout will often do this with a full stomach, when they cannot be hungry; many times this is the most effective way to fish for trout.

The blood of all animals must remain at a certain pH for the life of that particular animal. The blood of trout is almost exactly pH 7.2. If it should drop below this figure and the blood become acid, the fish would die from acidosis. This proposes a rather difficult problem to solve, because all the blood of the trout passes through the capillaries of the gills continually and is exposed to the circulating water, being divided from it only by a very thin membrane through which ions can readily diffuse. Why then, when water is acid, does the blood not become acid and the trout die? I put this problem up to a number of physiologists without getting any satisfactory answer from them. However, I have recently secured an explanation of this from Dr. Gifford Pinchot which seems to answer the riddle. The blood passing the gills covered by acid water is made acid, but this blood goes at once to the kidneys, which make ammonia compounds from the proteins of the food which are used to neutralize this acid, and maintain the blood at the normal pH 7.2 point. The kidney is the regulator of the blood acidity. I found that trout will avoid waters of pH 5.8 if possible, and will soon die in waters of pH 5.2. This shows that their ability to neutralize the acidity of the blood which is made acid in the gills is limited, and that they cannot do it beyond pH 5.2. It seems evident that this process involves the consumption of considerable energy on the part of the trout, because it is universally found that trout never grow as rapidly, or as large, in acid waters as they do in alkaline waters. In order to make sure of this I tested the water of a number of hatcheries where the growth of trout was well known and had been observed for years. The following list shows what I found and makes clear that the composition of the water has a marked effect on trout growth.

A further proof that acid waters exert a serious effect on trout is given by the fact that when trout are suddenly moved from alkaline waters to acid waters they are generally seriously affected by the change. If it is great in amount, and the trout are small, they may all be killed by the change.

The state of trout waters tested parts per million

	Lime		
Places of Fast Trout Growth	Oxygen	CO_2	as CAO pH
Bellefonte Hatchery, PA.	8.4	9.9	136	7.8
Cortland Hatchery, Cortland, N.Y.	8.9	7.7	76	7.8
J. M. Cook, Johnsville, N.Y.	9.4	3.3	70	7.4
Ed. Cumings, MI.	9.2	2.2	123	8.2
John Rhinesmith, Midvale, N.J.	10.8	4.4	28	7.3
Ph. Staats, Kent, CT.		1.1	93	7.7
E. W. Surber, Kearneysville, W. VA.	8.6	35.0	170	7.0
N. J. State Hatchery, Hackettstown, N.J.	9.2	6.6	77.7	7.7
Places of Moderate Trout Growth				
Windsor Locks, Conn., State Hatchery	10.2	5.5	33.6	7.0
Conneli Ponds on Neversink River		5.5	11.2	6.1
Tuxedo Hatchery, Tuxedo, N.Y.	5.8	12.0	25	6.4
Montagu, MA., State Hatchery			8.4	6.9
Sunderland, MA., State Hatchery			8.4	7.0
Neversink River at Hewitt's Camp:				
Above dam	8.25	2.2	8.4	6.7
Below dam	8.90	2.2	8.4	6.7
Conkling Brook, Hewitt's Camp, Neversink River	8.8	2.2	11.2	6.8
New Hatchery, Hewitt's Camp, Neversink River	11.4	1.1	11.2	7.4
Upper Willowemoc River, above Willowemoc, N.Y.		5.5	11.2	6.8
Places of Slow Trout Growth				
Blooming Grove Club Hatchery, July 15th			11.0	6.0
Same, November 27th	10.2	12.1	24.5	6.3
Hewitt's Camp water supply (fatal to trout) . . .	5.1	15.0	19.0	5.8
Eden Hatchery	8.0	14.3	11.2	6.0
Spring at Hewitt's Camp (bad trout growth and health)	5.3	14.3	16.	6.0
Peekamoose Creek, at Morrell's	8.8	2.6	8.4	6.6
Jenney Brook Hatchery, Napanoch, N.Y.		8.6	5.5	6.6

Pennsylvania moved sixty thousand small trout from alkaline water to a hatchery with acid waters, and they all died in twenty-four hours. I, myself, have had this trouble with trout several times. Evidently it may take some time for trout to get into working order the mechanism by which the acid blood is regulated. With larger trout the effect is not so marked as with young fish. Pennsylvania now has all its streams recorded as to acidity and alkalinity so that no trout grown in alkaline waters will be placed in acid waters. Trout raised in acid waters can be put in alkaline waters without danger.

The dissolved carbonic acid in the water can be a very important element in the life of trout. Where the lime salts are low in the water and all the carbonic acid is present in the form of free acid, I have found that it cannot exceed 14 parts per million without disastrous effects on trout. But when there are ample lime salts in the water, the carbonic acid is then present as bicarbonate, and in this case it can reach the amount of 35 parts per million without injuring trout, but in this case the eggs of some kinds of trout will not hatch. I have a spring at my camp which feeds a fair-sized trout pool. I found that trout could winter in this pool but that they died in summer although the water was still cool. By testing I found that the carbonic acid was about 8 parts per million during the winter but rose to 14 to 15 parts during the summer. This change was finally found to be due to the carbonic acid which came out of the roots of the forest trees during the summer, when the trees were in leaf. As soon as the leaves went off, the carbonic acid dropped. A limestone filter in the water running to this pool enabled me to carry trout all the year. In examining waters to raise trout it is important to take the carbonic acid into account.

Lime salts in trout waters are most important for growth, as it is thought that trout get the lime for their skeletons from the water they are in, rather than from their food. It is certain that waters high in lime salts grow larger and stronger trout, although this might be due to more food or the alkalinity of the water. Schleperclaus in his *Lehrbuch der Teichwirtschaft* gives his conclusions on the lime salts in fish waters. He says that from 2.8 to 14 parts per million of lime, calculated as calcium oxide, gives a low biological activity and low fish yield; from 14 to 56 parts per million, a medium fish yield, and from 56 to 140 parts per million, a high fish yield. My experience would tend to confirm this estimate. We can't expect high fish yields of trout in waters low in lime salts. The Catskill streams run from 8 to 10 parts per million in lime salts and are too low for best trout growth.

The injurious effect of sewage on trout waters is due almost entirely to the consequent consumption of the oxygen in the water, although, of course, chemical pollution of any kind will kill trout. Domestic sewage may not injure a stream although I know of several which it has ruined. At Tuxedo Park, years ago, the sewage used to empty into the Warwick Brook at a long, deep pool near the outlet from the Park. I used to fish this pool every spring and get a number of very fine large trout from it. While it is not pleasant to eat trout grown in sewage water, they are not injurious, as the sewage does not get into the flesh of the fish. At another place, in the Willowemoc, at Parkston, there is a sewer emptying into the bottom of the stream where there are almost always good trout to be caught. The sewage of the town of Liberty, N.Y., although it passes through a filter bed, has greatly injured the stream it empties into. If domestic sewage is not sufficient to consume an appreciable amount of the oxygen in the water, it may greatly increase the insect life in the stream, due to the organic matter it supplies.

These facts may serve to explain puzzling observations by fishermen on trout streams. In warm, summer weather when air temperatures may reach from 85 to 90 degrees F., it is often found that trout will bite well until noon, while in the afternoon they cease entirely and fail to rise even in the evening. This is because the water has warmed up during the day to a point beyond that at which trout care to feed. When the sun goes down, temperatures drop unless there is hot air coming in from some other place and the water slowly cools during the night. By morning the water in a wooded area will have cooled down ten or twelve degrees and be just right for trout to bite well, as they did not eat during the time the water was too warm. Quite often very good trout fishing can be had in the early mornings in hot weather. In such weather I go fishing only in the morning if I want to get fish and not just exercise.

I am often asked about tables or calendars which claim to indicate good fishing times by reference to phases of the sun and moon, and whether they are of value in indicating good times to fish. I always answer this in one way. They are of no value whatever as a prediction of good fishing periods. The times they indicate may, of course, and often

do, tell when the fishing is going to be good, but this is not on account
of any gravimetric pull by the sun or moon; it is because they happen
to correspond with the times fish do bite well anyway. I tested these
tables out most carefully myself and found no regular correlation whatever between them and the times fish bite. The same results have been
reported from other really careful tests I have heard of being made. This
is so because the gravimetric pull due to the moon, or the sun and moon
combined, is of very small amount, of the order of a fraction of a mil-
limeter of mercury pressure. If anyone will watch a barometer for any
considerable time, almost any day, he will notice changes in the pressure
of the air of the order of from one to several millimeters of mercury
every little while which are due to the winds, probably, and are many
times as great as anything made by the sun and moon. The barometer
has much more effect on the biting of trout than any "Solunar pull" can
ever have. Water temperatures as described above also greatly influence
the feeding of fish, as do the periodic hatches of the insects of the stream.
Many of these occur at certain dates, independent of any weather. I
have seen them in a snowstorm, with fish rising all over the water. The
Solunar Tables are for the fisherman and not for the fish.

Under the heading "Solunacy," the *Salmon and Trout Magazine* published in its issue of January, 1947, the following comment on this
theory, which is reproduced by permission of the copyright owners:

"It is curious how belief in this exploded theory persists. Records of
the rise in the Houghton Club's water are sufficient to show that it does
not work over here. Yet surely a feeding theory dependent on the moon
cannot be confined to the American Continent? Is it that the 'periods' (two
major and two minor) cover so much of the twenty-four hours that it is
difficult for the rise to avoid coinciding with one of them? Or is it simply
that this is the only country where records are available by which the
theory can be checked, and that consequently the credulous are inclined to
treat the chance coincidence as a result of the moon's attraction?"

The production of trout in streams will, of course, vary greatly with
the type of stream, the character of the water, and the kind of bottom,
stony streams and those with aquatic vegetation being the most productive of fish when the minerals in the water are of the right type and

amount. Many studies have been made of the weight of trout grown in streams, which show that it may vary from 30 pounds per year to the acre of water, down to as little as 6 pounds in poor streams. Narrow streams produce far more fish per acre than wide streams because the larger part of the fish food grows close to the banks of the streams. A growth of 15 pounds of trout per acre per year might be regarded as a fair average amount of trout grown in most streams. If the fish were removed when they weighed ¼ pound this would mean sixty fish per acre or, when they weighed ½ pound, thirty fish per acre. When we consider the length of an acre of stream of various widths it works out as follows:

Width of Stream	Length of One Acre	Mile Length per Acre
10 Feet	4400 Feet	.83 Mile
25 Feet	1760 Feet	.33 Mile
50 Feet	880 Feet	.16 Mile
100 Feet	440 Feet	.08 Mile

This means that a stream 5 miles long and 10 feet wide would furnish only 6 acres of water and 90 pounds of trout, or 180 half-pound trout.

A stream five miles long and 25 feet wide could furnish 15.1 acres of water and 226 pounds of trout, or 452 half-pound trout.

A stream five miles long and 50 feet wide could furnish 452 pounds of trout or 904 half-pound trout.

A stream five miles long and 100 feet wide would furnish 904 pounds of trout or 1,808 half-pound trout.

This shows clearly why our waters are fished out so easily when they are of the type where all the fish caught must grow in the stream itself. Many streams fortunately do not rely entirely on the trout produced in the stream itself for their entire fish supply. Often there are big areas downstream from where the fishing takes place that also grow trout, which run up into the stream during the fishing season. It is these migrating trout which have given the fishermen the impression that far more trout are produced in a stream than is really the case.

Where stocking has been practiced by Fish Commissions it has been shown that only a very small part of the trout put out are usually caught by fishermen unless the fish stocked are of catchable size, and are put in the stream shortly before or during the fishing season. When this is the case, as much as 80 percent of such fish may be caught by fishermen. The longer the period elapsing between the stocking of the fish and the actual fishing for them, the fewer will be taken. My own experience on the Neversink led me to do my stocking every week or two weeks, putting in the fish a few at a time. In this way by far the larger number stocked were taken by my anglers. This method is, of course, absolutely impractical for Fish Commissions to adopt, as they could not possibly make the necessary deliveries of the fish. The State of New Jersey employs forty trucks for delivering fish from its Hackettstown Hatchery and there are no streams stocked more than 150 miles from the hatchery and the bulk of the waters lie within much closer distances. In states of larger area, such as New York or Pennsylvania, the distances are too great and the mileage of streams too large for such effective stocking as is done in New Jersey.

Where the bags of the fishermen have been investigated through the whole season in many states, it is always found that by far the larger part of the fish caught come from the natural reproduction of the streams themselves. Hatchery trout which have survived the fishing season and lived to the next spring are invariably thin and in poor condition so far as I have been able to observe. They generally do spawn in the fall of the year they are put out and in this way add to the fish in the streams, but they do not furnish any good fishing the second year even if they do survive the winter.

There is only one answer to making better trout fishing for everyone and that is to reduce the number of fish each fisherman takes per day and season. As trout caught can be returned to the water with very small loss of fish, the fishermen can catch their fish, return them to the water, and have them to catch another day. I believe that four fish a day for a fisherman to take home is enough. All the rest should be returned to the water. With our present New York State limit of ten fish this would give potentially two and a half times as good fishing as we now have with no additional work. This is the only answer to better fishing.

I have been studying these problems for the last twenty-five years and have had every opportunity to experiment on my own waters. I am perfectly certain that good or even passable trout fishing through a season can be obtained in no other way.

The improvement of streams in various ways can add greatly to the carrying and productive capacity of trout waters. We scarcely yet know just how much greater output of trout we can get by making our streams better homes for them. From my own experience I would guess that the output of trout per mile of stream, as streams are today, can be doubled, but this involves the expenditure of much money, and the upkeep of stream improvements will also prove a heavy annual expense, because all streams are subject to freshets, at times, which may damage some of the stream structures. It is most difficult to make these stream improvements permanent, without running the cost up beyond what is practical. However, improvements of moderate cost, together with suitable provision for good winter quarters for the trout, can be made to double the trout grown in most of our streams at present. If this is done, and the daily bag reduced to four fish a day per fisherman, we might easily have five times as many trout to catch as we now have, and this would help greatly to provide some sport for the ever-increasing numbers of trout fishermen.

I have now had over twenty-five years' experience in stocking all kinds of trout in the Neversink River. They have been raised in every conceivable way—in hatchery pools which were kept strictly clean, in pools which were not kept clean, in ponds where the fish got limited amounts of insect foods. I have fed the fish all sorts of diets and put them out in normal condition and also much fatter than normal. I have watched these fish during the season and also caught them the following spring and the year following that. I have secured fish from numbers of other hatcheries for stocking. I can truthfully say that I have never stocked any fish in the Neversink, except wild fish grown on natural diets, that did not lose weight more or less rapidly during the season, and were thin the following spring and in bad condition, without making any growth. I do not believe we can grow hatchery fish which will make good long-lived stream fish unless we feed them largely their own natural diets and give them plenty of room in the water, without any crowding. Trout must be fed on the minute organisms in early life which are natural for them, or they never learn to feed on these foods. Without these microscopic foods they never get enough food to grow well in wild streams.

Many anglers have seen large trout leap for small white or yellow butterflies and have been unable to interest these trout in any fly they could present to them. It became evident to me that large winged flies in some way did not appear like butterflies to the trout, and they therefore ignored them. I studied this problem carefully and came to the following conclusions. The butterflies did not rest on the water; they sometimes touched it but were always moving. When they did touch the water they only did so very lightly and were away again. I could not imitate this procedure with any flies I had in my box. How was I to do this? I went back to my camp and tied several flies, finally making what is known now as the Neversink Skater. This was tied on a No. 16 light Model Perfect hook, which is the lightest hook I know that will hold a big trout. The big fly was tied as a hackle and not a winged fly because large winged flies do not cast well on the fine leaders which it is necessary to use in large, still pools. The fly had no tail, because this would interfere with its movement over the surface of the water. It was tied sparsely because I wanted it to cast easily and not have too much air resistance. It was made as large in diameter as possible, with the longest hackles I had. The outside diameter of some of these flies was two inches while some were slightly smaller. Even then, they were really not as large as the butterflies the fish were taking.

When I had completed some flies which I thought worth trying, I went down to the river to a pool where I knew there were a number of large trout. I wanted to make a fly which would take them at any time of day because I had seen them jump for butterflies at all times, and they would take the right fly if I could make one. My first attempts were made right in the middle of a sunny day in July. I found it most difficult to cast these large flies until I used enough line to supply sufficient energy in the cast to propel the fly forward when the line was checked in the air. As soon as I got out about forty feet of line the fly cast easily and well, and could be made to alight on the water like a feather and be jumped and dragged over the surface without getting wet or going under. It ought, therefore, to make an impression on the fish similar to a butterfly.

When I had perfected my casting so that I thought I could manage the fly reasonably well, I tried the pool in which the large fish were concealed under a ripple of current among larger stones, where the water was perhaps thirty inches deep. When the fly had made only two jumps over the water, a large trout of about four pounds leaped out of the water right over the fly like a porpoise and missed it entirely, and before it had time to come again a smaller trout repeated the maneuver. Neither fish touched the fly at all. I had enough sense to rest these fish and move lower down where there should be other fish. This time another big trout jumped for the fly, and I just touched it without hooking it. This showed they were not playing but wanted the fly. If the fly were fished well, it was evident they could be caught.

I wanted someone else to see this sport, so I left my rod and returned to my camp to get my son, who was taking a midday nap. The fly was then cast in the same place as at first, but drawn more slowly to give the fish more time. This time, when the trout rose, it took the fly solidly and was landed after the usual playing. Then my son claimed a try, as he was sure he could do this stunt. He also jumped two fish before he landed one. We kept on in this same run for an hour, to see if this method of surface fishing would put these trout down, or whether they would fail to be scared by this kind of fishing. The latter proved to be the case, and only bungled casts scared the fish. We caught six large trout in this run, right in the middle of the day, and hooked one more. Next day these same fish rose again as if nothing had happened. This would certainly not be the case with any other method of trout fishing I know. After fishing out this run we tried under my dams and found that the big trout would come out from under them and even take these flies in the white water. We also found that this type of fishing is effective in big, still pools, although it is much harder here to make the fly move properly on the surface than where there is a slight current. I had developed a way of dry-fly fishing which would raise and hook large trout in all kinds of water at almost any time of day. This seemed to me to be a real advance in fly-fishing.

One will ask, why not use this way of fishing all the time? The answer to this question is simple. Only the larger trout are effectively caught by this method, and in most streams there are so few large trout that one might fish long distances without raising or seeing a fish. Besides, casting a long line with upraised rod and jumping the fly is very tiring to the arm and one cannot do it for long together. Also, this method requires at all times a fairly long cast and many places in a stream are only suitable for short casting. I only use this type of fishing where the water is right and where I have good reason to think there are larger trout. Ten- or twelve-inch trout will jump at this fly, but it is so large that it is difficult to hook them. Another reason for not using this method of fishing continually is that these Skater flies become damp after a time, and when this occurs they will not stay on top of the water and move properly, and have to be carefully dried and set right or a new fly put on. They certainly are not a durable fly.

I use these Skater flies of several colors and find that one kind is better at one time and place, and at another time a different pattern is better. I carry them tied as a Divisible, brown with white wisp at the head, white, cream-colored, and badger, gray with black center, and all brown. I think I prefer the cream color and the Divisible to the others.

I find that few fishermen can cast well enough to fish this fly properly although I have taught a number of people to do it, and some of my friends swear by this fly and believe it is the best ever made. It certainly will raise more large fish than any other dry fly. You won't find it on sale in any tackle stores, as few suitable feathers are available.

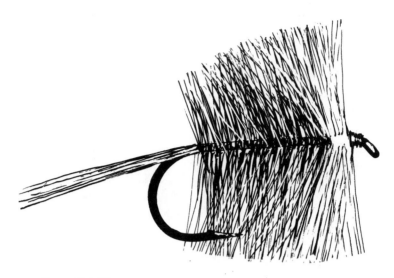

Brown Bivisible

The Point of View

George M. L. La Branche

The capture of a splendid ouananiche under circumstances most trying is somewhere described by a well-known writer, who, in his inimitable style, exhibits himself before his readers running through his entire assortment of artificial flies, first one and then another and still another, and all without avail. We see him casting, casting, all impatience, determined, perhaps exasperated. Surely some sort of lure is predicated. But what? Ah, he has it! A live grasshopper. Then follows the pursuit, the overtaking, and the capture of the grasshopper, the impaling of its unfortunate body, its proffer to the fish, a desperate battle, and, finally, the contemplation of the finest fish of the season safely landed. The thrilling moment! Which was it? Why, of all moments, that one in which he captured the grasshopper! The story affords a fine illustration of what I call the "point of view," but until after the revelation that came to me with my first success with the dry fly, I did not fully appreciate its finer and deeper meanings.

Certain pleasurable excitement always attends the taking of a good fish by the true angler. Yet, after all, the quality of his gratification should be measured by the method of capture. In angling, as in all other arts, one's taste and discrimination develop in proportion to his opportunity to see, study, and admire the work of greater artists. Even as a knowledge of the better forms of music leads, eventually, to a distaste for the poorer sorts, and as familiarity with the work of great painters leads to disgust with the chromolithograph-like productions of the dauber, so, too, does a knowledge of the higher and more refined sorts of angling lead just as surely to the ultimate abandonment of the grosser methods. One who has learned to cast the fly seldom if ever returns to the days when he was content to sit upon the bank, or the string-piece of a pier, dangling his legs overboard while he watched his cork bobbing up and down, indicating by its motions what might be happening to the bunch of worms at the hook end of the line; and, even as casting the fly leads to the abandonment of the use of bait, so, too, does the dry fly lead to the abandonment of the wet or sunk fly. There can be no question but that the stalking of a rising trout bears to the sport of angling the same relation to its grosser forms as the execution of a symphony bears to the blaring of the local brass band. It appeals to the higher and more aesthetic qualities of the mind, and dignifies the pot-hunter's business into an art of the highest and finest character.

I am thus brought to the consideration of the pot-hunter and the fish hog. Many angling writers there be who have not hesitated, nor have they been ashamed, to describe the taking of great numbers of trout on separate and many occasions. They feel, no doubts that such narratives entitle them to consideration as authorities on the subject. I quote from one—who shall be nameless—his bragging description of a perfect slaughter of fish. After telling of twenty-five or thirty trout taken during midday, naming at least a dozen flies he had found killing, he concludes: "All my trout were taken from the hook and thrown twenty-five feet to shore. Thirty, my friend claimed, yet when I came to count tails I found forty as handsome trout as ever man wished to see, and all caught from six in the evening until dark, about seven forty-five. I had no net or creel, therefore had to lead my trout into my hand. The friend at whose house I was staying claims I lost more than I caught by having them flounder off the hook while trying to take them by the gills and by flinging them ashore." And this fellow had the temerity to add that some poor devil (an itinerant parson, he called him) annoyed him by wading in and fishing with a "stick cut from the forest." Had Washington Irving witnessed this fellow's fishing I doubt that he would have been moved to write: "There is certainly something in angling that tends to produce a gentleness of spirit and a pure serenity of mind."

There are men calling themselves anglers!—save the mark—who limit the number of fish to the capacity of creel and pockets, and to whom size means merely compliance with the law—a wicked law, at that, which permits the taking of immature trout. It is not an inspiring sight to see a valiant angler doing battle with a six-inch trout, and, after brutally subjecting it to capture, carefully measuring it on the butt of his rod which he has marked for the purpose, stretching it, if necessary, to meet the law's requirements, and in some cases, if it does not come up to the legal standard, rudely flinging it away in disgust—to die as a result of its mishandling. Happily, this tribe is not increasing, because of the persistent efforts of true sportsmen who do not hesitate to denounce it publicly whenever opportunity arises. Perhaps it is permissible to hope that the pot-hunter and the fish hog may in time disappear, but, if this desirable end is to be brought about, true sportsmen must not shun their duty but must wage unceasing war against them.

Books on angling abound in word-pictures descriptive of the strenuous battle of the hooked fish to escape its captor, many such pictures being so vividly drawn that the reader fairly imagines himself in the writer's waders, his excitement ending only when the captive is in the net. It is meet, therefore, that some consideration be given to the point of view of those anglers who believe that great merit attaches to him who lands a good fish on light tackle.

There can be no question of the excitement attending the playing of a good trout nor of the skill required in its handling, and this excitement, in proportion to the ideas of the individual, is a greater or less measure of the sport; but, given the opportunity, it is my opinion that, in the hands of a skilful angler, the rod will kill nine out of ten fish hooked. Be that as it may, can the degree of skill, even with the lightest tackle, displayed in the landing of a two- or three-pound trout (a fine fish on our Eastern streams) bear comparison with that required in the capture of a six-foot tarpon on a six-ounce rod and six-strand line? A six-foot tarpon will weigh about 120 pounds, and the line will bear a dead-weight strain of 12 pounds. Compare this with the three-pound trout taken on a gut leader, the weakest link in the angler's chain, which will lift a weight of two or more pounds, and the futility of beguiling one-self with the belief that the trout has any advantage will be apparent.

The playing of a trout is undeniably part of the sport, but, however difficult one wishes to make it, it is but secondary to the pleasure derived from casting the fly and deluding that old trout into mistaking it for a bit of living food. It is this art, this skill, this study of the fish itself and its habits, that places dry-fly fishing for trout far ahead of all other forms of angling. It has been said that there is no sport that requires in its pursuit a greater knowledge of the game, more skill, more perseverance, than fly-fishing, and that no sport holds its votaries longer. I am quite of this opinion. "There is no genuine enjoyment in the easy achievement of any purpose," and in fly-fishing a full measure of satisfaction is obtained only when the taking of a single fish is accomplished under conditions most difficult and trying.

The true angler is content only when he feels that he has taken his fish by the employment of unusual skill. The highest development of this skill at the present state of the angler's art is the dry-fly method. I do not deny that there are many anglers who have carried sunk fly and even worm casting to a high degree of specialisation and refinement; yet It seems to me—nay, more than that, it is a positive conviction with me—that no manner of sunk fly or worm or bait casting bears any sort of favourable comparison to the manner of the dry fly. I know that in this country, at least, the dry-fly man is accused by his sunk-fly fellows of being affected, dogmatic, fanatic. Yet it is not so. The dry-fly man has passed through all of the stages of the angler's life, from the cane pole and the drop-line to the split bamboo and the fur-and-feather counterfeit of the midge fly. He has experienced throes of delight each time he advanced from the lower to the higher grade of angler. I insist that I do not make my words too strong when I say that in all of angling there is no greater delight than that which comes to the dry-fly angler who simulates a hatch of flies, and entices to the surface of the water a fish lying hidden, unseen, in the stronghold of his own selection. Let him who doubts put aside his prejudice long enough to give the premier method fair trial, and soon he will be found applying for the highest degree of the cult—"dry-fly man."

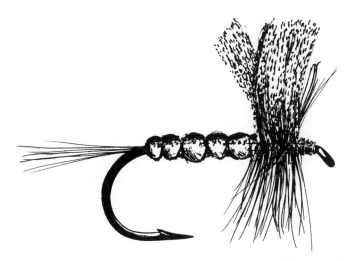

Bridgeville Olive

Sunshine and Shadow

RAY BERGMAN

This experience took place on the Neversink River at Oakland, New York. When we got there a green May fly hatch was in progress, aud although we tried all sorts of patterns, including all the colors of natural fowl and some dyed, we couldn't take a trout until we put on a fly made with mottled, light-green wings, light blue-gray hackles, and a succulent-looking whitish-colored body. On the same stretch seven days later we had a similar experience with a hatch of bluish-gray flies. In this instance two flies produced, and they were quite different in appearance from our standpoint—the Badger Bivisible and the Light Hendrickson. However, the Light Hendrickson proved most consistent, taking three fish to every one taken by the Badger. This was logical and consistent, as the fly on the water resembled the Hendrickson and not the Bivisible. Therefore it should have been better.

Under certain conditions trout do not see clearly. What the conditions are we shall now investigate. Bear in mind that this is theory although it has been applied to actual fishing, and as far as the writer is concerned it aids considerably in bringing success. But let us start at the beginning.

"Trout are selective to color and shape in inverse ratio to the intensity of light." In other words trout are more selective in the early morning and in the evening and on dark days than they are when the sun is shining brightly on the water. For this reason, if the trout will feed at all during the middle of the day, then a bright day will be the best sort of a day on which to fool them.

Before you rise up in arms over this paragraph I ask you to go back over your fishing experiences and see if you haven't had the following typical experience with flies many times. The early-morning fishing proves disappointing, and until the sun hits the water here and there, you don't do much better. But the moment the high and low lights made by reflections from the sun, or the sun itself, cast bold rays on the water, you begin to rise trout. While you don't take fish fast or see any spectacular rises, somehow you keep getting a fish here and there and have a really fine day. And then in the evening, after the sun has set and you expect fishing to be at its best, you suddenly find that you have a tough time fooling even a couple of ordinary specimens, if any at all. You change patterns time after time and cast, cast, and cast, but only occasionally do you strike the right fly and make a really good catch— that is, good compared to the number of fish breaking the water.

To explain how this might happen, let us start at the beginning. Under certain circumstances and on clear days trout cannot evaluate the size, color, or shape of objects on the surface of the water. These certain circumstances are caused by bright light. Let me show you what

I mean by making a simple experiment. Let us hold a fly directly between the sun and our eye. What happens? Color vanishes, shape is obscured, size becomes an uncertain quanity. About all we are conscious of is a black or purple indefinite shape and an uncontrollable eyestrain. But as we move the fly from the direct line between our eye and the sun, we see color and shape become more distinct and eyestrain become less. Further movement of the fly brings it to a position where the fly can be seen fairly well and eyestrain vanishes. In this position we cannot elaborate the little details of our artificial, but we get a good general effect. The vision is not so clear that we can tell exactly what the fly is, but it is clear enough so that we could make a good guess. Now if we stand with our back between the sun and the fly, we will note that we can see it very plainly indeed. We can see each hackle point, the hook, and the barb. We can also distinguish the pattern without effort.

In making stream experiments along these lines we find that when the fly is directly between the eye of the trout and the sun we get very few rises but that it makes no difference what fly is used. The fish, if they rise at all, will take a Scarlet Ibis as well as anything else, even though the natural on the stream may be gray, black, brown, or any other color.

In the area where the fly is somewhat indistinct and yet where the light isn't strong enough to cause bad eyestrain (the second position), we find the trout rise readily and are not particularly selective. This is because in this position they see quite well, but not so well that they can distinguish the little departures from the naturals.

In the third position, where the trout looks at the fly away from the sun, we find that we need to exercise excessive caution and use the right fly in order to get results. The fly and the cast must be about perfect. This is in direct contrast with the first position, where one doesn't need to worry either about the cast or the fly, or the second position, where any reasonable care is exercised.

In my opinion we have here the reasons why so often we have good catches during the sunny hours of a bright day, even when there isn't a general rise to naturals, and why so often when the tremendous evening rises occur we have such a difficult time to take fish. It is the rises occurring when the light is dull that cause most of our troubles and that make so many fly patterns necessary.

In my estimation, fishing on sunny days, when the fish in a stream will rise at all during this time of the day, requires less effort and fewer patterns of flies than fishing on dull days and only in the morning and evening. It is not necessary to fish in direct sunlight to get results. Reflections may easily form that distraction which prevents the trout from seeing too plainly what you are offering them. Understand, I'm not insisting that this theory is unassailable. I know that it is and could tear it apart without too much effort myself. But I do know that experience has consistently upheld my views in this respect, so that I consider them worth while passing along to you, to make use of or ridicule as you like.

Remember that on gray days there is no area where the fly is indistinct, and that this applies to any day when the sun does not cast a clearly defined shadow. On bright days, even under the shadow of the trees, the water may catch the reflection from a rock or cliff or the leaves of trees on which the sun is shining brightly, and so obscure the vision of the fish when a fly floats by in that are affected by the reflection.

All these things must be taken into consideration when choosing the most advantageous position to fish from, and the combinations you run into are many and complicated. In fact the subject is so big that it would take a lifetime of experimentation on this idea alone to definitely arrive at some perfect conclusions. I will say this, if you can ascertain the exact location of a large trout, the depth of water he lies in, and then figure out the angles of sunlight so that you can place your fly in that area of sufficient but somewhat indistinct vision, you stand a good chance of taking him, perhaps not the first time you try, but eventually, if you keep at it and make sure you have the thing figured out correctly. At any rate I have given you the thought. Some of you may go further with it; most of you will simply read it and then forget it; the rest of you will no doubt consider it mere twaddle. All I can say is that the original idea came from the mind of one whom I considered one of the best anglers of my time.

Just what constitutes a good fishing day? Ask a dozen anglers, and you're likely to get a dozen different answers. Of course each one will insist that his choice is the best. It is, because at these times he has had his best fishing. I have my own choice—right or wrong. It is a bright sunny day with a snappy, cool air, and a northwest wind. This has been my favorite ever since I've started fishing, and I've never had any occasion to change my mind. I don't care if it blows a gale as long as the skies are blue and the air invigorating. This sort of weather makes my blood move faster. I feel vigorous, optimistic, capable of moving mountains. But when I put the cold light of registered facts on experiences, I find that I've had poor fishing on such days as well as excellent fishing. As a matter of fact no matter what type of day I pick out I find that both good and poor fishing have been experienced on them. Nevertheless I still prefer the snappy day, probably because I feel so good on such days, and besides they really do show a positive record of providing more good fishing than poor. But enough of this. Let me tell you of some experiences along these lines.

First, the Neversink at Oakland, New York. The time, May 30th. Weather, cold and squally, sometimes blowing so hard that it was impossible to cast except during a lull. We had been fishing on the Mongaup but hadn't done a thing, so on the way home thought we'd go Oakland way and take a look from the bridge. By the time we reached the bridge the day had grown worse. It was much colder, and the periods between terrific gusts were shorter. We had no hope of seeing any action, but because we had plenty of time we parked by the bridge and leaned over the railing to look at the Ledge Pool, which could plainly be seen from this point. A white slash in the center of the hole caught my eye. It was a considerable distance away, so that really I couldn't tell what it was, but some inner sense told me it was a rise. I didn't say anything to the others at the moment—just kept my eyes glued to the tail of that pool where I had seen that peculiar streak of white. Then I saw another, and immediately after that two more. It was enough for me. Without wasting any more time I made a beeline for the car to get my rod. As I went I shouted to the others: "There's something doing down there." They looked at me as if I'd gone crazy. I didn't blame them. Instinct rather than sight had told me that those white streaks were caused by trout.

So we went down to the pool and assembled our rods. While doing so we saw a half dozen of the slashes; and now, being so close to the pool, I could see that there wasn't any mistake about their being the rises of fish. Then I saw the reason for them. There was a large hatch of green mayflies in evidence. The wind was blowing so hard that it made many of them skate over the surface of the pool, and the trout rising to take them sometimes had to chase them across the surface when the squalls struck. In doing this they make a slash of white spray, which the wind caught and accentuated.

The only fly in my box that in any way imitated this mayfly was the Bridgeville Olive, a nondescript fly of the fan-wing type I had adopted and named becaause it had brought me success on the Neversink on the stretch just below Bridgeville. It really should have been called the Green May because it imitated this fly very well indeed. My first cast with it was a failure. A strong gust of wind struck the ledge on the opposite side and backed across the stream with a vengeance, fairly throwing the fly back in my face. This made me cautious, so I waited until a momentary lull occurred before making the next cast. The fly alighted perfectly, but I had misjudged the currents and got an immediate and bad drag. I tried several more times from the same position but could not get a float that did any business—I presume because of the drag. The fish were feeding in midstream, and to get the fly to them required a cast that put the line on three currents of different speeds.

There was only one thing to do. Out in the center of the stream was a flat rock that divided the main current of the deep hole. It was a mean place to get at, but I felt sure one could get a perfect float from that position, and determined to make a try for it. I made it and found that from this location I could not only put the fly over the rising fish, but could also fish the extreme right-hand side, which had been absolutely unreachable from the first position.

Then, after taking all this time and going to all the trouble, I make a fiasco of a splendid opportunity. Although in six casts I rose six good fish, I never had a chance to feel them. In each case I struck too hard and too fast, missing four completely and leaving a fly in the mouth of each of the other two. This seemed to end any further chances. Either there were only six trout feeding in the pool, or else I had put the rest down. At any rate, even though the natural mayflies kept floating down with ever-increasing numbers, they did so without any molestation.

It took fifteen minutes to reach the next place where I could do any fishing. I saw a few rises here and there, but the water was very high and I could not wade out far enough to reach them. Coming to a hole where I knew a large fish lived, having had previous experiences with him, I was just about to try for him even though he wasn't rising when out the corner of my eye I saw one of the slash rises some distance out in the swirling current. It could be reached by a long cast from where I stood, but feeling sure that it was impossible to make a satisfactory float, I decided to make an attempt to get into better position. This took another ten minutes, but it was worth it. There was a shallow spot of small area some twenty feet below and to the left of the rock near which the trout was rising. From his place one had all the control of the short cast, something of distinct advantage any time and of particular advantage on this day with the wind so troublesome and the water currents so contrary.

All during this time the wind buffeted and howled, and the trout kept rising. He hit so viciously that several times the wind took the spray from his rise and sent it flying several feet in the air. Watching my chances with the wind, I sent the fly out on its mission, confidently expecting to take the fish on the first cast. But I found that a normal cast in line with the side of the rock and slightly above did not float the fly close to the rock where the fish seemed to be rising. While trying to figure out how to make the right float, I saw that the trout was not lying at the side of the rock but in front of it and that the occasional slashes were caused when a fly got by him and he rushed after it.

As I made the cast to this point the wind took the fly, deposited it just above the rock, then skated it alongside. I saw the trout come for it, and as the slash was completed I felt the pleasant sensation of a heavy fish fighting.

This entire afternoon was a succession of incidents similar to this. The greatest difficulty was getting in a location where you could reach the rising fish and then waiting your chance to cast it between squalls.

The fly hatch was continuous until sunset, when they disappeared and the trout stopped moving. I kept three fish that weighed a total of ten and a quarter pounds, and this at a distance of about seventy-five miles from New York City.

According to common belief this shouldn't have been a good fishing day. It was positively wintry. The next week I went back again, and it was just the sort of a day the average person would call perfect. It was warm, partly cloudy, and there was a light breeze. And yet there wasn't a fly hatch to speak of and we didn't't see a trout rise, either to a natural or to our own flies.

Only twice in the years since have I found this water just right for dry-fly fishing. On each occasion it was very windy and cold and mayflies were hatching. On one of these occasions I left my fly in the mouth of a brown trout that jumped clear of the water after feeling the sting of the strike. I'm positive it weighed six pounds or better. I'd be willing to wager that right now, if you got to this stretch of river at just the right time, you'd have some rare sport. This sort of thing happens all the time. It is where luck plays such a part in the game. A fish or a number of fish suddenly decide to feed, and as suddenly decide to quit. If you are there at the right time you make a good catch or at least have the opportunity to do so. But get there before or after and you might swear there isn't a fish in the place. This is more likely to happen on the large streams. The small, intimate brooks are usually not so temperamental.

But you can't lay down any positive rules about the weather and fishing. When you get dogmatic about it, nature often slaps you down. However, I must say that a day when the humidity is low has usually been best for me when fishing with a dry fly. Of course this is weather when the skies are blue, when you feel like doing things, when you do not easily perspire and feel uncomfortable. Mostly this sort of day comes with a rising or steady barometer, but I have also experienced them, with good fishing, on a falling barometer.

In many cases a strong wind with cool air and a rising barometer has made excellent dry-fly fishing. Often it knocks many flies from the bushes and trees and this makes the trout surface-minded, at least in places where bushes or meadow grasses overhang the water.

This overall condition is not confined to any one locality or section of the country. Almost always I have found the sort of day you wax enthusiastic about a good day for fishing with dry flies. When the day is muggy and dark I have found other fishing methods more productive, for instance wet flies, streamers, spinners, or bait. Of course this hasn't always held true, but it has worked that way with me the great majority of times.

Water temperature has a lot to do with the way trout rise, but to arrange their reactions to the different temperature degrees into a consistent table is well nigh impossible. I would say that on the whole 70 degrees Fahrenheit marks the top. Sometimes you can get good fishing at this level or even up to 72 degrees, but it depends on the character and setup of the stream and the type of trout. When it goes higher it is usually very poor indeed. About your only chance then is to find where springs cool certain areas or where cold-water streams enter the lake, river, or creeks. To illustrate this, let us go to the lower Neversink again, in the middle of summer after a long, hot, and dry spell. The water was so warm that you could bathe in it without gasping at the first plunge. We knew that we couldn't possibly catch any fish in the usual haunts, so we headed for a small, cold brook where I had had some rare sport with brook trout at another time under similar conditions.

This brook entered at the shallow part of a very deep and large pool. One never knew if the fish would be there, as they didn't use the place regularly—only on certain occasions. To get at them without scaring them, you had to wade out and around and approach from the pool side.

On this day I was lucky. There were about thirty fish in the hole, about twenty-five brookies and five browns. You could see them facing the cold water of the little stream. I managed to take five before they took fright and disappeared. I waited three hours in the hope that they would return, but my wait was in vain. Where they went is a mystery, but I imagine that somewhere near by there must have been a deep spring-hole in the main river. Certainly they couldn't stay long in the main currents with the water temperature what it was. Incidentally, this same day I saw some fish breaking out in the big pool and finally succeeded in getting them on a salmon dry fly, of which I usually carry two or three for night trout fishing. They were smallmouth bass. I caught eight. Two of them were somewhat better than legal size—the others ranged between eight and nine inches.

The Eastern streams are yearly subjected to these intense heat spells. The miles of open, rocky streams absorb the devitalizing heat of long days, and the nights are not cold enough to balance the condition. Low water does not make fishing bad in itself. Trout will rise just the same when the water is excessively low as they will when it is normal if the water temperature doesn't get too high and you use the extra caution and skill needed for fishing under such conditions. If you don't believe this, take a thermometer with you and notice the difference in activity between the streams where the water averages 65 degrees or below and those where it ranges 68 degrees or above. And, let me tell you, it is always possible to catch trout in the upper reaches of the streams where the cold springs and dense shade offset the extreme heat of the sun on long summer days.

It is the effect of this extreme heat that so often, if not always, causes Eastern fishing to taper off at the end of June, and why, when the nights of late August become longer, with an occasional cool one, that the fishing sometimes picks up. Of course there is no set rule about it. It all depends on seasonal conditions.

Bumble Puppy

Some Big Fish on the Neversink

LARRY KOLLER

One day, a number of years ago, I was camped on the banks of a wonderful little mountain stream—again a feeder of the Neversink. For
many days in seasons past I had had good fun with dry flies over its
pockets and pools. As so often happens, one fine hole in the stream consistently rebuffed my every effort. It was a picture pool with the water
pouring in from a yard-high fall, churning itself among fat, mossy boulders; then flattening out its glide against a low ledge, then swinging
around and around in a whirlpool eddy. The pool was deep, its bed a
mass of black boulders; the sunlight barely flickered though the heavy
overhead arch of hemlock and beech, leaving most of the hole in deep,
mysterious shadow. An ideal spot for trout, I had always thought, but
whatever trout were there I failed to disturb.

On this day I had made camp in the evening, barely getting set up before dark. After a solid snack I turned in early with a firm resolve to be up at first light for a full day on the stream. But sometime during the night the steady strumming of spring rain had roused me and I lay awake, for hours at least, it seemed, tormented by the fine mist coming through the little pup tent to pinprick my face with tiny needles. I was late in crawling out; too late, I was soon to learn, for as I wrestled with bacon and eggs in the half shelter of the tent, two fishermen came splashing down the stream, one of them carrying, almost dragging, a heavy trout that must have weighed a full three pounds.

I knew almost before I asked where this great fish had been taken. "Yep, right up by the falls," the lucky lad said; "grabbed a big night-walker almost as soon as it hit th' water! Tried like hell to get back under a ledge, but I hauled 'im right outa there!"

It was some satisfaction at least to learn that finally a clever (or lucky) fisherman had succeeded in taking a fish from the falls pool. Certainly I never had been able to raise a fish there for a couple of seasons past to any of my flies and it so happened that I lacked the opportunity of working the hole on a rise of water. But with the big trout gone at last other fish worked their way into the pool and before the season slipped by it was possible to raise other nice fish there to the dry fly. Just how often an incident like this happens to other fishermen I can't imagine but it must be a frequent occurrence with any fly man who prefers the smaller streams.

This day I traveled a few miles further upstream, up into the Oakland Valley, where if anything, the stream is even more picturesque than below. It was new water to me, but since I hadn't caught any trout as yet it made little difference. I entered the stream near the head of a little island, thinking that the division here might give me two smaller streams to work on rather than the full volume of the river. The stream was a bit above normal level and slightly discolored and for this reason I felt that the bucktail should be a good choice. I now held a heavier, more powerful rod and, not content with a single fly, I tied in another bucktail midway up the nine-foot leader. But, I remember, I had absolutely no confidence in taking or even raising a trout. I was more anxious to try out the new, stiffer rod on the big water than any-thing else.

My first casts were at the head of a long heavy riffle where the water swung around the head of the island and chuted down in a hobbling rush into a flat fast run. Depth must have been three to four feet through these rapids, and in the run below at least five feet of water raced over the rocky bottom. My instincts were to pass on, down to the quieter water below, but with the new rod in hand I began casting at once. The two flies dropped heavily beyond the middle current and swung quickly downstream. Hurriedly I jerked them back in a rapid, cross-stream retrieve, anxious to pick up for the next cast. The rod worked smoothly, laying out the heavy line to distances that to me were great—probably no more than fifty feet—but the casting was effortless, the flies dropping easily just where I directed them.

On my fourth or fifth cast and with a stunning suddenness, a heavy trout leaped high, clear from the water and over the flies. He missed, of course, but his appearance was so startling that my hands shook as I retrieved line for the next cast. However, I thought better of making another cast at once and I sat down on the bank to recover my breath. I tried to remember then just how I had been handling line and flies, just which fly had been over the fish when he rose, but I had been so intent on the casting I couldn't for the life of me remember what had hap-pened to bring this fish above the surface in such a vigorous leap.

Steadier now and with the fish rested, the bucktails swung over the fish in short jerks. Again and again I worked over the trout's posi-tion, even changing the angle of presentation by moving upstream in the effort to bring the flies over the fish more slowly. But nothing I could do would bring him up and it was with heavy heart that I moved downstream. In a half-hearted way I worked the flies over the riffle and, just above the beginning of the deep run, another trout smashed thunderously at the tail fly, throwing spray above and before him in his eagerness to seize the big brown bucktail. With the sharp reflex of youth I sank the big hook home, tying my tackle solidly to a three-pound brown. Without pause or hesitation the fish ran hard for the deep water, then, pausing momentarily, he came clear in a great jump, splashing silvery drops in the yellow sunlight, his golden sides and ocher fins gleaming beautifully above the surface. Twice more he jumped, fighting one moment to free himself in the air, the next instant boring deep into the sheltering rocks at the bottom of the run. I held him hard, forcing the fight, leading him reluctantly from the heavy current into the shallow backwater near shore. Once more he jumped and then he lay quietly, finning gently over the small round stones at my feet. But as soon as he discovered me he rushed off, quick as light, to the very middle of the deep run and minutes passed before I could once again lead him to the shallows and the net, now a thoroughly beaten fish.

Once on shore, with the fish safely moved from the river, I could pause to gloat over his gleaming sides, his deep brown, thick back and the rows of irregular vermilion spots aligning his body. I was proud of this fish, my first big Neversink trout, and it is difficult even today to describe the emotions of that moment. There is little doubt that I felt some release from frustration, and new hope. Still, this was but one fish and thus far I could not analyze the reasons for this initial victory.

I went on then, working the water downstream hoping to raise another fish, fearing that I might bungle the raise, pondering over each movement of line and flies that had brought up the two good fish in this run. Almost hesitantly I cast over the stream again, afraid of making some movement that might either put down a fish or fail to interest one. The flies swung down and across, swimming in little jerks, simulating as best I knew how the motion of a terrified minnow, but for several casts nothing happened. I waded out to the bank and moved down to the next run, fishing now only the heavy, fast water, wasting no time on any spot which did not appear to be like the runs from whence the trout had come. Between two heavy boulders, where the flow was great and fast, I dropped the flies. The line slipped from my fingers and the last loop pulled tight with a little tug, jerking the rod tip slightly. As my fingers touched the line to retrieve, another lusty trout came clear, cleaving the run below the bucktail in a rainbow leap over the flies—another miss! I waited him out for a minute or two, then again curled the flies over and above him. This time the dark body rose just to meet them and I felt the quick, sure tug of a heavy fish.

I struck solidly and surely and felt the line tighten in my fingers, the rod strain in my hand. At once the fish leaped, a splattering, slashing jump that took him far across the stream. Again he jumped and again, fighting now right on top, and suddenly he was gone. Perhaps I had been too eager, too strong on the strike, and had hooked the fish lightly; at any rate, he was gone and I could add another charmed spot to my mental notebook.

The morning passed in this fashion. The trout were enthusiastic about the bucktails; too much so, for I failed to hook more than one fish of five risen. But by noon I had six wonderful fish filling the basket and it was time to call it quits for the day. Every fish I had netted came to me with the brown bucktail in his jaw; several had jumped for the white dropper fly but none had taken it well enough for me to save for the creel. I suppose that I should have removed the dropper fly after it proved to be ineffective, but I enjoyed seeing it dance over the riffles on its way down and across the stream, and in a way it helped to keep the cast always in sight.

Before leaving the stream I cleaned and ferned the catch and stupidly, I can see now, failed to make any but a cursory examination of the stomach contents. I did find two fish with freshly taken minnows but more important, I neglected to carefully the insect life which podded out all the fish. This could have been the tip-off on future fly-fishing but perhaps I was too excited about this first successful day on the river to give it much thought. I was to regret this for a long time to come.

Five o'clock on a Sunday morning in mid-May found me trekking up the Oakland Valley to Eden Falls, where the river breaks over a stratum of rock to form a pool several hundred feet long, boulder lined, deep and fast, with froth-flecked whirlpools on each side. Big browns lie here in the fast run, safe in the deep crevices unseen from the bank.

I had left my car in the woods after driving in as far as possible. Nevertheless I still had a two-mile walk ahead of me. Grouse roared wildly out from beneath my feet; two deer bounced up the hillside, crashing over blowdowns, and with a clattering of loose rocks disappeared into the laurels. A grandpa porky, puffing and grunting from his long climb up the hillside, stopped in the middle of the trail to eye me suspiciously before shuffling away, his quills bristling aggressively.

The day seemed perfect. I had waited until the river and weather were right. Plenty of fly hatches were in the air; the water was clear and of normal height. The warm sun beat down through the new foliage, bringing out little wisps of steam from the damp leaf mold.

My hopes were high—today I could not fail even though days past had been fruitless. My kit held each lure that had ever taken a trout for me since the very first. All kinds of bait, every useful pattern of fly— each should have its chance.

The pool at my feet was deep in shadow. I threaded on a minnow, hoping to attract a big fellow still on the early-morning feed. Carefully I cast across the run, manipulating the rod tip to effect a swimming motion to the bait. Soon a quick flash, a sharp tug, and I had my first strike! Letting the fish mouth the bait for a moment, I set the hook. After a short run there broke from the surface a beautiful—bass!

Throughout the morning the performance was much the same. Only two trout graced my basket, natives and rather small, both taken on bait. Flies were definitely a flop with me, having failed to bring a single brown trout to creel.

By midafternoon, with two miles of stream behind me, I was ravenously hungry. Picking a flat rock, I stretched out for a few minutes, perhaps longer. When next I looked downstream, there was a fisherman working toward me, whipping the water rapidly. A greenhorn, I thought, wearing out his arm. But no, somehow he seemed familiar. Old John, sure as shootin'. As I watched, instantly interested, there was a splash, a vicious tug at his rod tip, and then he leaned far back, arching his rod to set the hook.

Wild with excitement, I dashed down and netted the fish, a sixteen-inch brown. Slowly and with great care I extricated the fly: a common Gordon, though about twice as large as any I ordinarily used. My greatest surprise was his leader. It was about six feet long, mounted with three flies, but of unusual thickness, probably about ten-pound-test, untinted.

Naturally I asked him if that was his first fish.

"Gosh no, son. Feel that basket."

I did, and nearly dropped it. I took out every one, each an elusive brown trout, straightening those that were too long for the bottom of his ample creel. Eleven fish I laid side by side, not one less than a foot long, and two over seventeen inches. A limit catch, if I ever saw one.

With his famous reticence, he reeled up his line and leader, preparing to quit.

"Had tough luck downstream," he told me. "Lost my fly book. Kinda hungry, too. Forgot my lunch this mornin'."

What an opportunity! Plenty of eats in my coat pocket, and the Lord only knows how many flies!

Food loosened up his tongue a little after I had explained my problems and failure to catch these darned trout for so many years. He looked at my flies with evident disgust.

"Son," he poked at me, "you're one of these newfangled fishermen who uses all the doodads that are meant to ketch mebbe a ten-incher. You don't even know how to fly-fish to raise a decent trout in this river or to hold him if you do. I've fished this river for thirty years or more, and never needed all that stuff to ketch me a mess of fish. Now jest use that head of yours for a minute.

"These trout are mostly all good-sized browns and plenty wise. They feed all day long in this fast water, but you never will see a raise. You boys all fish the glassy water where a fly will float good but doesn't interest any fish. The trout that do lie there are only resting.

"When fish are feeding, they move up into the fast water right from the rapid. Then when something comes along in the line of eats, it has to be big enough to make it worth their while to dash after it. Once they start, they don't have much time to look it over—it's now or never.

"That's one reason why I use a heavy leader. 'Tisn't often that a fish in this fast water can inspect the leader. And I use one that's strong enough to land 'em. No use to go to all the trouble of hooking 'em and let 'em break off with a fly in their mouths."

"But there must be more to it than that," I argued. "I've used big flies and only caught chubs and bass."

"Well, there's a little more that you didn't give me a chance to tell about, son. You've been fishing the wrong places, and too, flies have to be handled right. I cast across and bring 'em back with my rod held high, so the flies will skip on the top. That's the way these here 'water crickets' swim, and that's what the trout feed on mostly.

"Now about that leader again—you have to use a heavy one to support the three big flies when you're skipping 'em on the surface and to straighten out the cast. With the flies on top, there isn't much of the leader that's on the water anyway. But no matter what kind of leader you get, don't use one with dropper loops. It makes foam on the surface, and the trout can see that. I loop my snell around the leader above a knot, where it won't slip."

I still wasn't quite satisfied, though tremendously interested. It didn't seem possible that such simplicity in angling could be the key to success on this hard-hearted stream. There must be something about his flies.

"Nope, nothin' special, except that I can't get big enough flies at the stores. It seems that everybody else uses a lot smaller sizes than when I first started fly-fishing; so I have a young feller tie 'em up for me. The Gordon is my best bet, 'cause it looks something like the 'water crickets.' Any ordinary fly will do, though—Female Beaverkill, Light Cahill, or Mallard Quill—as long as it's large. Big without being bulky—sparse, I guess you'd call it.

"Now there's another little trick that I can't tell you about, but I'll show you. Come along."

He led me upstream to a long run, broken by big boulders and very fast. Casting directly across, he retrieved rapidly, rod tip high and his hand shaking in a sort of palsy motion. That must have been what he meant to show me. It gave the flies a darting, erratic motion as though struggling across the current.

No raises were forthcoming from this run, but I wasn't in the least discouraged. Further upstream I tried my hand at it, and soon became absorbed in the novel departure from my usual style—so much so, in fact, that I missed the raise of a brown that would easily have weighed a pound. Excitement so claimed me in the next few hours that I failed to land a single fish, though I raised many.

I left the stream that day with an empty creel. My excitement and inexperience in this type of fly-fishing were responsible, but I had no regrets. Failure that day was lost in anticipation of better days to come, now that knowledge was mine. Subsequent trips have proved the old-timer's logic. Very few are the lickings that this stream hands me now, thanks to these wet flies and his not-too-modern method of handling them. The dry fly has never given me as consistently large fish in any waters, nor an even chance of landing a heavy trout.

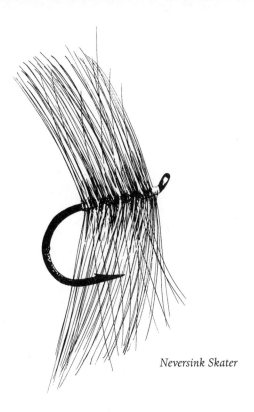

Neversink Skater

With Hewitt on the Neversink

JOHN ATHERTON

One of the most pleasant assocations of my fishing career was with Edward Hewitt on his Neversink water. The many days spent at the old camp with the rearing pools down in front, the long roof of the hatchery under the slope at the side and, across the meadow, the Camp Pool showing dark against the hemlocks, have brought with them an apprecation of how complete can be the angler's reward, not in mere numbers of trout, but in a renewed appreciation of those completely satisfying moments which every true angler experiences from time to time.

Perhaps it would be a trip to the Big Bend in that incredible old Buick with the holes in the top for the rods, and the rough woods road that would be taken so vigorously by Mr. Hewitt, a driver whose speed and dexterity hardly comported with his advancing years. The wonderful pool itself, with the current running deep along the vertical rock, and the clear water like a reading glass over the sand at the tail. There you could see the trout so well that it was a great treat as well as great sport to bring one up from the bottom to your fly.

There were many lunches on the high bank above Mollie's Pool, where we could watch a big trout feeding below in a pocket near the bank while we broiled a small one on a stick. There was a real whopper under that old fallen tree and we planned our strategy to outwit him.

The Little Bend was a great attraction as well. We would drive up to York's Ford, wade the river, and follow an old path along the far bank through the rhododendrons. In late June and early July, it was like walking through a great conservatory a half mile long. The heavy clusters of blossoms brushed us as we passed and left their petals like snowflakes on our shoulders. At the bend, the river pushed its current against a long submerged ledge which overhung deep water and hid the big trout in its shadow. But they moved out at times, and when we saw the little dimples drop down with the current, we would try not to be too clumsy in our casting. The trout in that pool were wary; I imagine that the ones which finally came to our flies were the less experienced, and I always wondered, when we unhooked them and sent them back with our blessing, whether they communicated their adventures to their brethren.

Mr. Hewitt had greatly improved his water and his fishing by building a series of dams, and when he put in a new one which made the Shop Pool, a large rock at the head became a favorite hide for good fish. It was difficult to resist a few casts in passing and I rarely went by without a try or two. There was always a trout there, so the spot was always fished with enthusiasm. If we caught its tenant, it was only a short time before another would be using the same lie. The fly had to pass the rock within an inch or two, and the best place was where the water curled around it. The fly appeared particularly attractive as it rode the little crest and slipped past. A heavy swirl below the rock meant that the trout had been late in his decision and after overtaking the fly had turned to seize it.

Some of the finest water was in the Camp Pool. There the river ran along a vertical rock wall for a hundred yards before it slowed and flattened to a wonderful big tail. The trout loved the very edge of the rock, and the overhanging trees made it a grand place to show our skill, or lack of it. Once, there, I had been given a chance at a fine heavy fish that Mr. Hewitt had located. After considerable casting and several fly changes, and of course when I was least expecting it, the fish rose beautifully—and I left the fly in his mouth. My resulting confusion gave the old master at my elbow reason for a chuckle or two, but he was generous and didn't laugh too long!

He and I used to fish the big Flat Pool together. It was nearly eight hundred feet long, thigh deep except near the bank where it was deeper and wide enough for two rods. The fish were distributed along the banks of the pool, so we would take a bank each and work up the pool side by side. It was the perfect combination of angling and companionship as we cast steadily and passed our comments back and forth. The branches overhung the water as much as fifteen feet, sometimes nearly touching it. It was great fun to get the fly well back in a difficult place and see the boil that indicated a good fish. The big spiders worked well for this, and I was shown how to cast them to bring out the trout that were difficult to approach.

Mr. Hewitt has made a great many contributions to angling, one of the most noteworthy being a willingness to try unorthodox methods. The invention and use of the big spider, the "Neversink Skater," is a good example. It was invaluable for fishing under the bushes where the line had to be driven in with considerable force. The greater air resistance of this fly always caused it to come down gently.

He tied his skaters on a light No. 16 hook and the diameter of the hackle was from 2 to 2½ inches. No body or tail was used. It was simply a pair of hackles wrapped around the hook shank. The favorite color on the Neversink was red-brown, and the hackles were as stiff as could be found. He kept the fly moving in quick jerks, bounces, and draws, which proved very deadly to large trout.

The big trout under the fallen tree at Mollie's Pool was in a tiny eddy beyond a swift current. It was very difficult to get a fly to him at all. The big spiders came in handy here. When the cast was thrown, the spider was immediately made to jump across the eddy, the line being held clear of the current as much as possible. The unavoidable "drag" was thus converted into a distinctly attractive movement which enabled me to hook that "Aunt Sally" solidly on several occasions, only to lose him in the dead tree each time.

Probably the best place of all for the skater was under the dams. These low dams made fine holding pools out of otherwise unproductive riffles and flats. They were built two logs high, and faced on the upstream side with heavy planks running from the top of the dam to the stream bed at a long angle. The falling water dug holes back under these dams, making fine hides, and there were always big trout in them for us to try to lure out.

As the sun left the water in the evening, the fish would move out gradually and begin to feed. We would cast the big spider up close to the foam and broken water, even into it, and work it back in jerks. Frequently a fish would leap fully out and take the fly in his descent, a thrilling sight and one of the reasons the big spiders make such exciting fishing. Sometimes a fish could be teased into a rise, with many casts. Or one might approach the fly repeatedly, even rise and miss it; but usually if the trout was not pricked he was not put down.

This fishing took nice judgment and manipulation. If the fly was moved too fast, the fish was apt to miss it or be lightly hooked; if too slowly, he might not become excited enough to go for it. Sometimes bouncing or bumping the fly had a deadly appeal. A breeze helped, as well as a downstream or quartering cast. With a fairly long rod, and a light line which aided in keeping line and leader free of the water, only the fly touched lightly in little hops here and there. Needless to say, this could hardly have been done on a long line.

During the summer evenings the fish almost invariably rose in the big flats just before dark. Mr. Hewitt had developed a surprisingly effective method for these difficult risers, using a small, very thin and streamlined wet fly with the hackle clipped off top and bottom and a thin, sloping wing. Even this dressing was sometimes reduced in size if the fish came hesitantly. As the trout were usually cruising, it required nice judgment to place the fly where they could see it. It was almost like leading a bird by swinging the gun ahead of him.

It was really a joy to cast with the tackle used for that fishing. Mr. Hewitt spliced a long leader of about fourteen feet to a light line which was handled by an eight-foot rod of quite soft and slow action. He used a deliberate swinging cast, similar to that with a two-handed salmon rod, and it made for particularly delicate fishing. I grew to love that last hour on the flats those long evenings, and ten o'clock suppers were our rule.

Occasionally very small dry flies, about No. 20, were used during those late hatches but as I remember it the wet fly seemed to produce the best results. In fishing the flats during the day, when trout came poorly to the dry fly, Mr. Hewitt usually employed a wet fly like the one described and fished it close to the banks, underneath the branches. He cast nearly straight across stream, or at a slight angle up or down, and the fly had to be presented within a few inches of the bank in most cases to raise the fish. He usually added a very slight motion to the rod in retrieving.

It was on this lovely clear river that I got my fill of catching big fish and realized how disappointing it can be. My largest brown trout was taken in the Shop Pool at high noon on a bright day. He came to a small variant, out in the open water, and for some moments I was under the impression that it was only a medium-sized fish. Then suddenly he was very heavy on the light gear and made two or three fairly good runs. The rest of the battle was a grim tug-of-war, with the trout swimming around me, head down, trying to nose into the bank to rub out the hook. After about ten minutes of this I lifted him out with my hand, having no net. As I returned him, I can only guess at his weight but he was about 4½ or 5 pounds. A friend of mine who hooked a 4½ pound brown trout one day on the Big Beaverkill below Roscoe said that it was in the net within a minute or two without ever knowing that anything was wrong until it was too late.

Of course, a big fish can be a different story in heavy water, such as the Pit or the Feather River in California, where I have frequently scrambled downriver in pursuit of a fleeing rainbow for a battle that left me nearly as exhausted as the fish. But in our more easy-flowing Catskill and New England streams, a trout of 1½ to 2 pounds seems to me the very best to catch. And I would greatly prefer a day in which the rewards were three or four medium-sized fish than one spent in pursuit of a single big one. The angler who has a passion for big fish only, at any cost, is missing a great deal of the charm of the sport by not simply taking things as they come. Fishing, to me, should be a relaxed pursuit, and the angler who hurls himself at his quarry, covering miles of water in a day or hotly stalking a single fish for an entire weekend, will probably return to find me asleep on the bank after having watched his flying coattails disappear around the bend.

The Neversink taught me the true meaning of many things and I emerged from those experiences a more philosophical man. And both my wife and I learned much of angling from the many days spent on those clear waters under Mr. Hewitt's tutelage.

To Max,[1] particularly, he imparted a practical knowledge of stream-craft, casting, and fishing with a patience and interest equalled only by her appreciation. How much he had contributed toward making her an angler of prowess neither a big brown trout nor I realized until one day when I tried fruitlessly for an hour to deceive him. He looked over my fly a few times but each time turned it down with a nonchalance which was irritating to an already sorely tried angler.

When I finally decided to give up, Max, who had been waiting on the bank, waded out to try for him. Secure in the knowledge that if I could not get him after such long effort, she could not, I started off up the stream. I had gone but a few steps when I heard her reel screech and turned to see the fish slash madly across the pool. He had taken her second cast and thus two more males had underestimated the power of a woman.

---

[1] Maxine Atherton, the author's wife.

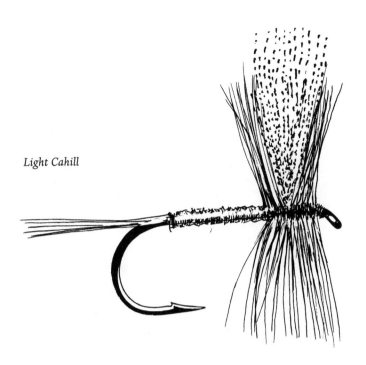

Light Cahill

The Quest for
Theodore Gordon

SPARSE GREY HACKLE

First there was Theodore Gordon, the consumptive exiled to the Catskills, whose cosmopolitan personality and passion for angling enabled him to project his spirit across the ocean into kinship with the great figures of contemporary British angling; he was, in fact, the father of dry-fly angling in America. He died in 1915.

Then there was John McDonald, scholar, writing genius of *Fortune* magazine, and devoted angler, who more than thirty years later rescued Gordon from oblivion by the keenness of his discernment and the ardor of his research. His labors culminated in 1947 in the angling literary milestone *The Complete Fly Fisherman: The Notes and Letters of Theodore Gordon.*

Then, some two years later, The Theodore Gordon Society (there is no connection with a conservation organization of similar name, which was formed some years later) was formed by four members of The Anglers' Club of New York: Lewis M. Hull (The Physicist), Guy R. Jenkins (The Underwriter), the late Edgar G. Wandless (The Attorney), and the present writer (The Reporter). Out of a chance conversation before the Club fireplace grew an expedition to the Catskills to photograph the house in which Gordon had died. On that occasion the four organized this most informal society, which eventually interviewed at length the surviving two of the three native fishermen who had been Gordon's only familiars in the Catskills, and later helped in solving the mystery of Gordon's last resting-place.

Finally, there was Virginia Kraft, then a talented writer-reporter and now an associate editor of *Sports Illustrated* magazine. In the course of authenticating Gordon's fly box for the then-new magazine, she formed a desire to know more about the man. Over the next several years she devoted several thousand miles of spare-time travel and investigation to finding and interviewing Gordon's few surviving, scattered, family connections. In this manner she accumulated what meager information still was available about that little-known recluse and today undoubtedly knows more about him than any other living person. Ultimately this knowledge became the key which unlocked the mystery of Gordon's burial place.

"THINGS OF THE SPIRIT"

It was a most unseasonable pilgrimage for a late November weekend, a sentimental journey to find the Catskill farmhouse in which Theodore Gordon had lived his last years and died, and to see again, before a New York City reservoir should drown it, the lovely Neversink that he had fished. Unseasonable, yet it had crystallized instantly and urgently out of nowhere during a chance conversation among four angling friends. Why is not clear; but perhaps they had subconsciously in mind the news lately come from England of the death of Gordon's dear letter-friend, the great angler Skues.

They left the city that weekend in a drizzle that worsened into sleet, but they were warm and dry, and some sympathetic bond not only joined but uplifted their spirits. So while the station wagon slogged along, they sang the songs grave and gay that everyone holds in memory; and this was remarkable, for they were not a singing sort of men. Even when, at Napanoch, the sleet changed to a blinding white wall of snowflakes in the headlights and it seemed as if tire chains would be needed, they still sang, and when they came at last to Claryville, and carried their heavy lading into the frigid cabin, they sang though their teeth chattered.

Three roaring fires, a gallon of scalding coffee, and a mound of sandwiches soon made things comfortable, and they wound up smoking and chatting before the fireplace. But the first night of an expedition is nothing more, spiritually, than what the Arab caravan men call "the little start," a mere getting of the expedition on the road. So after nightcaps as tall as a cowboy's sombrero, they burrowed into heaps of five-point blankets and slept the night away.

Then it was morning, "the great start," the spiritual setting forth, with fires rekindled and the pungency of coffee summoning the sleepers to add to it the fragrance of that best smoke of the whole day, the pipe before breakfast. It was afternoon when the pilgrims finally took the road to Gordon's habitation. As the car picked its way through the deserted, ruined village of Neversink huddled amid slopes desolated by the dam builders, no reminder was needed that the shortest days of the year were at hand. The Physicist shook his head in despair as he read his light meter, and the others were depressed by the obvious approach of the day's end.

When they came to the spot, they were doubtful, for the house had been torn down, but a deer hunter who came by assured them that upon this foundation had stood the Anson Knight house, in which Gordon had lived out his last days. All this part of the valley had been condemned now for the reservoir, and the city had pulled down the dwellings at once to keep out squatters. Soon the place where Theodore

Gordon had lived and died, as well as much of the river he had loved to fish, would sleep beneath a hundred feet of water.

The building site was across the road from the river and above it. A long knoll behind it was mantled with a dense windbreak of evergreens. A somber sky pressed down on the dark pines, and a pool in the river that had been bright crystal last summer now shone like black polished flint through the naked branches. The raw, wet air eddied in sullen gusts.

Sleet crunched underfoot as the pilgrims climbed the little pitch to the house and stood on the wall of a foundation filled with a mean, pathetic jumble of rubbish. Yonder still stood the rotting, unpainted barn and here were the weed-grown steps up which the dreary angler must have plodded so often; but the spirit of Theodore Gordon had gone from the place and it was only a littered, dreary site.

Before they drove away, someone produced a flask and they stood together in the road looking back at the spot they had left, murmuring brief toasts to the great angler as they sipped the spirits.

"Do you suppose Gordon took a drink, on occasion?" queried The Reporter.

"I am sure that he did, but Herman Christian and others who knew him agree that he was most temperate," replied The Physicist. "In one of his later letters to Steenrod, Gordon refers to 'my bottle of whiskey which I never use' but in an earlier article he recalls a weary walk home from fishing with a companion whose flask, 'a miserable caricature of a thing,' was so small that it provided no sustenance. Theodore Gordon was gently born and reared, and lived in many places, and I think we may safely assume that he knew how to enjoy the good things of life."

It was almost dark when they got back to their cabin. A conflagration was started in the outdoor fireplace, and while it burned down to a bed of embers, The Attorney made a salad. Then, muffled to the ears, he went out to the fire with a long-handled fork in one hand and a great steak in the other. He threw the latter on the embers and a rich aroma streamed down the wind so that a benighted hunter, a hundred yards away, stopped short and then struck out for home at a quickened pace. The Reporter brought the cook a drink, and they stood together looking at the river.

"The shades of all the great anglers who knew the Neversink must still frequent this place," said The Reporter. "They must be enjoying that savory scent, right now."

"'The gods of the place'—a pagan concept," replied The Attorney. "This steak is ready."

After dinner The Reporter went out to the woodpile, but before he carried in his load he paused to look and listen. Despite the snowy gleam of the ground, iron winter darkness lay on the land—an empty, desolate land unrelieved by even a point of light, from the peaks of Slide Mountain to the river gurgling half-frozen at his feet. But yellow lamplight streamed through the window; and inside the cozy cabin, redolent of good food and tobacco, they were singing an old college glee as they washed the dishes.

"Like a blackbird in the spring . . ." mourned the silvery tenor, the notes harmonizing sweetly.

"Oralee, Oralee, maid with golden hair," sobbed the counter tenor, and the baritone throbbed like a bronze bell. Soft and mellow, the music faded into the icy darkness, making it seem even more cold and empty. The Reporter gazed at the pool below him and imagined a frail little man casting with a nine-foot rod amid springtime greenery, placing a tiny dull-colored fly with consummate artistry. He carried in his wood, then mixed a stout drink and carried it back outdoors.

"'The gods of the place,'" he quoted softly. "A libation to the gods of the place." He started to pour a libation in the manner of the ancients, then changed his mind and turned back to the cabin. He held the door wide and stood aside for a moment as if in invitation, then went inside and put the drink on the stone mantelshelf of the fireplace, in the shadows.

When the work was done the four sat smoking by the fire and their conversation was of Gordon, weaving into a varicolored fabric the threads of information gathered from the recollections of The Underwriter and several others of their acquaintance who had known Gordon, and from the collected letters which are almost our only record of him. They spoke of his frail physical aspect, his habit of rolling cigarettes between thumb and finger of one hand, of the mysterious "Fly Fishers" to which he several times refers in his writings as his club, and of Skues's coinage of the pen name Val Conson. It was getting late when the fire finally burned low and the room turned chilly.

"Throw on some wood," urged The Physicist with a shiver. "It's cold in here. How Gordon must have suffered winters, in that primitive farmhouse."

"He did," affirmed The Underwriter. "It runs through his letters; he detested the cold. He was an outdoorsman, and loved the woods on a crisp, sunny winter's day, but he hated dark, raw weather like today's."

"Coldness and loneliness run through his writings," chimed in The Physicist. "Note how recurrently he says things like: 'It is too cold to work'; 'It is wild and lonely up here'; 'It is a dreary day'; 'This is a cold, raw day, damp and windy'; 'Now it is overcast, raw.' And in December 1905, he wrote in *The Fishing Gazette*: 'It is rather dreary in the country at this season. The birds have gone for the most part, the hum and buzz of insect life has ceased, the leaves, which recently were so beautiful, are on the ground, brown and withered. On a still day, Nature seems to be dead or at least in a comatose state. Even the light of day is hard and cold. As I write, the wind is shrieking and tearing at this frail wooden house as if determined to carry it off bodily.'

"The loneliness of this city-bred, cultured man imprisoned in a rude mountain settlement all winter was pathetic, and I think there was intense feeling in his remark to Skues: 'I am very lonely tonight and am writing to you for the feeling of companionship,'"concluded The Physicist.

"And now Skues is dead. What a reunion they must have had in Valhalla," mused The Reporter.

"A pagan concept," reiterated The Attorney. "It's getting late; let's turn in."

They wasted no time in their preparations for the night, but before he went to bed, The Reporter turned back to look at the glass on the mantelshelf. It was empty.

What the world knows of Theodore Gordon, the anglerepistolist, comes principally from his published letters to R. B. Marston and G. E. M. Skues in England, and the youthful Guy Jenkins; and from the recollections of his friends in the Catskills. Of these there were three; but one, Bruce Leroy, died long before without ever having recorded his impressions of Gordon. The other two were Herman Christian and Roy Steenrod, both living as this is written (1969). Herman Christian resides in Grahamsville, New York, and Roy Steenrod in his native community of Liberty, New York. Both are in retirement.

The nature of Gordon's friendship with each of his three Catskill friends differed in subtle ways. Christian and Steenrod agree that Gordon "thought a lot" of Bruce Leroy; Leroy named one of his sons after him. Yet, judging from Gordon's letters, he called him Bruce only occasionally. It is impossible to evaluate this friendship now because all we know of Leroy is that he inherited a prosperous farm at Leroy's Corners, two miles from Bradley, but preferred hunting and fishing to farming.

Herman Christian was Gordon's familiar; they lived only a quarter of a mile apart during Gordon's last years and saw a great deal of each other. Specifically, Christian fished with Gordon far more than did any other person. Gordon called him Christian, and Herman still refers to his friend as Mr. Gordon.

But Gordon never called Roy Steenrod anything but Mr. Steenrod and after ten years of correspondence still so addressed him in the salutations of his letters. Roy always refers to him as Gordon, but I think he addressed him as Mr. Gordon. Yet Roy feels that he was closer to Gordon than any of his other friends: "He told me more than anyone else in the world."

The following interviews are taken almost verbatim from my stenographic notes of a series of interviews with Herman Christian and Roy Steenrod, condensed but not altered in meaning. They are given here in the present tense, the form in which they were originally written soon after the interviews were completed in 1950 and 1955 respectively.

HERMAN CHRISTIAN

Herman Christian lives on his 176-acre farm contiguous to the Big Bend pool of the Neversink River below Hall's Mills, so remote that the bears come into the woods to gather the juneberries (shadblow). He makes a living out of a little of everything—bees, maple syrup, timber, a small garden, trapping, hunting, fishing—"but my best crop is trout flies." At sixty-eight he carries his lean sinewy six feet two inches erect and moves with the lithe surefootedness of a master woodsman, trapper, and hunter that he is. He gives the impression of military bearing and one is not surprised to learn that he has been a soldier. A hawklike profile and piercing eyes give him a forbidding look, but when he smiles, his expression becomes warm and friendly.

For many years he had the reputation of being able to dance more dances, kiss more girls, and whip more men than anyone in his valley. But more than that, he is still known throughout the length and breadth of the Catskills as a peerless fisherman with the dry fly and particularly with the wet fly. Theodore Gordon himself paid tribute to his ability to find and take big fish. The following is Herman Christian's own story of his early life and his friendship with Theodore Gordon.

"I was born in Eureka, New York [in the Rondout Valley]. My father died when I was two years old. When I was fourteen I went to work on a farm near Halls Mills [in the adjoining Neversink Valley] for three dollars a month. When I was sixteen, in 1898, I lied like hell and enlisted in the regular U.S. Army. I was assigned to the Tenth Infantry and with that organization served a year in Cuba and three years in the Philippines. Afterward I returned to the Neversink Valley. Later I became a guard at Great Meadows [New York] Prison and through an advertisement in *Field & Stream* magazine became manager of the fly-tying department of the Pflueger Tackle people in Akron.

"I was a fisherman from boyhood; fished the Neversink the first time when I was nine years old. I came with two men and we camped alongside the pool above the Big Bend. I never dreamed that I would own it sometime, but it was a part of the farm I bought thirty-three years ago. I subsequently sold the river frontage to Ed Hewitt.

"In 1896, the year I went to work on the farm, I caught my first brown trout on a line I had set for eels. He was nineteen and a half inches long and weighed two and a half pounds; I sold him for fifty cents.

"I do not recall when I began fishing with flies; I know I was using them in 1897 or 1898. Around 1906 I wanted to get Theodore Gordon to tie some flies for me—in those days he was generous in giving his flies to fishermen he knew. I asked Bruce Leroy about it, and he said that Gordon did not give flies to everybody, and suggested that I get some good feathers for him. I got some blues and gingers and took them to Mr. Gordon, and we became acquainted.

"He called me Christian. When he moved from the hotel in Neversink Village to Anson Knight's [near the Neversink Bridge; Gordon died there], they did not deliver his mail to him, and I used to bring it to him every day—I lived on the other side of the bridge, about a quarter of a mile from Knight's. He would receive ten or twelve letters a day. Mr. Gordon used to come and see me often. He went out very little in winter, but if he went out at all he would come to my house. He wanted to board with us, but I had two little girls, two and four years old, and my wife didn't want him because he had TB and had the habit of spitting on the floor when he was tying flies.

"I used to go up and talk to him a couple of hours at a time, two or three times a week. 'Gosh, Christian,' he would say, 'I'm glad you came up. It got lonesome here.' Sometimes he would give me a drink. He never drank much, but he always had a bottle of cognac or something to give a drink to anyone who came in. But when I was fishing with him I never smelt liquor on his breath.

"Whenever I located a nice big fish, the next day I'd take Mr. Gordon down to fish for it. I wouldn't take a rod myself; I'd ten times rather see him catch it. But almost always he would insist on my fishing a little with his rod while he rested. He would not fish at all, no matter how many fish rose, until the fish he wanted began to feed. When he got him, he would usually stop fishing. He never kept more than three or four fish but always good ones. He liked to give a brace of fish, or a brace of partridge or woodcock, to the Smiths who had a summer home nearby. I think Mr. Smith was a customs appraiser—they were not local people. In all my experiences with Mr. Gordon, he would never fish more than a couple of pools in an afternoon, usually only one. If he could not get the one fish he had gone for, he would not care to fish any more.

"Ed Payne made Gordon a rod about 1895; Gordon tied him thirty-nine dozen flies to pay for it. About 1912, when he was staying at DeMund's Hotel in Neversink, I took him down some feathers and he went in and got this rod and said, 'I don't know anybody who would appreciate it as much as you would,' and gave it to me. I still have it and occasionally use it. It is nine and a half feet, three pieces, and of course soft, wet-fly action. [This rod is now in the collection of The Anglers' Club of New York.]

"As time went on and his illness became worse and worse, he fished closer to home, and less. The winter and spring before he died, he was so sick that he did not tie me one single fly.

"Leroy said somebody ought to get hold of Gordon's relatives and tell them of his condition; he said Gordon had a cousin living in Newburgh, New York. I started writing letters, and it took me to Haverstraw, New York, and finally to East Orange, New Jersey. I finally turned up a cousin and talked to him on the telephone, and he came up and I went to Anson Knight's with him.

"Mr. Gordon was in bed. He got up and dressed and said to his cousin sharply, 'What did you come up here for?' His cousin sort of passed it off. We visited for a while and then came back to my house, and then I took him to the train. Mr. Gordon died five or six days later.

"Theodore Gordon as I knew him did not weigh much over ninety pounds and was maybe five feet two or three inches. He was a hell of a good shot and had keen sight and hearing, but he could not tell the direction the sound came from when a bird got up behind him. He liked to get some exercise, but he could not take much owing to his health. He was a man's man in every way.

"He used to use the bamboo tip-case of his Payne rod for a walking stick. He did not need a stick, but he would take it and go strutting down to see the Smiths." (This tip case was of whole bamboo, hollowed out and fitted with a brass screw cap. For a nine-and-a-half-foot, three-piece rod it would have to be thirty-nine inches long, or considerably too long for a man of five feet two inches. The rule is, two inches added to half the user's height; a total of thirty-three inches in this case. Furthermore, the tip case now with the rod shows no sign at all of having been used as a walking stick. Since it is scarcely possible that Christian invented this little sidelight, apparently Gordon carried the case as a swagger stick, under his arm.)

"He smoked one cigarette after another—rolled them between his thumb and one finger and never licked them; he would give them a twist and they would stay tight. He would only smoke a few puffs, then throw it away and roll another.

"I do not know when Mr. Gordon came to this valley. I know he was here in 1896 or 1897. At different times he stayed at Billy York's hotel in Claryville, at DeMund's, and at Herron's in Neversink, and for the last three years of his life he lived at Anson Knight's in Bradley [across the river from Neversink Village]. He always stayed in as good accommodations as there were in the locality, and so far as I can tell, he always had money enough to live on.

"While his mother was alive he used to stay winters at the Liberty House in Liberty, New York, with her, and in summer he would live in Neversink, Claryville [at the forks of the Neversink], or Bradley, close to the river. He would go from river to river in earlier years, staying a week or two at each place. In later years, probably because of his failing strength, he no longer went from one stream to another.

"He spoke to me quite a lot about his mother and what a care she had been to him. He would tell me about the English chalk streams, but I never understood that he had been in England. I do not know that he ever belonged to any club around here and do not know what club he referred to as the Flyfishers in his letters.

"He was a great friend of Bruce Leroy's, and sometimes he would stay with him. Bruce was always getting feathers and raising feathers for Mr. Gordon, and when Gordon would buy a good rooster he would give it to Leroy to keep for him. He would just pick out the feathers occasionally; Gordon never kept chickens.

"Mr. Gordon was a very fine fisherman. He did not cast a particularly long line in spite of the big rods he used, but he cast a particularly nice line, and he could cast the fly right where he wanted and put it down the right way. As I said before, he usually fished only to rising fish but sometimes, if he wanted exercise, he would fish when there were no rises. It should be remembered that in those days it was common to see a pool covered with jumping fish; it was nothing to take three or four out of one pool." (The terms "jumping" and "bugs" were very widely used by the older generation of trout fishermen; nowadays the words are more likely to be "rising" and "flies" or, perhaps, "naturals.")

"Mr. Gordon studied the insects and used to carry a little thin bottle of alcohol in his pocket; if he caught a bug he would take it home and try to copy it. He never used a marrow spoon"—this point was raised because of Gordon's friendship with Skues, who advocated the marrow spoon for extracting stomach contents from a dead fish—"but he would cut a trout open to see what it had been feeding on.

"There was a beautiful big pool at York's Ford that since has filled in; it was four or five feet deep in the middle and had a pothole fifteen feet deep at each end. Mr. Gordon went up there many a day to get the big trout that lived there. One day when the drakes were on, the big fish came up and Gordon said he took his fly 'like a blackberry.' When he 'squeezed the handle of the rod' to tighten on him, the fish was off; he was using drawn gut. Later, the big trout was caught at night in one of the nets that had originally been used to snare passenger pigeons. Bruce Leroy saw the fish taken" (and helped to catch it, according to Ed Hewitt). "It weighed over six pounds."

"If Gordon could get someone with a horse and buggy to drive him, he would be tickled to death to go up to the Big Bend or York's. He did not fish much downstream from Anson Knight's house, although there was a dandy night hole down there, only about three or four feet of water in it.

"One time I saw a couple of good trout in a hole about a mile below Neversink. It was a nice pool; the upper end was nice fast water, and there were some rocks for the fish to run under. I took Mr. Gordon down there, and he got one fish, a sixteen-inch fish, and I think I got the other one in Hewitt's Camp Pool, in the middle or latter part of June, at night on a No. 6 dun fly—dun hackle, dun-colored muskrat fur or seal's fur body, with hackle palmered down over it, and wood-duck wing. It was twenty-nine and half inches long and weighed eight pounds four ounces. I caught another one in the East Branch [of the Delaware] that was three inches shorter and two ounces heavier.

"Gordon did not fish at night, but he would go quite often for an hour or so after supper, in July and August. I remember once he caught a fish that weighed two pounds; he came to the house and wanted to know if I would take it down to Smith's.

"Mr. Gordon used the Light Cahill and the Quill Gordon to imitate the drake. He tied them in three shades, and so do I. As the season advances, the hatch gets lighter in color. He would put on a big fly, Quill Gordon or Cahill, and fish for big fish just like any other trout.

"He used to fish the dry fly for bass just the same as he did for trout, down on the East Branch of the Delaware, between the towns of East Branch and Cadosia. He would take a boat and fish the big eddies [in the Delaware watershed a long, deep river pool is called an eddy] with big bushy dry flies. He would locate a rising fish and cast to it. When he located a big fish, he would study the stream, the bugs, etc., just as he did for trout. He went after one big bass that turned out to be a brown trout thirty inches long that he said would have weighed ten pounds, and that sounds about right." (Gordon released the fish, which is mentioned in his published works and letters, because the trout season was closed.)

"What Mr. Gordon did not like was to have his leader float. He certainly did hate a floating leader; he would not fish with one. He always soaked them well in water and was careful not to get any deer fat on them when he greased his line. He usually put a little kerosene on his fly.

"As a flytier, there is one outstanding fact about Theodore Gordon. He never taught anybody to tie; he never showed anybody anything, even me. When I went to his room, if he had a fly in the vise half-finished, he would take it out and lay it on the table. I used to show him flies that I made and sometimes he would say, 'That one ought to take a fish,' but he never would say anything about the way they were tied. He liked me, and he would make me flies, but he never would let me see him make a fly. (The foregoing positive statement was directed against a once-famous Catskill tyer, Rube Cross, who, Christian angrily said, told people he had learned to tie from Theodore Gordon.)

"Mr. Gordon tied the Quill Gordon, Light and Dark Cahill, and the pig's wool flies in light, medium, and dark colors. He used a wire over his quill sometimes for protection, not for color. He invented the Quill Gordon and the Gordon and a lot of other flies that he did not name at all. Many of the 'special' flies now in common use were invented by him." (A dig at Rube's famous Cross Special.)

"The story of Gordon's Bumblepuppy is that there was a fishing guide in Haverstraw who used a long cane pole to fish live bait in the weed pockets, for bass. Gordon tried to tie a fly that could he fished this way and after making three or four that were no good, he made one that caught fish. He made me one, but he did not make it big enough to suit me. I took it over to Loch Sheldrake and it caught fish, but no big ones, I made it bigger and a little different." (Hook 1/0 Model Perfect, mixed scarlet and white hackles, narrow brown turkey wing above thin white bucktail tied with butt of hair reversed, white chenille body, scarlet ibis tail.)

"I started to tie flies when Mr. Gordon got so he did not make me as many flies as I wanted. I could not get what I wanted in the store, so I started to tie my own. Nobody ever showed me anything about tying. I used my fingers—I still tie with my fingers and just put the fly in the vise a moment to finish it—and worked it out myself. The first time I ever saw anyone else tie a fly was when I was put in charge of Pflueger's fly-tying department, thirty-two or thirty-three women, in Akron.

"Some time around 1886, private people brought 2,000 brown trout from the Caledonia (New York) Hatchery and stocked the river. In a few years every hole in the river had three or four big fish in it, and it was nothing to see forty or fifty fish jumping; you could look them over and take your pick.

"Bruce Leroy and I stocked the river for twenty years. We would get all the farmers around to sign over to us their allotments of fry and fingerlings from the state, and we would meet the train with a horse and wagon and take the cans to the river and stock the fish.

"The Neversink was a fisherman's paradise around 1900. I cannot see much difference now in the river itself. But in 1900 it was nothing to see fifty trout jumping in a hole, and you could fish the river for a month without seeing a man unless it rained; then a few farmers would come down to fish with bait.

"The drake is the great fly in the Neversink; we do not have the Green Drake and the Coffin Fly [Gray Drake] of the Beaverkill. The male of our drake is a sort of smoky dun color, and the female is a big fly with spotted wings and a yellow body. The Quill Gordon imitates the male and the Light Cahill, the female. They come on about dark in great multitudes and fly upstream, and they look as if they had tails on each end—they have feelers sticking out in front."

(I am totally at a loss to identify this fly. I know the Neversink no longer has the Green and Gray Drakes—[E. guttulata]—although the old-timers said they occurred as far upstream as just above the Neversink iron bridge, when the banks were cultivated fields instead of second-growth, as they became. Christian's flies sound vaguely like the Hendrickson, which should be on much earlier than Decoration Day, however. The feelers sound like stonefly or caddis. And Ed Hewitt used to use and sell a wet fly with mottled brown and tan wings—female pheasant was Jack Atherton's guess—and a grayish-tannish body with, it seemed to me, a few shreds of green wool in it. Ed called it a stonefly, but I always thought it more resembled a caddis; it was tied with "down" wings, for one thing. It was a deadly fly on that river. After he died I checked with Farlow in London, who used to tie them for him by the gross; they had no record of the pattern. And none of those in the Anglers' Club who bought them by the handful had a surviving specimen. But I will say this: the Light Cahill, with almost whitish body as developed by W. A. Chandler and/or Rube Cross, is a really sterling fly on the Neversink, all summer long.)

"The drake comes on just about Decoration Day and is on all through June. I have seen them so thick you could not put your finger on the water without touching one. Usually they won't come out until dusk, but if it is a cloudy day, they may come on about noon and hatch three or four times during the afternoon. The fly is just about the size of a nice No. 11 artificial.

"I think you can never get a big fish to come to a dry fly except when the drakes are on. They won't pay any attention to little flies at all. I have caught three or four fish over twenty-two inches on a dry fly, and it was always when the drakes were on. That is about the limit in size that I have caught on a dry fly.

"Even in deep water, a big fish that is feeding will come up for a natural fly and not go down again very far; he will only go down maybe ten inches. You can almost always get a jump out of a fish that is feeding with a head and tail rise. And if you see a fish jumping today, you can go back tomorrow and see him jumping in the same place, at the same hour."

ROY STEENROD

When Roy Steenrod retired in 1952 after serving twenty-six years as a New York State fish and game protector, the affiliated sportsmen's clubs filled the biggest dining room in Sullivan County at a testimonial dinner which was the more impressive because a goodly number of those present had been pinched by him for hunting or fishing violations sometime during his career. He had won their respect and liking, as indeed he has that of all the regulars who fish in the western Catskills.

But it is the boys who best know and like this well-spoken, smiling, even-tempered man who does not now like to be reminded that in his youth he was a hot professional motorcycle test rider and a holy terror in a fistfight. As a master flytier (he created one of the best American brown trout flies, the Hendrickson) and lifelong fisherman, hunter, and woodsman, Roy has been counseling and instructing Boy Scouts almost from the beginning and holds the prized Silver Beaver of the organization for his services. And he has been teaching fly-tying and woodcraft in the state conservation seminars for boys at the DeBruce Hatchery ever since they were started.

A strictly homegrown product of Liberty, New York, Roy was born in 1882 of old American Revolutionary stock. He caught his first trout, right in Liberty, at the age of five and soon began taking all-day fishing trips, carrying a frying pan and a slice of bread so he could bring his catch home inside him. So it was natural that when, in 1904, he went to work in the United States Post Office, he should have become acquainted with Theodore Gordon through selling him foreign money orders with which to buy English fly-tying materials.

Roy feels that he was closer than any of Gordon's other friends, and one cannot interview him without sensing that this devoted friend is continually choosing what he will and will not reveal and is holding back personal and family matters which he undoubtedly feels it would be a breach of confidence to disclose.

More than all, Roy has one unique distinction. He is the only person to whom Gordon gave fly-tying instruction, aiding him from time to time with hints and tips which he was "on his honor not to tell anybody" and suggesting that Roy learn to tie without a vise so he could tie a needed pattern on the stream.

For it is a fact that Gordon jealously guarded his fly-tying knowledge, which, Steenrod thinks, he gained from books except for his exchanges with Skues.

Gordon's books, which his executor gave to Steenrod, testify to their owner's reticence and secretiveness. All but one of these are replacements of those destroyed by fire in 1913 while they were stored in Liberty, and as he died in 1915, there was not much opportunity for them to have become used. But even his old, well-thumbed copy of Francis Francis's *Book on Angling*, which he owned and used for many years, is devoid of any marginal comments, penciled notations, underscorings, or other reflections of their owner's personality. Apparently this does not reflect orderliness, which was not an outstanding trait of the owner, but secretiveness. "That one thing about Gordon—he never put anything concerning his fly-tying methods or patterns anyplace where anyone could get hold of it," Steenrod explains.

The Gordon books owned by Steenrod are: Perry Frazer's *Amateur Rodmaking*, the gift of Mrs. C. F. Clark of Michigan, whose husband had been a copious Gordon correspondent (I believe it was Mr. Clark's large collection of Gordon letters that Mr. Clark's widow burned as rubbish, after having kept them for many years, a couple of months before John McDonald traced her down); two copies of George LaBranche's *The Dry Fly and Fast Water*, one a gift to Gordon from Will T. Williams of Lebanon, Pennsylvania, another correspondent, and then to Steenrod "with the compliments of his friend Theodore Gordon" and the other inscribed "to Theodore Gordon, Esq., an angler and one whom I am glad to call my friend, this little book is inscribed with the best wishes and compliments of George M. L. LaBranche"; Emlyn Gill's *Practical Fly Fishing,* inscribed "to Theodore Gordon with the deepest appreciation of the unknown correspondent 'Whirling Dun' for the beautiful flies sent to him through *Forest & Stream*"; Ronalds's *Fly Fisher's Entomology* (rebound by Steenrod), which apparently was bought secondhand in England, for it bears a penciled signature, "Rev. H. Corles (?)" and a notation referring to the gray drake on an Austrian river; Halford's *Modern Development of the Dry Fly, Dry-Fly Entomology,* and *Dry-Fly Man's Handbook;* G. M. Kelson's *The Salmon Fly* "from R. B. Marston to Theodore Gordon with best wishes, Christmas, 1914"; Francis Francis's *A Book on Angling,* fifth edition, and Leonard West's *The Natural Trout Fly and Its Imitation.*

"Gordon came from the South," Steenrod recalls. "He had no particular Southern accent, but he had the manners of a Southern gentleman, talked often about Savannah, had quantities of mail forwarded to him from that city, and kept hackles in envelopes bearing his name and a Savannah address; apparently he had been in the banking business there. He did a lot of writing, and I often wondered whether he had been to college or had picked up his education himself. He did not get out often or mix much with people, but he was very fond of Bruce Leroy, and sometimes he would take trout to the A. W. Smiths, city people who had a big summer home near Herron's on the Neversink where Gordon boarded for a time.

"If Gordon liked you, it was all right, but if not, you had better keep out of his way; he was kind of a cranky old cuss. When I was working in the post office, I had Wednesday and Saturday afternoons off, and I seldom missed walking over to Bradley [about five miles] to spend the afternoon with him. When I did not, he would worry about me.

"Gordon's mother was a little bit of a woman, about as big as he was—five feet two inches. She used to come up to Liberty, and he would come over from the Neversink and visit with her for a week or two; she never went over there. His only relatives were apparently the Pecks in

Haverstraw, New York, and the Spencers in The Oranges, in New Jersey. One of the Pecks (probably Gordon, his favorite nephew, named for him) came to Liberty to fish with him a couple of times. At the end, when Gordon got so bad, he would not have a doctor, and I could not do anything with him. I got out of him the address of Robert Spencer in New Jersey and wrote to him to come up. Two brothers came up before Gordon died, and they came again afterward." Steenrod still has Spencer's letter of acknowledgment in which he agreed that he would not disclose that he had been sent for, and would not come to Bradley on the days when Steenrod would be there.

It will be noted that both Steenrod and Christian got in touch with Gordon's family shortly before he died. Both of their accounts are much too detailed and circumstantial to be figments of a failing memory; it is obvious to me that these contacts were made at approximately the same time, and that the cousins got in touch with each other and arranged to visit Gordon circumspectly so as not to alarm him.

"The only people present at Gordon's funeral besides myself were two men and two women, apparently relatives. Bruce Leroy was not told of the funeral and felt terrible afterward that he had not been present, and my recollection is that the same was true of Herman Christian," Steenrod continued.

"Gordon's mother was not present either, a fact upon which a letter from Gordon to me may shed light: 'My mother sleeps most of the time. The question is—has she strength enough to carry her through? I doubt if the doctor thinks so. She is surrounded by her nearest relatives, except myself, and the doctor thought my presence would excite and inspire there, and I could do nothing but be in the way.'"

One indication of Gordon's interest in Roy was his practice of asking him to write reviews of fishing books. "Then he would tell me: 'Young man, you had better not jump at conclusions.' When Emlyn Gill's book came out, he asked me to write a criticism of it, on which he made that same comment. He did not think much of the book," says Roy.

As a matter of fact, Roy inherited some of Gordon's correspondents. He had considerable correspondence in later years with R. B. Marston, the great editor of *The Fishing Gazette* in London, and with the

widows of W. T. Williams and C. F. Clark, both of whom are mentioned
in the published Gordon letters. One of Roy's regrets is that he did not
preserve more of this correspondence, particularly with Gordon.

"Back around 1905 my correspondence with him was heavy, but it
was only in the last few years of his life that I kept his letters. Even so, I
have a lot that were not published. These were later given to Miss Kraft
and are now in her possession."

These letters and Roy's close friendship with Gordon enable him to
clear up several puzzling points in the published letters, including the
identities of "C. M.," "the fat lady," and that mysterious stream the
Ringip, which the closest study of Catskill region maps fails to show.
"C. M." was Charles Messiter of Young, Messiter & Dodge, who had a
general store in Liberty; he hunted with Gordon. "The fat lady" was
Mrs. Anson Knight, with whom Gordon boarded in the last three years
of his life. And the full text of the letter which mentions the Ringip
makes it clear that Gordon was not talking about the Catskills, as the
date might indicate, but about Rockland County, New York. "It is wonderful the fishing and shooting there is to be had within 40 miles of New
York," Gordon wrote. "Three or four years ago a young relative of
mine . . ." And in that anecdote he mentions the mysterious Ringip.
Incidentally, the name is twice clearly written as beginning with the
letter "P," but one cannot decipher whether it is "Pingip" or "Pinqip."
The name is probably an old or local one, and the stream just possibly
may be the one in Rockland County now known as Cedar Creek, still a
good little trout stream. The confusion was heightened by the fact that
there is a Cranberry Pond in Sullivan County and a Stony Clove over
beyond the Esopus, as well as in the Haverstraw area; both were mentioned in the cryptic letter.

The one mystery which Roy cannot, or more likely will not, solve is
the identity of the woman with whom Gordon was photographed
fishing the Neversink, and the circumstances of its taking. He says that
the published picture (in McDonald's book) and another, unpublished
picture of Gordon and his friend reclining on the stream bank and
apparently taken on the same excursion, turned up in one of Gordon's
books after his death. Although there is no name on it, he thinks a pro-

fessional photographer took it since it is a proof, brown in tone. But photographer's proofs are purposely not chemically fixed to make them permanent, and to have lasted so long it must have been "retoned" to a sepia tint, a photographic fad popular in Gordon's time. Roy is definite in saying that the picture was taken in the Neversink, several hundred feet above the old Neversink bridge, in the run alongside the road by the stone wall in front of Chandler's house. (All that is now under a hundred feet of water in Neversink Reservoir.) But that is all he will say; and all that Christian would say was that "Gordon was disappointed in love and the girl in the picture is the one; she was not a local girl—I don't know who she was." So probably we shall never know the identity of this intrepid sportswoman, and maybe it doesn't make much difference.

In discussing Gordon as an angler, Steenrod has the opinion that Gordon would not rank with the best present-day tyers in technique, but he says that Gordon's flies were unsurpassed in effectiveness because in his day he was one of the very few who understood the nature of the dry fly. He was meticulous about the quality of his hackles and about hooks, and he labored endlessly to achieve the exact shades to match the body colors of natural insects. "He continually asked me to get different colors of silk and wool for him from my sister's embroidery shop in Liberty," Roy recalls. He fell heir to Gordon's tying materials and still has many boxes of the Hall's eyed hooks that Gordon preferred, Gordon's tying vise, which Roy still uses, and a big bag of crewel wool in scores of shades.

"He was a good fisherman and, particularly, a careful stalker. He paid a lot of attention to the sun and things like that. He used a big rod but with a very light line; and although he did not cast far, he cast very delicately and put his fly on the water 'just so.' I think he learned to fish in Rockland County, but at that time he was mostly a bass and pickerel fisherman. He learned his trout fishing pretty much in the Catskills. The first I ever heard of him in the Catskills was around 1895.

"I think he fished downstream, wet, almost entirely until he fell under the influence of Skues and began fishing upstream. Then he fished half wet and half dry—in or just under the surface. Many of the flies which he originated and in which he specialized, such as the Quill

Gordon, Catskill, and Gordon, represented classes of flies rather than particular species, but on some flies he was particular as to the color of the hackle, and on the body color it had to be a perfect imitation. His Quill Gordon was what we called silvery—almost invisible, 'water-colored.'

Naturally, it is impossible to talk long with Roy about the old days without getting some comments about the fishing as it was then.

"In LaBranche's time there was mill after mill up the North Branch of the Callicoon from Hortonville to Callicoon Center—one dam after another, with big rainbows in the rough water under the falls.

"I fished often from Neversink to Hasbrouck, and there were eighteen- and twenty-inch fish there all the time," Steenrod continued. "About a mile below Neversink, opposite Frank Hall's farm, the river came right down against some big rocks, and there were a couple of ten-pound fish there all the time." (This was below the present reservoir dam; there is scarcely any water at all there now.)

THE GRAVE OF THEODORE GORDON

"Time moves slowly in angling," John McDonald wrote in *The Complete Fly Fisherman*. But it moves rapidly in every other aspect of life, so that it was ten years after McDonald had published his opus and three after Miss Kraft had finished her investigations that the determination to clear up the one outstanding unknown fact of Gordon's history, the place of his burial, crystallized into action.

The situation which faced the researchers, Miss Kraft and the present writer, was that, first, there is no official, governmental record of Gordon's burial place and no record of any kind except in the files of the quiescent and obscure corporation that still operates the cemetery in which he lies. Second, there was no unanimity of recollection among the few aging people who might have known where Gordon was buried, including his relatives. And third, the recorded facts were meager and inconclusive.

The town clerk's records in Neversink Village showed the burial place as simply "New York." The fortunately preserved records of

McGibbon and Curry, the Liberty undertakers who had handled Gordon's funeral, showed that his body had been shipped via the Ontario & Western Railroad, the day after the funeral, consigned to Gordon's nephew Robert Spencer of South Orange, New Jersey, and that it had been received by one Frederick Bommer, otherwise unidentified.

It is curious how a fixed, mistaken idea can arise and become accepted so firmly as to persist through the years, coloring and misleading all thought connected with a situation. In this case it was the conviction among a number who had had some connection with Gordon, including the undertaker and Gordon's friend Roy Steenrod, that the nephew Robert Spencer had retained an undertaker in The Oranges, Frederick Bommer, to inter Gordon's remains somewhere in or near South Orange.

The situation was further clouded by the "recollections" of friends. One aged woman was positive that the services had been held in the little church in Claryville, which is famous among Catskill anglers for having a wooden trout as a weathervane, and that Gordon was interred in its churchyard; she remembered looking in through the church windows to watch the services as a little girl. The established fact that at the time of Gordon's death an unusually late spring had left snow piled up to the windows of the house in which he had died and that the ground had been too solidly frozen for grave digging cast doubts on this recollection.

A number of others were sure Gordon was buried in Haverstraw, New York, where his relatives the Pecks lived and where he himself had stayed for several years. And an aged relative said that "he was was buried in the family vault in some old New York cemetery," the name of which she could not recall.

Having checked the official records, the next step obviously was to check the cemeteries in and around South Orange, New Jersey, and New York City and Haverstraw, New York. New York and Haverstraw were checked by Miss Kraft by telephone, but invaluable assistance in checking the South Orange cemeteries was volunteered by Mr. John Knapp, a long-established funeral director of that town. He even went to the length of having a cemetery employee make a personal check of the headstones in Robert Spencer's burial plot on the chance that Gordon might be in the plot without being in the records. All of these investigations were no less valuable for having drawn complete blanks.

The next obvious step was to identify Frederick Bommer and discover who had taken over his undertaking business and records. Here the investigators drew another blank. Telephone books and directories of The Oranges in or around 1915 were found not to be available. The licensing of undertakers in that area had not begun until 1927, so there was no help in that quarter. It was noteworthy that Mr. Knapp, who, as he said, "thought he knew everyone who had been in the business around here for the last forty years," could not recall a Frederick Bommer. The suspicion began to grow that Bommer might not have been an undertaker but merely a truckman who had transported Gordon's remains to some pier on the New Jersey waterfront from which it had gone by steamer to Alabama, where he had lived in his youth and where he had family connections.

"I believe his mother is the key to the situation," Miss Kraft said during a discussion. "They were very close; she protected and overprotected him all her life, as long as she was able. She visited him each summer in the Catskills almost up to the time he died. He never married. I wonder if they aren't buried together."

Her records showed that Fanny Jones Gordon had lived in South Orange, and that she had died late in 1915. A look at the vital statistics in the South Orange Village Hall was obviously in order, and the present writer went over there for that purpose. Miss Mary Scully, a longtime employee in the Village Hall, a native of South Orange, and one of those people who know and remember everything and everybody, made short work of the search.

"Fanny Jones Gordon, aged 86 years 1 month, residing at 444 Hillside Place, South Orange, died of a cerebral hemorrhage and arteriosclerosis December 23, 1915, and was interred in the New York Marble Cemetery."

And what—and where—was that? Neither the telephone book nor the classified directory listed it. But Miss Scully called up a friend who was a funeral director, and he, after consulting some sort of directory or handbook, came up with the information that the cemetery was on Second Avenue and Third Street, Manhattan, and even furnished the telephone number of the superintendent. For good measure, he added the rather confusing information that several blocks away there was another cemetery, the New York City Marble Cemetery, not connected in any way with the other except that the superintendent was the same man!

This superintendent, Mr. Eugene Restucci, proved to be most obliging and helpful. His own records were complete, but he had been superintendent only since 1941, and his predecessor, he noted, had kept only fragmentary records or, usually, none. Mr. Restucci looked through what records were available and found plenty of Gordons in both cemeteries, but no Fanny Gordon or Theodore Gordon either. He called up the office of each corporation and quickly got negative reports.

But could not the headstones be checked? They could not, for like many oldtime New York cemeteries, both of these consisted entirely of underground vaults, each containing the ashes or remains of as many as forty people, and without identifying markers of any kind except that the name of the owner of the vault is inscribed above it on the cemetery walls. The only record of those interred in it would be in the books of the owning corporation.

Had not a New York City burial permit been issued? No. None had been necessary since a death certificate had been issued by the town clerk of Neversink Village.

By this time Mr. Restucci had become interested and volunteered to help.

"How much do you know about this whole thing?" he asked.

"Well," I said, "we know that the body was shipped from Liberty, New York, by train and received at the Weehawken terminal by a New Jersey undertaker named Frederick Bommer.

"Frederick Bommer!" Mr. Restucci exclaimed. "He was no New Jersey undertaker! He had the job here before I did; he was a New York undertaker and the superintendent of the New York and the New York City Marble Cemeteries until he died!" And yet we hadn't found the grave.

"Sometimes people are careless," said Mr. Restucci. "I am going to try the offices again." Forthwith he called the secretary of the New York Marble Cemetery, who read to him over the telephone the following information from the corporate minute-book.

"At the first meeting of the directors in 1916 it was reported that among those interred in the New York Marble cemetery during 1915 were Fanny Jones Gordon and Theodore Gordon, both in the vault of George Gordon, No. 26."

There remained only to go to the scene. New York is an old city which grew from a small area, so that numerous cemeteries that were originally established in the outskirts have long since been engulfed. But even when they are filled, and all known relatives have disappeared, it is so difficult to "abolish" an old cemetery as to be virtually impossible. So long as there are funds for perpetual care, and space for further interments, the cemetery continues as a living entity even though its corporate soul may consist of nothing more than a set of books in a drawer of a lawyer's desk.

The New York Marble Cemetery occupies the interior—what otherwise would be the backyards—of a square block of tenement houses, small stores, humble dwellings (several of them over a century old) and a municipal lodging house for vagrants. The block is between Second and Third Avenues and Second and Third Streets, a distinctly shabby neighborhood in 1957 but vastly changed from the ghetto of fifty years ago that centered around it and made infamous such streets as Cannon, Rivington, Delancey, and Hester.

The only outward sign of the cemetery is a locked iron gate in an arch between two buildings which leads into a passage closed at the farther end by another locked gate.

Through the gates a stretch of high retaining wall and a fragment of grassy turf are visible. The little half-acre cemetery itself is flat and unencumbered, well grassed, neat and seemly; the retaining wall and the absence of backyards deprive urchins of both incentive and opportunity to invade the premises.

A week before the forty-second anniversary of Gordon's death on May 1, 1915, Roy Steenrod and I went to the sloping shore of Neversink

Reservoir, behind and above the site of the old Anson Knight house, and there gathered an armful of laurel. We gathered another beside the Brooklyn Fly-fishers Club water on the Beaverkill, where Gordon had loved to fish and where he had been a permanent permittee.

I had a wreath made from this doubly symbolic greenery, and on May 1, 1957, Miss Kraft and I hung it below the marker which stands at the head of the vault, on the wall. Later in the month when Roy Steenrod was in New York as the guest of The Anglers' Club at its Spring Dinner, The Theodore Gordon Society along with Miss Kraft, John McDonald, and Roy, visited Gordon's grave and the occasion was recorded by photography.

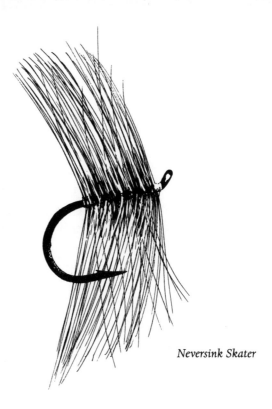

Neversink Skater

The Golden Age

SPARSE GREY HACKLE

Golden to me was the decade on the Neversink that ended with 1940. Edward Ringwood Hewitt had some five miles of the river between Neversink Village and Hall's Mills, and his fishing "camp" was an old farmhouse on high ground overlooking the largest flat along that part of the valley. Here the "rods" who rented annual fishing privileges used to assemble at the end of the day for unforgettable nights of fun and companionship and fishing conversation.

And what a goodly company was there, the choicest spirits of the angling age, the finest sportsmen, the best fishermen, the liveliest wits, the best-stored minds; the kindest and most helpful, too, as we novices quickly learned, and of course the best of teachers. Here was no stupid

113

competition for big baskets, no vulgar boasting and lying, none of the boozing and gambling that are traditional in some camps. These were the spiritual descendants of Walton, Norris, Hills, Prime, and Marston, and the atmosphere was the sublimated atmosphere of The Anglers' or The Flyfishers'.

Around, about, and over all was Ed Hewitt, the very monarch of this happy state, discoursing, informing, arguing, teaching, demonstrating—and criticizing. One still remembers his caustic comment—before witnesses, too—that "your fly is all right; the trouble is on the other end of the rod." We always fished our best under his eye and tried to hide our shortcomings from him.

As when, for instance, he took Tom Howell and me to fish in Molly's Pool, one sunset. Ordering us to put on fifteen-foot leaders, he handed us each a No. 16 variant with the most miserably invisible blue hackles imaginable, and clipped off top and bottom, to boot.

"Cast to the edge of the foam," he ordered. "Sparse, you stand here," and he placed me sixty feet below the dam. "Tom, you come over here; I'll show you." Tom was a visitor and it was all new to him.

No honest angler needs to be told that sixty feet is a long way from home plate even with a good rod, which mine was not. I tried and tried but each time fell far short. Apprehending that momentarily my mentor would turn his gaze and his disapproval my way, I wound up with all my strength and threw a mighty backcast and a still mightier forward cast. My line went into the bushes behind me and broke off at the leader knot.

I was undone if he looked my way now, but fortunately I had a leader soaking and another variant. I went frantically to work. I was just finishing my Turle knot when Mr. Hewitt exclaimed:

"What are you doing, Sparse? Don't change that fly!"

"Just tightening the knot, Mr. Hewitt," I replied humbly and not quite mendaciously.

Then my troubles were over, for Tom hooked one of Ed's huge browns. The fish got a move ahead of him and, probably because it was used to being caught and knew all the dodges, headed for a little side stream around the dam below. Then I saw one of the Neversink pictures

I shall never forget, the spectacle of Ed Hewitt, seventy years old, running like a deer in his old wading stockings to intercept the fish and at
every second step leaping with both feet together to make a splash and
scare it back.

It was fun to wade belt-deep, side by side with Mr. Hewitt, up the
middle of the glassy Flat Pool casting (he right-handed and I left-
handed) to the fish that lay along either bank under the alders. It was a
far shot on water that excused no errors, and it took more eyesight than
I had even then to see the little sipping rise with which a four-pound
brown would take a tiny wet fly or a thinly tied variant. Ed got all the
fish, as I recall, but I got most of the fun.

It was even more fun to pursue the variation of night fishing that
Mr. Hewitt developed for his water, which was improved with numerous low, sloping dams having deep undercuts beneath them in which
any number of big fish harbored during the daylight hours. As the light
failed, they would come out and begin feeding under the foam where
the water came over the damn, and then for a brief period one who was
a good angler could have rare sport fishing a close-clipped variant to the
edge of the foam.

When it became dark, the big fish would drop down still farther and
feed below the foam, and then we would use a No. 13 Hewitt wet
stonefly on the same fifteen-foot 4X gut leader. This was cast up and
across, and as it came down, the rod point was raised and slack drawn
in so that the fly was kept jogging along without drag—not an easy
thing to do by guesswork in total darkness.

The fish did not hit hard but sucked in the fly, and it was largely by
sixth sense and divination that one had to judge when to tighten. Then,
if the angler were fortunate, he would feel a gentle pluck quickly
building up to a powerful pull. The succeeding action was always violent and almost always brief, for these were strong, heavy fish. There
would be a tremendous splash and a hard vibration of the rod tip,
another heavy splash simultaneous with a hard jerk, all within a space
of two seconds, and then the angler would reel in and put on a new fly.
With the exception of Mr. Hewitt, we seldom landed those fish.

But the thrill still lingers in my memory. I love to recall the July evenings I used to spend standing knee-deep on a smooth, sandy bottom that dived abruptly down to six feet close below the dam, watching the starry sky and the white, white lace of foam where the water fell, hearing the night sounds in the black woods towering over me on the steep far bank, tasting the mellowness of Kentucky burley in my pipe, and still concentrating every taut faculty on taking up slack at the right speed.

Particularly do I treasure the memory of such an evening, the last time Ed Hewitt and I night-fished together. It was just sunset when we drove down to the Meadow Pool in his ancient Buick touring car with the top aluminum-painted to reflect the heat and holes cut in the back curtain through which to shove rods. In front of us was the great wide dam of the Meadow Pool, the blue water of its undercut covered with a tracery of white foam, with room on the brilliant white sand below for four or five to fish abreast.

From a distance which was daunting to me but merely respectful to Mr. Hewitt we cast invisible blue variants, clipped so they floated in rather than on the surface, for an hour or more, he with his usual success and I with mine. Although he cast with an ungraceful chopping motion, the result of an old shoulder injury, and seemed to sock the iron into his fish like a Nantucket harpooner, there was nothing wrong with the way Mr. Hewitt's line went out to its target; and as long as I knew him, I never knew him to break a leader. So while he caught fish, I watched, mostly; that way, each of us was getting what he best enjoyed.

A rain squall came suddenly over the mountain and hammered at us. I glanced at my companion, but he continued to ply his rod and paid no attention to the downpour that quickly soaked us. He was in his seventies at the time, and I decided that if he could stand it, I could.

The rain was tapering off when Ed remarked, "Hello, it's raining; let's get in the car." He stumbled as he waded out of the pool, but as he quickly recovered and paid no attention, I thought nothing of it. By the time we had stowed the rods, the shower had stopped and darkness had fallen.

"Let's go up in the tail of the Camp Pool," Ed suggested and drove the hundred yards or so that we had to go.

We started fishing with our same fine leaders and the little No. 13 stoneflies. Usually that was the best bet on that water, but tonight the fish would not take, although we knew they must be there and feeding. When I next heard from Mr. Hewitt, he was halfway up the pool.

"Hey, Sparse, they want something big. Put on a heavy leader and a salmon fly."

He had changed fly and leader in the dark and had been experimenting. I followed suit and was still fumbling when I heard a heavy splash and a savage exclamation from my companion. "Ha! Got him!" he cried with as much exaltation as if he had not hooked a fish all summer. The fact was that fishing was to Mr. Hewitt what whiskey is to a drunkard; he couldn't get along without it. Four or five times during the course of every day you would see him drop his work, hastily slip on his old wading stockings and go down to the river with his rod. In a few minutes he would be playing a fish, and in a few minutes more he would be back at work.

And yet, that night, he experienced as much wild elation over hooking a big fish—a fish which he tossed back carelessly after playing it in—as I would have who, naturally, never caught anything.

It was near midnight when Ed finally called it quits and we went back to camp, where he and I happened to be the only occupants at the time. As we sat on the porch steps and took off our wading gear, I was astounded to see him coolly dump a quart of water out of each of his wading stockings. He had filled them when he stumbled at the dam, thus completing the soaking that the shower had begun. But quit while there was fishing to be done? Not Ed Hewitt!

We changed to dry clothes and then he made a pot of tea for himself and for me broke out a bottle of Edradour, a fabulous pot-still Scotch twenty-five years old that no words of mine can describe. We ate a sandwich, then went into the common room, where my friend made a couch out of pillows on the window seat.

"Sparse," he said when he had arranged it to suit him, "You've been after me for a long time to write my reminiscences, and I finally made a start. Listen to this."

And then, while I smoked a pipe and sipped my whisky, he read me the bright narrative which became one of the best chapters in his fascinating autobiography, *Those Were the Days*. I can hear his voice yet and see the tackle-littered common room in the lamplight, and I cherish this memory, for the camp is gone now and all that lovely stretch of river where we fished is underneath Neversink Reservoir in sixty feet of water, and Ed long ago crossed that other River to fish from the far bank. That evening was a fragment of the Golden Age, both of the Neversink and of me.

Quill Gordon

Neversink Fishing

ERNEST SCHWIEBERT

Neversink fishing has been decimated since completion of its reservoir, but its tradition remains as rich as any river in the Catskills. Its fame is secure as the home river of Theodore Gordon, the bachelor fly-fishing genius who evolved the Catskill style of fly-dressing and adapted British dry-fly theory to American waters. Gordon is considered the father of American trout fishing, and his writing was collected by John McDonald in *The Notes and Letters of Theodore Gordon*. The book verifies his major role in the evolution of American trout-fishing practice. It gives us important insights into the frail, tubercular little man who invented the Gordon Quill and other classic flies. Gordon fished the Neversink faithfully the last years of his life, suffering the harsh winters beside his potbellied stove to dress exquisite flies for wealthy clients, and died in the old Anson Knight farmhouse near the Neversink in 1915.

The river has also been home water to great anglers of other generations. Edward Ringwood Hewitt had his famous mileage above Bradley before the reservoir was built. Most of his pools are under water now, except for the few cribbing dams that remain above the impoundment on the mileage of the Big Bend Club. Hewitt wrote ten books and pamphlets on fishing, capping his career with *A Trout and Salmon Fisherman for Seventy-Five Years*. The old master was a tireless innovator in fisheries management and fly-fishing, and carried on a cantankerous, lifelong partnership astream with the equally famous George LaBranche, whose *Dry Fly and Fast Water* is another Catskill classic.

The fly-dressing tradition known as the Catskill school began with Gordon on the Neversink. It continued in the delicate flies dressed by tiers like Herman Christian, William Chandler, and Roy Steenrod. Although it was Gordon who developed the Light Cahill from the older Catskill patterns, Chandler is responsible for the pale modern dressing, and Steenrod was author of the famous Hendrickson.

Two other great anglers were regulars on the Neversink in the last years of their lives. John Atherton often fished with Hewitt, and his experiences on the river are recorded in the pencil drawings and passages of *The Fly and the Fish*. The late Larry Koller lived at Monroe near the river, and fished it regularly from a hunting camp at Long Eddy. His books, like the *Treasury of Angling*, are filled with fishing pictures and experiences gathered on the Neversink.

The river is born in two branches high on opposite shoulders of Slide Mountain. Its clear little West Branch drops down a lovely valley through the Forstmann estate and the beautiful Connell mileage. These upper reaches are all private water, tumbling musically down pale-gravel riffles and sliding through ledge rock pools. There are wild brook trout with darkly-mottled backs and bright-spotted flanks and orange fins. The main river also supports them as far downstream as the reservoir, perhaps the largest river south of Maine that still holds wild brookies. These headwaters are all private except for a brief mileage available on the tumbling East Branch above Claryville, where the country church has a wooden trout for its weathervane.

There is a lot of public water left between the dam at Neversink and the big private estates below Bridgeville, where the late Ray Bergman described a great afternoon of Green Drake hatches in his classic *Trout*. However, the flow released from the reservoir is erratic, often insuficient to purge its boulder-strewn bottom of silt and sustain its once-great hatches. Fishermen can still find first-rate sport around Bridgeville and Fallsburgh when conditions are right, particularly in April and May, during the heavy hatches of Gordon Quills and Hendricksons.

There are many memories from the Neversink. Len Wright shared his mileage with me on the upper river one cold April weekend, catching wild trout on small wet flies in its sweeping riffles and flats. There was a brace of heavy two-pound browns from a deep flat on the Connell water above, while phoebes caught tiny Trichoptera flies above the riffles and deer browsed in abandoned orchards.

Still the most persistent memories of the Neversink are those hours spent with Larry Koller on his hunting-camp water below Bridgeville. There were afternoons with sunlight slanting through the pines, following hen grouse and their broods along paths deep in fiddleback ferns. The last evening I took a big brown fishing the ledges above Long Eddy, with cooking smells of a woodcock cassoulet drifting down to the river. Koller is dead now, and no longer fishes the river or stalks whitetails or walks up grouse on the ridges. His friends ended his funeral in that simple hunting camp above Long Eddy, and scattered his ashes into the river.

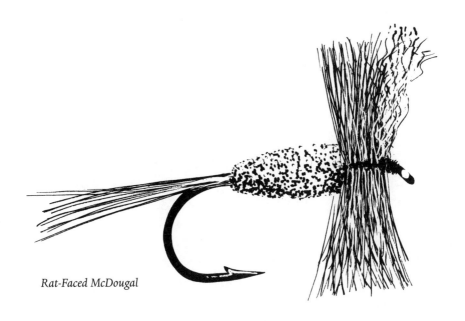

Rat-Faced McDougal

The Woman Flyfishers Club

AUSTIN M. FRANCIS

Jane Smith was sitting in the Icelandic Airlines lounge at the Reykjavik airport waiting for her husband and their flight back to New York. It was the summer of 1975, and they had been fishing salmon on the Leirasveit. Another fisherman came along and, noticing her rod case, engaged in the usual where-and-what-luck conversation. He further noticed that she was wearing a gold pin with a fly on it.

"What kind of a fly is that?" he asked.

"A Rat-Faced McDougall," she answered.

"Is that a club emblem?"

"Yes, the Woman Flyfishers Club.'

"What is this club anyway, a woman's lib organization?"

Mrs. Smith pulled herself erect in her seat and, in measured tones, replied, "We are a club incorporated in 1932. Our members are all dedicated women fly-fishers. We have our own clubhouse and water and we fish all over the world."

The Woman Flyfishers Club was conceived by Julia Freeman Fairchild, Frank Hovey-Roof Connell, and Mary Ashley Hewitt as a way of extending the enjoyment they got from fishing with their husbands, two of whom were members of the Anglers' Club of New York. As recalled by Mrs. Fairchild, one day in 1931 they were seated on the porch at "Wintoon," the fishing preserve assembled by Clarence Roof in the early 1880s on the West Branch of the Neversink. "We started talking about how much fun the men had in their club," said Mrs. Fairchild, "and we said, 'Let's form a club of our own!' So, a small group of us got together at the Hewitts' downstream on the main Neversink and made up a list of women we knew who enjoyed fishing. Later that year we had the details worked out and on January 28, 1932, we were officially incorporated with thirty-three founding members."

The Woman Flyfishers Club, with Julia Fairchild as its first president, was an instant success. The following year they raised their dues and took in twenty-two more members. Quite a few of the members had husbands or fathers who fished and who owned private water or belonged to fishing clubs; so even though they had no headquarters of their own at first, they received invitations right away to fish many of the choicest streams of the Northeast. Ironically, the husbands rarely got to fish each other's water, which led one of them, Dr. Whittington Gorhan to nickname his wife and her club mates "The Lady Wanglers."

Mrs. Fairchild and her directors had been searching from the outset for a "home pool" for their fellow members, and in 1936 they found it on the upper Willowemoc, above its junction with Fir Brook. As she remembered it:

"The property belonged to Mrs. Walter Bolling of Alabama and was about to be sold for taxes. She was very ill at the time and the negotiations were tedious and prolonged, but we finally got possession. Along with the lease we inherited a caretaker who could talk more and do less than anyone I ever knew."

The Bolling place contained 265 acres and one mile of stream. Three more miles of private water were made available through the courtesy of the Wilowemoc Fishing Club. By 1937 the women had hired a new caretaker, fixed up the house, stocked the stream, and they were in business. Until 1946, the Willowemoc was the home of the Woman Flyfishers Club. Then Mrs. Bolling came back, terminated their lease, and reclaimed her house. Said Mrs. Fairchild, "We had a lot of fun there and left it with regret, especially as we had no home to go to and the future looked dim."

To the rescue came Ed Hewitt, who had a soft spot for women anglers. He had heard of some water in the valley next to the Neversink and quickly arranged a merger for the homeless anglers with new landlords in a "little red house" on Sundown Creek, a tributary of the Rondout. Unfortunately, the fishing turned out to be disappointing, especially as the stream had not been posted until the Flyfishers took over, and they would often arrive "just in time to see a poacher sneaking away with a heavy string of trout trailing a large hook festooned with worms."

Discomfort on the Sundown led to restlessness, to continued searching, and finally to the West Branch of the Neversink, less than two miles upstream from where the club was born. In 1950, Frank Connell graciously offered the upper end of her Neversink water complete with clubhouse to her fellow members, and the women anglers came home to their native stream. They are there still, over eighty members strong, having recently observed their sixty-seventh anniversary.

A member of the Woman Flyfishers Club excites a great deal of curiosity when it is revealed that she belongs to the first-ever organization of female fly fishers in the world. She is often asked, for example, how she got started fishing. It used to be that a female fly fisher took up the sport because she grew up in a sporting family, or was drawn into it by romance. "What started me fishing?" pondered a woman angler. "Love wielding a fly rod; four years later I cast well enough to marry."

Mabel Ingalls, a granddaughter of J. P. Morgan and member of the Flyfishers, did her first fishing around at summer camp in the Adirondacks. She remembered catching two small fish, on dropper flies on a backcast. "I really started fishing seriously through boyfriends," she said.

"Only 'boyfriend' didn't mean the same thing then as it does today. These were just nice boys who were friends; sex was not involved, certainly not. But all kinds of fun things were—like camping, hunting, and fishing.

"We fished with a group of young men who had gotten out of Harvard, been in the war, and were back in New York in business. Two of them would ask two of us, or maybe there would be three boys and three girls. We took the West Shore Railroad at noon on Saturday, because they all had to work Saturday mornings, and we got off some place near Bear Mountain, fishing various places the boys had been going to alone. They knew the streams."

Reflecting on their outings and relationships with male anglers, Julia Fairchild said, "I think there is an equality of sexes in fishing that is entirely different from any other sport. We never had the slightest feeling with any of our fishing men that we weren't just as good as they were. In fact, it never occurred to any of us that we were men or women; we were fishermen."

In spite of this equality there are certain personality traits commonly associated with men and outdoor sports that a woman must possess if she hopes to be a successful angler. She must be self-reliant. "One of the things Julia was very firm on," said Jane Smith, "was that we were women who were not dependent on anybody but ourselves. We were expected to take care of our own equipment, to know what flies we had, to clean our own fish in places where they didn't have somebody to do it for us. This made quite an impression on me; we didn't come up and forget our wading sneakers."

A Flyfisher is also expected to cope with the physical stress and discomforts of an outdoor sport. She should have an appetite for hiking, wading, and long sessions of casting. She knows how to have fun in spite of rainstorms, biting insects, cuts, and bruises. In short, she is a good sport, a rugged individual.

If women anglers are so little different from men anglers, and so at ease in their company, why should there be any reason for them to start their own club? What is the rationale for a women-only fishing club? "I think it is the same for women as for men," said Jane Smith. "There is a certain kind of fellowship that seems to be present if there is only one sex. Once you get rid of the men, there's a kind of letting down of effort to appear anything but what you are."

Angling by its nature is a sport for escapists. "It's my secret life,' said Tappen Fairchild, and he introduced his wife, Julia, to a world of privacy and solitude. She and her fishing friends embraced this world and intensified its pleasures by forming their own club. In it, they enjoy the freedom to be themselves, to abandon care, and to recapture the joy and innocence of their youth.

Grey Fox

Incident on the Bushkill[1]

A. J. McClane

Fishing with Beedle was never dull. When he was Commander of the First Army, we were frequent visitors at A. F. Wechsler's mountain retreat—a 10,000-acre estate that straddles the Neversink and Bushkill Rivers. The Bushkill is a pretty little stream that meanders through heavy forest. It becomes club water about halfway down after it leaves the Wechsler property. Occasionally we'd meet a club member who strayed into Wechsler's water, but it was a tacit agreement that if anybody got lost, the respective owners wouldn't push the panic button.

[1] Reprinted with permission of Scribner, an imprint of Simon & Schuster Adult Publishing Group, from *Fishing with McClane* by A. J. McClane. Copyright © 1975 by A. J. McClane. All rights reserved.

For a long time we politely ignored that top pool of the club section. We'd fish to where the Bushkill Club posters began, then stand around admiring the trout rising on the other side of a single barbed-wire strand. Just about dark one evening, Beedle rationalized that we more or less had an invitation to fish the club water and anyhow, a big brownie was working on mayflies in midstream and to present the fly properly, one of us had to get below the wire to be in position. We both volunteered. I don't think we'd been in that pool five minutes when all hell broke loose.

First it was sirens. It sounded like thirty police cars. Which it was. Then horns started to blow. Then powerful lights—obviously spotlights—sweeping the treetops.

"Geez, these guys mean business!" said Beedle. "Let's get the hell outta here." We floundered up a muddy bank and headed across the wire, reeling in our lines as we ran. We could hear people shouting. "Let's advance as far upstream as we can," commanded the General, always the tactician. "Nobody will know we were near the place."

Judging by the number of voices echoing along the Bushkill, the entire First Army knew where we were. Beedle plowed through the bushes and I followed. Before long we were surrounded. Flashlights closed in from all directions. We stood there blowing like two beached whales. The woods were full of cops and Wechslers (and that is a formidable family).

The first state trooper to reach us was a big guy who pointed his light in our faces. "Which one of you is General Smith?" A brilliant question.

"I am," said Beedle in that basso profundo tone saved for dress parades.

"Sir." The trooper snapped to attention. "I have the honor of informing you that President Truman announced your appointment as Director of the Central Intelligence Agency, and you are to proceed to Washington at once. Sir."

Now you'd think Harry would have sent Beedle a coded message by pigeon or quietly dropped a CIA agent in the Bushkill by parachute. That brown trout was five pounds if it was an ounce! I'll say one thing—he took it like a true general. All he said under his breath was (delete expletive).

Cinberg

The Great Days

R. PALMER BAKER

The Catskill angling tradition flowered during the days of the Great Depression. Years later, in *Fishless Days*, Sparse Grey Hackle recalled the period as a golden age. On Hewitt's water, between Neversink Village and Hall's Mills, he remembered there "was no stupid competition for big baskets, no vulgar boasting and lying, none of the boozing and gambling which mar some fishing camps." Here were to be found Hewitt's "Neversink Rods"—Dick Hunt, Rogers Lamont, Joe Bamford, George LaBranche, Tom Collins, Reg Cauchois, Steve Dawley, H. G. Pickering, and Sparse himself. The joy that these men found in their fishing, however, must have been tempered by the state of the country and the world in which they lived, in the same volume there appears a famous story called "Murder." The hero methodically exhausts and kills an enormous trout on 5X gut. Suddenly he realizes this is just what the Depression is doing to him. He leaves his fishing to "catch the midnight to Pittsburgh"—where, by way of happy ending, he gets a contract.

Hewitt died February 19, 1957, in his ninety-first year. Apparently he never lost his affirmative outlook on life, but he had seen his own four-mile stretch of river flooded out by the dam except for the Big Bend at the top. Pickering described the water in the June, 1957 issue of the *Bulletin*. The right bank, looking upstream, was precipitous and inaccessible to outsiders. At the lower end of the stretch was the Dugway Pool, where "a dry fly rightly floated over the right current would take a good fish, two pounds, three pounds—if you knew how to do it." Then came a rapids and the dam at the foot of the Home Pool, the Camp Pool, and then Molly's Pool, where a creek emptied into the river on the westerly bank. Pickering said this was a pool that "called for art." Then came the Flat Pool, where the fish "knew their stuff, and the angler needed to know his.' And finally the Big Bend Pool. This survives. The rest, as Pickering wrote, is drowned "beneath the dammed (damned) waters of progress."

The short stretch of river above the reservoir and the East and West Branches above Claryville also still survive, largely preserved by private ownership. It is the river below that has suffered, its trout fishery virtually ended by the reduction in stream flow during most of the year. Down to Oakland, some sixty miles from the New York City line, it produced magnificent fishing for the big browns that used to stage up from the lower Delaware. Ray Bergman tells us in *Trout*, which was published in 1938, that on a squally afternoon, the 30th of May, he hit a rise of fish that lasted until evening and of which he kept three with a total weight of 10¼ pounds. There are sports writers, jaded by fishing around the world, who cannot contain their excitement when they speak of the fish that used to break them off in the rifts below Bridgeville.

These were the great days.

Early Stone Fly

Salar Sebago

LEONARD M. WRIGHT, JR.

One late-April afternoon four seasons ago, I decided to fish the reservoir itself, and chose a stretch where a sizable brook flowed into it. I was playing a hunch that the schools of smelt that spawn up this brook after dark would be resting nearby, and so would a lot of hungry predators. After covering two hundred yards of shoreline without a touch, I decided to sweep that area again, only this time farther out by wading up to the top of my chest-waders. This maximum effort meant shedding my fishing vest with attached net so that the fly boxes in the side pockets wouldn't get soaked.

I had worked well down the shore again and was beginning to congeal from the lengthy and near-total immersion when I felt a solid pull and then saw a large swirl. The fish just held there a few seconds, wagging his tail—probably confused at having been brought up short—then took off for deeper water. At the end of that first sprint, he performed a somersault two feet above the surface and I could see he was BIG. When he ran down the shoreline to my right, I backed slowly into the shallows, letting him run off the reel, and, when I reached knee-deep water, began applying serious pressure. This goaded him into two more jumps, and after a few more zigzagging runs I felt I had taken the starch out of him.

However to make that agonizing, five-minute trek back to my vest and net would be asking for a lost fish. I spotted a gently inclined patch of gravel about a hundred feet below me and decided to head in that direction and attempt a beaching. When I'd towed the fish down there and started to back up on dry land, he would have none of it. He wasn't as pooped as I'd thought. On my first two attempts, he panicked when he hit the shallows and made short runs, but on my third try I got him on his side and, keeping pressure on him by backing up steadily, used his flappings to swim him five feet up onto dry land.

At my feet lay a bright, male landlocked salmon with a scimitar tail that was so stiff I could carry him by grabbing the wrist of it the way one can with a mature Atlantic. He measured exactly twenty-four inches, and at four pounds, fourteen ounces he was handily the biggest fish of any species I'd ever taken from Neversink waters. It took all my willpower to keep from carting him off to the taxidermist.

While I felt this capture was a milestone of sorts, I couldn't say it was a complete surprise. Landlocked salmon had been successfully introduced into the upper Neversink over a decade earlier.

Back in the mid-1970s, a state fisheries biologist—the same one who's since settled in the Valley—paid calls on most riparian owners asking if it would be all right for state crews to enter their land to stock landlocked salmon fingerlings in the river. This caused quite a stir because landlocks, with the possible exception of Atlantic salmon, are the most glamorous of freshwater fishes.

A few owners wanted assurances that this wouldn't harm existing trout populations. And everyone wanted to know what sort of salmon fishing we could expect if the program succeeded.

The answer to the first query was that trout and salmon were usually compatible, rather than competitive, species. The salmon would leave the river at about six-inch size and do the rest of their feeding and growing in the reservoir.

It was admitted that we couldn't expect much river fishing for them. In most systems, a limited number of landlocks will run a short way upriver just after ice-out, and a scattering of fish may ascend a few miles if there's sustained high water in the summer. The major upstream migration would be a spawning run in October after the season had closed. The reservoir, which was open to the public and which the state felt was currently underutilized, would be the main fishery.

Of course, our consent wasn't necessary—state conservation personnel can enter private properly at any time to check on licenses and on possible fish and game violations. However, it was tactful and considerate of the department to tell us in advance, before we stumbled on crews stocking our waters with alien fish.

I'd caught landlocks in Maine and had found them game fish that were second only to their bigger cousins, the Atlantics. They took flies readily (if in a feeding mood), fought hard, jumped high, and made delicious eating.

The landlocked salmon, *Salmo salar sebago*, looks almost exactly like its larger, sea-run relative, *Salmo salar*, except that it often has a few more black spots. The two fishes are taxonomically identical. The more detailed dissections fail to reveal any physical differences, which lead biologists to believe that landlocks split off from Atlantics quite recently.

There must be a distinct difference in genetics, however. Landlocks will not seek out salt water, but will settle for a deep lake or impoumdment and do their growing up in this smaller, freshwater "ocean." Then, too, landlocks will take and digest food as they run upriver in spring or summer, while Atlantics won't. But, except for these two characteristics, their freshwater lives are similar.

Both are born in rivers and lead essentially troutlike existences until they reach six inches. This usually takes two years, but in stingy environments it can take three, even four. When this size or age is reached, the fish turn silvery, are called "smolts," and, usually in May or June, migrate downstream—Atlantics to the ocean, landlocks to their lake.

In both environments, it takes two more years of feeding and growing to attain sexual maturity. At that point, they seek out their natal river for spawning. In most Canadian rivers, Atlantics start their upriver trip as early as June, giving anglers up to four full months of river fishing. Landlocks are not nearly as accommodating. A few spawners may start nosing their way upriver in September, but most come up in a last-minute rush in October and November.

During their two-year lake-feeding period, landlocks will grow to two or three pounds, which is impressive since it took them that much time to reach two ounces in the river. The ocean is a far more lavish provider and an Atlantic salmon of the same age will weigh about ten pounds. However, both fish have the opportunity to grow much larger because, unlike the Pacific salmons, they don't necessarily die after spawning. Since they are true trouts (remember, the first names are Salmo), they can live on to feed, grow, and spawn several times. Both species have a life expectancy of eight years, and most are only four at first spawning. The world-record landlock weighed twenty-two and a half pounds. Atlantics have been caught weighing in at over sixty.

During the first two years of the stocking program, late-spring plantings were made with fingerlings raised from Atlantic parents of the Grand Cascapedia strain from Quebec. This gamble was taken because it was not until the third year that true landlocked stock became available. It turned out to be a poor bet. Over twenty years before, Hewitt had stocked the Neversink with fry from Scottish Atlantic salmon, and only a handful were caught or even seen in the next few years. Apparently, smolts of Atlantic parentage can't be tricked by the deep reservoir and keep on heading for salt water—either over the Neversink dam spillway or through the ten-foot-diameter water supply pipe that is armed with lethal generator turbines.

The first genetically suitable fingerlings weren't stocked until 1977. Some twenty thousand were placed in the West Branch exclusively, beginning way up in the narrow reaches seven or eight miles above the confluence. One stocker told me how they carefully tucked each tiny fish behind a protecting rock. "We planted them like kernels of corn."

This and subsequent stockings were a venturesome, even visionary, effort. Landlocks have only once been established outside their original range (in South America, of all places) and some efforts have failed even within it. Native populations were limited to northern New York, the top half of New England, and on up into New Brunswick and Quebec. Even within this limited perimeter, only some of the lake-river systems supported salmon populations.

The reason for this is that landlocks demand a highly specialized environment. First, they need a deep, cool lake with enough oxygen in the lower layers of water so they can escape the summer heat-up by cruising around at twenty- to fifty-foot depths where temperatures stay in the fifties. Nearly all qualifying lakes in the upper Northeast also contain healthy populations of smelts—another formerly anadromous species that was presumably cut off from the ocean by the same event that isolated landlocks.

Unfortunately, there are not now, nor have there ever been, lakes or rivers where landlocks are truly abundant because habitat requirements limit their numbers. Most deep, cool lakes lie at high elevations, up near the headwaters of rivers or lake-chains. At these altitudes, inlet streams are characteristically small, providing limited nursery acreage for parr and smolt to stock the lake below. Even systems that receive supplementary stockings of hatchery smolts deliver a discouraging fish-per-fishing-hour ratio. Perhaps, as is the case with muskellunge, scarcity has made landlocks even more admired and sought after.

During the first few years of this program, fingerlings were stocked in the West Branch only, but after a while in the main stem as well. Samples collected by electrical shocking revealed that fish planted into the less-fertile headwaters took three to four years to grow into six-inch smolts, whereas fish stocked in bigger water smoltified at two.

In a year or two, everyone reported hooking into small, bright fish that were obviously miniature salmon. They were most often taken from fast, almost white, water and these silvery slivers would leap several times before they could be grabbed and released. Anglers were catching yearling parr as well but most confused them with the small trout they closely resemble.

A few years later, mature landlocks were seen and a few actually caught in the lower reaches of the river. Then, in the early 1980s, came the banner year when many salmon ascended the river in mid-June and stayed up for two or more weeks. The river had risen four feet and stayed high for several days. When it fell back to fishable height, upriver anglers started catching bright fifteen- to twenty-inch salmon as far as three or four miles up the West Branch.

All rejoiced, convinced that this blessed event would recur after every high water now that the fish had been established. It was not to be. Occasionally, a few landlocks will nose two or three miles upriver after a summer spate, but for some inscrutable reason that major run has never been repeated.

I do catch a few larger-than-smolt-sized salmon on my water each season, but they're not a significant addition to the fishery. Some of these, in the eight- to thirteen-inch category, are fish that simply forgot to smolt and remain troutlike in size and coloration due to a lapse in instinct. A few times each year I hook into, even catch, an obvious reservoir dweller that has moved up on high water and settled into a lie of his liking. The best of these measured just over twenty-three inches and nearly caused coronary arrest when he jumped after being hooked halfway up Cliff Pool.

These accidental fish nearly always lie in the deepest water, and since they're not addicted to overhead cover, as big browns are, they're frequently seen hovering just above the gravel. Most of the few that are caught each season are taken on minnow-imitating streamer flies when river levels are up. However, salmon will surface feed when there's a decent hatch of flies, and I've taken several up to three pounds on a size 14 dry fly and two-pound-test tippet. Needless to say, many more have broken off.

Landlocks are the most sudden of freshwater fishes and usually hit a streamer with the wallop of a barracuda. They'll surge up through five or six feet of water and zip back to the bottom so quickly you'd miss the entire show if you blinked. Such takes nearly yank the rod out of your hand, and I have seen salmon of three pounds or less snap eight-pound-test nylon when an angler had a tight grip on his line and his rod tip low.

Quickness is also the hallmark of the fight that follows. Landlocks seldom run far—I've caught only a few that got into my backing—but they're nimble and powerful broken-field runners, darting this way and that so suddenly that if you're focusing on where your line enters the water you may catch their next jump only out of the corner of your eye.

Three or four clean, high leaps are only average performances. Some will erupt again and again like trampoline artists. It takes a prime, wild rainbow to challenge their acrobatics.

The Reverend Henry Van Dyke, America's most respected, perhaps even revered, outdoor writer back in Victorian days, positively gushed over the performance of this fish:

> Thou art not to be measured by quantity but by quality and thy five pounds of pure vigor will outweigh a score of pounds of flesh less vitalized by spirit. Thou feedest on the flies of the air, any thy food is transformed into an aerial passion for flight, as thou springest across the pool, vaulting toward the sky.

How any apostrophe as fruity as that escaped the editor's scissors I can't imagine, however it is pellucidly clear that the good reverend considered the landlock the Lord's most inspired creation since the fashioning of Eve.

After five or six years of planting young-of-the-year in running water, the state decided to shortcut this labor-intensive practice. Since the Adirondack hatchery could turn out six-inch smolts in a year, it was decided to put three thousand of these directly into the reservoir each May. Every fishlet was fin-clipped, alternating fins each year for generation identification, and catches soon proved that survival rates of these direct deposit salmon were far higher than among the more vulnerable two-month-olds placed in the demanding, fast-water environment.

The reservoir is usually ice-free by the first week In April, and landlocks have been caught as early as that. Salmon, however, like trout, rarely feed actively until the water heats up to 45 degrees, and fishing is far more productive two weeks later.

Then, too, smelt start spawning at these same temperatures and many salmon follow the huge schools inshore to the mouths of the brooks where smelt will ascend at night to lay their eggs. This is the time of great opportunity for the fly-fisher. When the salmon are within casting range in the shallows, a Grey Ghost streamer or other proven smelt imitation accounts for most catches.

Reservoir fishing holds up pretty well until surface temperatures climb up into the low sixties and hold there a few days. This usually occurs about Memorial Day, and after that the fish head out for deeper, cooler water.

This ends the fly-fishing for that spring, but a few diehards pursue landlocks all summer long. This means working the reservoir in a row-boat and trolling with lead-core line or a down-rigger. A few anglers drift-fish with a live alewife weighted down with split-shot so it will sink into fish-holding depths. Both systems seem to work and an occasional large brown trout can sweeten the pot.

I have tried this fishing a few times, but my heart is not in it, much as I love catching salmon. Long hours under a blazing sun thrill me not, and blank days are as common as catches.

On weekends I'll often count as many as two dozen anglers along the banks live-baiting or spin casting for trout and smallmouth bass, but I can't remember ever seeing more than four boats at any one time out over the deeps where the landlocks hang out. Motors aren't permitted by the Bureau of Water Supply and horny-handed toil is not as popular as it used to be.

Reservoir stocking is considered a success by the state despite the mediocre catches. Landlocks are nowhere numerous and there are few fisheries even up in Maine, where you're likely to do much better.

I have some misgivings about this new program, though. It seems likely that fewer of these fish will nose up into the river in spring and summer, and they may not even be attracted to the river at spawning time.

The late Dwight Webster, the foremost cold-water fishery biologist of his day, once told me that on an Adirondack fishery he supervised, landlocks stocked directly into the lake rarely located the running-water spawning area. Apparently, like Atlantics, these fish have to be imprinted in infancy by the specific and distinctive chemicals of their natal stream, otherwise it will exert little attraction.

This possibility doesn't seem to bother the state in the least. If the reservoir turned into a purely put-and-take fishery, it wouldn't make any difference to them as long as the boat and bank fishermen didn't complain. After all, how many riparian voters were there upriver? A dozen, possibly two, at most.

Still, the river keeps producing a good supply of smolts and I'm not convinced their numbers have peaked. Every fall, the retired biologist and I try to count the number of salmon that are spawning upriver. During the last few years about fifty pairs have made the trip. This means that over ten thousand eggs will be deposited, but that couldn't produce the nearly thirty thousand fry they used to stock.

Even so, this annual run makes a fascinating spectacle and nearly, but not quite, makes up for the sparse numbers of salmon upriver during the open season. They cut their redds mainly in the soft nibble bars at the tail ends of pools, the way brown trout do, and some of these fish are enormous. I have observed salmon of ten and perhaps twelve pounds spawning in early November. I've never seen such big ones in springtime.

While it is probable that most of these sprawners are river-bred fish, this is hard to verify. The river is often high at this time of year and the rippled surfaces make detailed observation difficult. Identification of a fin-clip, or lack thereof, on a fish swimming in the water requires close scrutiny.

A few years back, I recalled another point Dr. Webster had brought up. Not only did spawning Atlantic salmon sniff out their parental stream, but some studies showed that they homed in on the particular portion of it where they grew up. Since pH and mineral content change as a river moves downvalley, fish can apparently be further imprinted to a relatively short, specific stretch. In other words, a salmon that grew to smolthood thirty miles up the river would run up there to spawn, whereas one that grew up only five miles above salt water would stop running and spawn there. Dr. Webster suspected that trout and landlocks probably followed the same pattern, since they are closely related and such a characteristic would be beneficial to any species by spreading its young more evenly throughout the river.

Betting that the Doctor was right, I decided to try to lure as many spawners as possible to my stretch of water, Then, when the hatched-out fry grew into smolts and finally returned as spawning adults, they would stack up in front of my house. This would offer an advantage in closed-season October, but it could be a bonanza if high water and a cold snap fooled salmon into running prematurely in September, as sometimes happens.

Making artificial spawning beds is simpler than it sounds and I'd discovered how to create them by accident. I noticed that when I'd removed all the rocks and large stones near a cribbing for use as fill, trout invariably spawned in the residual small gravel, even when current-flow and pool position made the site seem unlikely. Apparently, the proper gravel size was an overriding attraction.

Every August, now, I chuck aside all stones larger than fist size in patches where the current quickens at the tail ends of pools. If a scouring flood doesn't undo my handiwork both salmon and brown trout find these prepared sites irresistible. In good years I have attracted as many as seventeen pairs of spawning salmon, plus a lot of browns, to my relatively short stretch of water.

The one September when we've had both unseasonably cool weather plus a good flush of water, the latter turned out to be too much of a good thing. A five-foot rise in river level, which ranks as a junior flood, scoured my prepared beds down to the large, forbidding rocks underneath.

My artificial beds will stay in mint condition through a three-foot rise, but that may not be enough flow to draw salmon up prematurely. We'll see one day. In theory my scheme should work but it will probably do so only under a rare combination of circumstances.

Still, I can prepare six-foot by six-foot beds with about an hour's rock tossing, and two years out of three they remain so inviting that fish programmed to spawn higher up are seduced into stopping. The resulting samlets must achieve better growth and survival rates in these slower and more fertile waters. Even if I've overestimated this benefit to the fishery, just witnessing these big fish working in the shallows or resting up in the adjacent pools makes the few hours spent one of my shrewdest investments of the year.

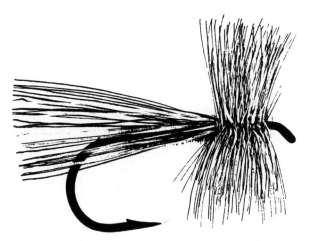

Fluttering Caddis

The Endless Belt

LEONARD M. WRIGHT, JR.

If water weren't so plentiful and ubiquitous, medieval alchemists would have lusted after it and present-day scientists would be enlisted in crash programs to create it that would dwarf our recent atomic energy and space-travel efforts. Happily, water is an everyday, everywhere miracle even though we take it for granted.

Yet consider for a moment what water is and does. It is far and away the most extraordinary compound known to science. It has so many unique properties and capabilities that only the few that have a direct bearing on trout behavior can be discussed here.

First, water is the universal solvent: it is capable of dissolving a greater number of substances in larger amounts than any other liquid known or imagined. This means that it can steal from the atmosphere and leach from rocks and soil a vast range of chemical elements or organic nutrients and distribute them to the plants and animals it nurtures below its surface. Second, no other substance has as great a capacity for absorbing and conducting heat. This gives it the dominant role in the heating or cooling of the earth's atmosphere from the torrid equator to the frigid poles (the Gulf Stream's stabilizing influence on the climate of northern Europe is a vivid example) and makes water, as an environment unto itself, highly consistent and strongly resistant to sudden and violent temperature fluctuations.

No wonder, then, that water is by far the largest component of every living cell—vegetable or animal. Even the most visionary science-fiction writers find it hard to imagine living creatures of any type or form without water.

Fortunately, there are 340 million cubic miles and billions of billions of gallons of water on and near the earth's surface. That's good news for the world in general, but the trouts are limited to a stingy share of this abundance.

Some 97 percent of all this water is stored in the saline seas and oceans of the world to which a trout has only occasional and limited access. One percent is locked up in solid state in the earth's snowfields and glaciers. Only 2 percent exists as unfrozen fresh water and the bulk of this is confined in lakes, ponds, and underground aquifers. Running water with the purity and temperature to support trout populations makes up a minute portion of 1 percent of the earth's total supply of water.

To grasp even a superficial idea of what this tiny, chosen fraction is like and of the basic conditions and limitations it imposes on the trout's everyday existence, you have to enter a stream with mask and snorkel. As you swim or drift downcurrent, peering through your face-plate, your first impression (if the water isn't bone-chilling, as it usually is) is that trout live in an enchanted and idyllic world.

What has appeared from the surface to be a rather prosaic pavement of stones turns out to be far more intricately sculptured with suddenly deepening pockets, undercut rock slabs and dark, mysterious grottos. Horizontal fountains of snowy bubbles pour downstream from rocks that break the surface in fast water. Pennants of pale-green algae flutter frqm the stream floor, contrasting sharply with the patches of near-black moss that blanket the sides of chosen boulders.

Fish, only occasionally seen from the streambank, appear in profusion. Thumb-sized sculpins hug the bottom, loose schools of striped dace dart around you, and large, dark suckers nibble the stones. Most exciting of all, here and there you encounter a solitary, uneasy trout opening his mouth, then his gills, in alternating sequence.

A fish that skitters away forty feet ahead of your approach from the bank now allows you to enter his living space when you're disguised as a log drifting downstream. He'll eye you suspiciously and increase his fin action when you're a dozen feet away, but he'll seldom bolt till you're within four or five feet the first time you drift past. You don't fit the specifications of mink, otter, merganser, or cannibal trout that are his usual underwater enemies and he'll give you the benefit of the doubt up to the last seconds. Try a second trip, however, and if he isn't still tucked away in his sanctuary, he'll flush the moment he sees you.

Attempt to make a quick movement with your hand or foot and you'll discover that water isn't nearly as "soft" as you'd thought. It's more like Jell-O than air, making fast motions impossible. For example, I have never been able to drive a spike with a five-pound sledge underwater while constructing or repairing log cribbings. I can't build up enough head-speed with the instrument to make a spike penetrate even soft wood. Water resistance increases geometrically as the speed of an object increases arithmetically. This means that it takes four times as much force to move an object through water at two miles per hour as it does at one, and sixteen times as much power at four miles per hour.

Though trout are better equipped to slip through water than you are because they are more streamlined and covered with friction-reducing slime, the above formula holds true for them, too. Small trout may appear swifter than large ones because they travel more body-lengths per second. But a large trout can overtake (and eat) a small one in an open race because muscle power increases slightly faster with size than drag does.

If you grab a rock and sink to the bottom of a pool, rolling over on your back, you can get some idea of the trout's-eye view of the above-surface world. Visibility is quite distinct directly overhead, but at wider angles objects become blurred. At about 45 degrees (actually, 47½) vision out of the water cuts off completely and the surface acts like a mirror. However, debris like floating insects or hemlock needles trapped in this peripheral quicksilver zone advertise themselves with sparkles of light out of all proportion to their size.

Come up for a breath now, then drift downcurrent, swivelling your head to see in all directions. You'll find our underwater view is limited to ten, rarely twenty, feet in each direction. You'll have the feeling that you're living in a small to medium-sized room with a low ceiling that travels with you and constantly changes—adding new wonders on one end and losing familiar ones on the other.

You've now experienced most of the few characteristics that free-stone trout stream environments have in common. Nearly everything else varies widely from water to water, even though they all start out with the same raw material: droplets of rain condensed from water vapor in the upper atmosphere and returned to earth by gravity. These raindrops are slightly acidic and have also picked up small particles suspended in the atmosphere, yet they can be considered as pure water for our purposes, or pure, at least, compared to what happens to them after splashdown.

Most raindrops either quickly re-evaporate or are used by vegetation—both considerable factors In summertime. But about 27 percent of the rainfall in trout-supporting areas enters our streams either as immediate runoff, delayed flows that have percolated through soil and gravel, or even later as trickles from springs—more gradual meterings from underground reservoirs called water tables and aquifers.

Obviously, watersheds vary widely in soil depth, soil type, and ability to store water. The most violent systems usually occur in rocky, arid areas where streams become rampaging torrents a few times a year and are dry arroyos the rest. Such streams, or temporary ones, are more like the concrete catchments one sees on the slopes of Caribbean islands than true waterways, and usually they too support no aquatic life. The exact opposite situation is found in certain chalk and limestone regions where rainwater filters down through hundreds of feet of porous rock before it is discharged from deep springs that are nearly constant in both volume and temperature the year around.

Most trout streams, however, fall somewhere between these two extremes and are fed by a combination of all three sources. Those that are created mainly by the first two—quick runoff and percolation through the soil and sub-soil—are called (and take your choice) rain-fed, freestone, or spate rivers and an estimated 98 percent of all North American running trout waters fall into this indistinct category.

Streams of this type lack easy identifying features because they differ widely in volume of flow, chemical content (or fertility), gradient, and in stream-bed composition to name just a few variables. There are no true twin streams in nature, and in fact, there are usually wide differences in tributaries that drain similar geological and ecological areas.

I know of two streams, for example, that are nearly identical in length, volume, and gradient that rise within a mile of each other at the same altitude, flow for some ten miles parallel to each other, and run not three miles apart until their confluence. If ever there were the setting for twin streams, this would be the textbook example. Yet one is easily more than twice as productive as the other in both trout and trout food.

The only visible difference between the two is the structure of the stream-bottoms. The poorer has a bed mainly composed of small rubble and gravel while the richer is paved with sizable boulders and slab-rocks of varying sizes—a bottom-structure with three obvious advantages. It offers more cover for trout and trout food, provides more stability in time of flood, and traps more twigs and leaves that many aquatic insects feed on. The branch with the mainly pebble bottom is extremely unstable in high water, losing both its trapped detritus and aquatic insect populations when its small stones are rolled over by quickening currents.

Unseen, yet equally important, is the difference in acidity, or pH, in these two streams. Rainwater reaching the richer one is apparently filtered through deeper layers of soil and gravel before entering the flow, thus picking up more nutrients and neutralizing most of the acidity acquired while percolating through the highly acid dead leaves and ever-green needles that carpet the surface of the forest floor. It has a pH of 6.4 while its poorer neighbor scores a scratchy 5.7.

If the differences between these two neighboring rivers seem sur-prising, the variety of conditions that can occur within each separate river should be astounding. I'm not referring to the spring-summer-fall-winter variations which are to be expected and which are usually gradual enough to give the trout time either to adjust to or avoid them. Almost equally violent are the possible daily changes that can take place in this roller coaster environment which the trout must feel keenly although nobody knows how uncomfortably. During a warm, sunny afternoon in March, for example, when the thawing snowpack streams down the hillsides in rivulets, the pH of the stream can plummet from a neutral 7 to a near-lethal 5.5 in a very few hours in the Northeast's acid precipitation belt. What this sudden change plus the rapid increase in current flow and the surge of silt particles that can clog a fish's delicate gills do to a trout's body chemistry and oxygen intake would appear to be catastrophic yet somehow, nearly all seem to survive.

Flash floods caused by thunderstorms in summer and early fall may have less effect on the chemical composition of the water—although they tend to lower the pH markedly. More important, they carry down vast quantities of silt and organic matter that hamper the trout's oxygen-supplying gills, increase water volume immensely, and easily quadruple both current speeds and pool depth . . . all this happening within an hour or so. Trout usually roll with the punch by swinging to the margin of the stream out of the main flow of currents and debris, but after this sort of sudden mini-flood, one finds many young-of-the-year landlocked in puddles left by the receding waters where heat, dessication, or raccoons will soon finish them off. One has to wonder, at such times, whether all of these fishlings were really genetic culls or whether some were mere victims of a quirk in the currents or of just plain bad luck.

Daily fluctuations in atmospheric pressure would appear to be trivial to a fish totally immersed in the far denser water, but anglers will tell you otherwise. A low, or falling, barometer is considered an almost certain sign that trout will cease feeding and that the fisherman's catch will be skimpy at best. And, according to the consensus, the faster and lower the barometer falls, the worse the fishing will be.

Why this should be so has mystified most anglers for years. After all, the difference between the lowest barometric reading ever recorded and the highest would affect the pressure felt by an underwater creature equal only to that felt by a depth-change of three feet, and the average fish-inhibiting drop would be the equivalent of a depth-change of only several inches. Since trout readily rise and descend far greater depths than this while happily surface-feeding on flies, it is hard to believe they feel acute discomfort during a small drop in the barometer.

However, a low, or falling, barometer is not an isolated phenomenon. Lessened pressure in the air above means that the water below can hold slightly less dissolved oxygen and other gases. And low or failing barometers are usually accompanied by cloud cover and, in many cases, by storms of varying intensity. The presence or absence of sunshine alone can have a drastic influence on a trout stream's essential make-up, due to temperature changes.

Indeed temperature changes, and the changes that are triggered by them, may be the most influential factors in the life and behavior of trout—especially in spring and summer when trout feeding and trout growth are at their peak. During June, July, and August, stream temperature can rise as much as 15 degrees Fahrenheit within a twelve-hour period and drop back that much in the following twelve. In clear, bright weather when nights are crisp and days sunny and the water is low and slow, I have taken readings on a first-rate Northeastern trout stream that ranged from 54 degrees at dawn to 70 at 4 P.M.—a time differential of only ten hours or so.

Since the trout is a cold-blooded animal (which really means that its body temperature tries to stay the same as that of its environment) it takes some time for the trout's body to absorb the heat from the rapidly warming water in the morning and equally long to adapt when the temperature starts dropping at the end of the day. In other words, during roughly half of any twenty-four-hour period, the trout must feel the water around it as quite warm and during the other half as distinctly chilly.

It has been determined that the optimum temperature for brown trout is 63 degrees F., slightly lower for eastern brook trout, and perhaps slightly higher for rainbow trout. By optimum biologists mean that the trout's metabolism rate and overall biological efficiency seem to peak at this temperature even though they may function nearly as well through quite a wide range on either side of this mark. Active feeding, for example, seems to start at about 45 degrees F. and usually comes to a halt when the thermometer registers 72 degrees or more.

The temperature itself, however, is only one of the factors that varies during these wide diurnal swings. Fot example, the density, or viscosity, of the water is changing, too. Not much, perhaps, but water at 54 degrees F. is nearly 1 percent more dense or more difficult to plow through than it is at 70.

Far more dramatic is the change in oxygen content of water as the temperature varies. Water can retain 20 percent more dissolved oxygen at 54 degrees than it can at 70—a violent swing of a vital requirement in trout survival.

Though water may have the most stable liquid known, this characteristic is sorely tried when it runs in a shallow sheet. Stones on a stream-bottom heat up rapidly under the direct rays of the summer sun and pass the calories on readily to the endless belt of water flowing over them. Only the steady discharge of springs from the water table keeps most trout streams from reaching lethal temperatures on bright summer afternoons.

The seasonal, and especially the daily, fluctuations in the trout's environment have increased in recent years. Because of timbering, agriculture, water abstraction, paving, and literally everything associated with man's use, occupation, and alteration of the land—watersheds are now less stable in temperature, flow, and chemical comnposition. So far, while trout may not have flourished under these conditions, they have at least survived in most rural environments. As our "civilization" of the land increases or intensifies, let us hope that the genetic plasticity or simple innate tolerance of trout allows them to continue to exist in a wild, self-propagating state.

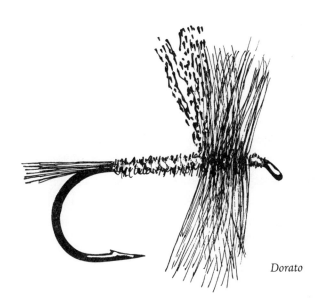

Dorato

Last Days Are for Dreamers

NICK LYONS

To be perfectly safe, I saved two days with which to end the trout season: a Thursday and Friday. I wanted to round off the year; I wanted some long hard fishing, away from the crowds, and some active trout. I wanted a tidy chord or coda to end what had been a very pleasant season—and two days, before the busy last weekend would be private and surely safer than one.

Last days always held surprise, high drama: a day in October on the Big Hole when every trout in the river wanted my Dave's Hopper for lunch; a late afternoon on the Ten Mile when trout after trout—you would not have believed the river held so many—busted up at streamers I chucked to them; and that cool evening on the East Branch, three casts from season's end, when an alligator of a brown, bigger than my arm, rose to take a huge chub I'd tossed back carelessly. Mysterious, wild, memorable things happened to me on the last day of a season.

Perhaps it was the onset of the cold, the start of the spawning mania, or the intensity with which I always fished at season's end. I thought of a dozen such days filled with excitement, as I drove upstate on Thursday, watched the autumn color grow richer, denser amid the green, as I headed north, toward trout country. Gash of scarlet, yellow of beech and maple, oaks red and tawny, the sun bright and cold, and I, at middle age, still trembling, like the kid I've always been about this fishing business, full of hopes and dreams.

But the Willowemoc was pinched and shrunken, clear as water in a glass; the trout were skittery phantoms, quick dark shadows, and all I caught was that image in the pond of all the colors of the mountain doubled and blurred, so there wasn't any recognizable form, only an abstract of color, a late Monet or Guston.

I was scarcely discouraged on the long trip back to the city. I still had Friday. It had been a long full year and I merely wanted to give it a coda, a tidy ending. The Willowemoc had been too low but the Neversink in the Gorge would be perfect—a brilliant choice: when the water dropped below the tops of the boulders there would be thousands of pockets, and the cool weather of late September would have the browns fighting for our flies. I picked up my old friend Sandy in the rented four-wheel drive and we met Justin near the Neversink at 10:30. I was achy and tired from the trip Thursday but no matter: I'd fished the Neversink twice this year and had grown to love the broad tumbling river, studded with boulders and long glides, tucked into the base of a deep, narrow, primitive gorge. The trout were wild browns, there were reports of four- and five-pounders in the deeper pools—and there was a wildness about the place, with its dark forests and huge stands of rhododendron and mountain laurel, which in May and June had been in luxurious bloom. The property belonged to Ben Wechsler and we were grateful for the invitation.

Our plan was to drive the four-wheel drive a couple of miles downstream, then trek downriver another mile or two and fish. Then Justin would drive the car upstream another mile and Sandy and I would fish up the last stretch to him. I couldn't wait.

"You shouldn't drive so fast," Sandy said as I whipped up the rutted dirt road, anxious to be there, to be on the water.

"I'm crawling," I said.

"I'd hate to get high-centered," he said as I scraped over a stone, "and have to walk back and get a tow truck. I'd hate to . . . SLOWLY, Nick!"

A turtle could not have been going more slowly.

"Slow and steady. SLOW-LY," Sandy said.

"You really ought be be more careful, Nick," Justin said.

"I'd like a long day on the river, is all," I said.

"I'd just like to get there," Sandy said. "I've been high-centered in some ugly places, some very ugly places, Nick."

So I crept at a ridiculous pace and we inched closer and finally got there and suited up and headed down to the river. Perfect. It was precisely the right level. It was clear, but the little rain the night before had given it a touch of color; it was low but this was a river that fished best in lower water. I had absolute confidence that I'd made a brilliant choice. Justin said he'd gotten six the week before. We'd get sixty today.

The Gorge was dazzling and I paused a couple of times—when Justin erroneously thought my heavy breathing was a sure sign of too much middle-aged paunch—to look at the fluttering birch and beech leaves, yellow and ocher, and the umber slopes, where tawny browns mingled with the remaining green. The bottoms of the pools were peppered with yellow and brown leaves and I hardly noticed the slight morning sun had given way to a chill gray and a steady drizzle.

When we'd gotten downstream as far as Justin thought I could walk, we each settled into a pool and began to cast. In a moment I forgot the fluff of scenery, the chance of putrid weather, and concentrated on the tiny tuft of white that was a Hair-wing Royal Coachman flicking up into the head of the pool and drifting down through the bubbles and foam of the Neversink. There ought to have been one there, and one there. I fished four pools hard and never saw a rise. So I switched to a Dave's Hopper at a gorgeous bend pool, where the white water bounced around a turn, washed in against a huge rock wall, eddied, and then shot downstream around a boulder. The twists of current and crosscurrent made it hard to keep the fly afloat but I kept flicking the grasshopper in against the rock, hoping so large a fly would draw some alligator up from the depths of that beautiful pool. On the tenth cast a respectable brown, about sixteen or seventeen inches, darted up out of the opaque depths, turned, swiped at the fly, which hesitated for a moment, sending that brisk charge of electricity up into my hand. Pricked and gone—but I cast a dozen times anyway and then headed upstream.

The gray and drizzle had settled in for the day and I figured it was the lousy weather system that was keeping the fish down. I waded the rocky pools with more difficulty now, tripping several times, falling on my face once, tossing my rod up onto the grass as my foot hit a submerged rock and I went forward, caught myself, banged my knee, and barely kept myself from a full-fledged dousing, which, in this weather, would have been disastrous.

By the time I got to the spot where we'd left the car I was exhausted. Sandy, my age, looked little different in shape from what he'd been thirty years ago, when we'd been in the army together; Justin, twenty years younger, was a mountain goat. I was tempted to volunteer to drive the car to the spot upstream where we'd all agreed to meet but had some last faint hopes that I'd raise a good one in the final stretch. Anyway, Sandy was afraid I'd high-center the car, especially without his sober counsel.

As I worked my way upstream the weather grew more and more foul and my high hopes changed to grim determination: not to collapse before I got to the spot upstream. I cast poorly. I passed up difficult pools. I tripped and stumbled and trudged wearily upstream. And at last, beyond the final bend, I saw Justin high on a rock, cross-legged, safe, reading. He'd caught nothing but his happy enthusiasm was undiminished: he'd fish the river all autumn; he'd snowshoe in during January. Sandy had caught four or five, raised a few others, one of decent size. He was humming.

My score was less impressive: seven flat-out falls, a busted reel, a broken net, a bleeding wound like a stigmata on my forehead smack between my eyes, a knee that felt like mush, bruised ribs, a back that ached so sharply I thought I'd be hunchbacked for life, a dribbling nose, two boxes of soaked flies, a wet sandwich, shin splints, and one small brown trout, about nine inches.

Without a word I stumbled up the hill to the car, disengaged myself from my fishing gear and from the season, and headed glumly for the highway, happy only slightly that we hadn't been high-centered.

Sandy, a tiger on the stream, began to doze; my mind grew furiously active. I dreamt of the bruised ribs and bleeding forehead that were the only coda I'd have this year. And, as I race-horsed back to the city, I dreamt of a first day in April, only half a year in either direction, when dun Hendricksons popped up out of cold, slate waters and rode the currents like little sailboats into the safe harbor of my dreams.

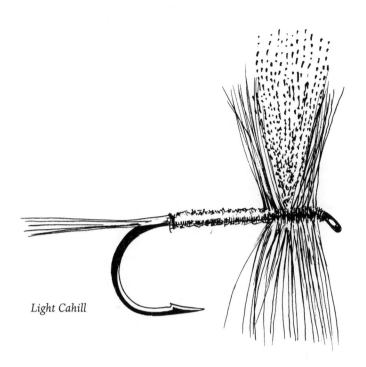

Light Cahill

A River's Tale

JUSTIN ASKINS

The Neversink Gorge is the hidden jewel of the Catskills. Wild and stark, its banks brilliant with rhododendron, the Neversink River sweeps and tumbles here for four boulder-choked miles. A little over an hour and a half from New York City, the gorge has been protected for more than one hundred years as a private conservancy and remains as primitive as a Western wilderness. This river is also my home water.

It was not always so. Ten years ago, knowing little about the Catskill rivers and even less about fly-fishing, I bought a small house outside Monticello, New York. A spinning rig had introduced me to the public sections of the Beaverkill and Willowemoc, but the lure of solitude drew me farther and farther from the heavily used waters. I knew nothing of the Neversink until I bought some Geological Survey maps that showed a virtually untouched river area not ten miles from my house. My interest piqued, I began to wander the fringe, walking my way down from Bridgeville, where Route 17 crosses.

One January morning I drove to the outskirts, loaded my pack, and began walking down a snow-covered road. In a few minutes I was in a stand of enormous hemlocks, listening to chickadees and an icy mountain stream. The effect of those first steps was immediate and electrical: The spell of the Neversink's wildness was upon me.

Soon some members of the local hunting and fishing club gave me permission to explore the area, and I took full advantage, returning often and looking longingly at that winterbound river. Then the club allowed me to join as a fishing member, and opening day became my obsession.

Several times I had tried to teach myself fly-casting, but the results were meager, my helpless flailing quick to frighten anything in the water. I was always looking around to make sure no one could see what I was doing, fearful that I would be turned in to the casting police and arrested for disorderly conduct.

Once I had access to fishing in the gorge, however, my secretiveness changed. Even on weekends, when members of the other clubs that rented from Benjamin Wechsler came up, few fishermen appeared. During the week, it was rare to see anyone near my favorite haunts— the series of pools near Hackledam and at the large pool above Denton Falls. I could cast with abandon, and my technique improved rapidly.

I knew very little of the Neversink that first year, but those two places opened me to further intimacy. Hackeldam was a particularly effective tutor. It offered deep, undisturbed stretches and chuting rapids, with everything in between. I learned that hair-wing flies like the Royal Wulff and Elk-hair Caddis would stay up in the fast currents, and how to keep them up for as long as possible. Soon, I could trick brookies with a 7X tippet in the quiet pools and hook browns in the broken water. My concentration was intense although a kingfisher's rattle or the hoarse call of a scarlet tanager might bring me back to a different world, of the rose-purples of wild geranium and fringed polygala, the soft whites of wood anemone and painted trillium.

Slowly I became more comfortable with the river. Sometimes I would look off to what remained of the Hackeldam bridge, built around 1800 by a Dutchman named Hackel. A settlement had grown up here, including a small concern manufacturing barrel staves and grain scoops. The power came from a dam Hackel had built on Wolf Lake Brook.

Other days, my mind would drift further back to when the Lenni Lenape had hunted through the gorge. The Neversink was traditional Delaware territory (probably for the Port Jervis band of Minisinks), and I delighted at how little disturbed the gorge remained from when Indians walked its banks.

That summer, I discovered the comforts of the Campground Pool above Denton Falls. There I would sit at a rickety picnic table laboring on my doctoral dissertation—appropriately, on Melville's landscapes—and watch for rising fish. I must have missed many, but when I noticed, I grabbed my rod, raced through the bluets and forget-me-nots, and began working an active trout. A phoebe had built its nest in the ledge across the river, and if I put down the brown with my ineptitude, I would often watch the small gray bird shooting and dipping along the far bank.

By autumn, I grew restless for new water, eager for fresh terrain, and I began to push farther into the gorge. Perhaps it was the sight of a bald eagle up from the Mongaup Valley, perhaps it was Wechsler's advice to try the canyon area, where the best fishing reputedly was. I'm not sure. But I felt an irresistible urge to explore.

One mid-October afternoon, with autumn bringing a richness of dark crimson, lemon yellow, and tawny orange to the mixed hardwoods, I crossed the river just above Denton Falls and began moving deeper into the gorge. Asters, fleabanes, and goldenrods covered the banks, with the occasional bright red of a cardinal flower breaking the whites, lavenders, and yellows of the other blooms.

I came first to a long, wide pool where the Neversink slows not far below Demon Falls. In that spacious and gentle water I've watched many rising trout, and I've been able to take a few if I approached warily and my fly was right.

Chimney Pool came next, where the Neversink turns sharply, rushing hard against a steep rock wall, a spot I have always taken as the beginning of the gorge. It was here one afternoon that Nick Lyons brought up an enormous brown on a grasshopper bounced off the far wall. I have had little luck with Chimney, but I know there's at least one big fish in its protecting waters.

Below Chimney I found my favorite place on the river, a stretch where I've pulled in a number of hefty browns. Scores of boulders push the river together here, and it twists and turns quickly, leaving dozens of small, tricky pockets. It's exhausting to wade, but its productivity can be sensational. I went back regularly, that first October, and one afternoon I brought up ten fish in a little over two hours.

The last trout that day taught me never to underestimate the escape strategy of a big brown. I had positioned myself behind a shielding boulder, looking to a tiny, calm oval that simply had to harbor something large. I was using a number 12 Light Cahill because it was easy to see, but each time I dropped the fly into that opening, the fierce current tore it instantly away. I moved closer. The water pulled at my waders. Leaning forward with little balance, I finally kept the fly there long enough for a powerful fish to shoot up and savage the Cahill. In the rushing water he seemed enormous, over three pounds for sure, and I had to let him run or lose him on my 6X tippet. Soon he was a hundred feet away. Now I had to work my way down through the turbulence, all the time keeping sufficient strain on the fish. For ten minutes, I struggled toward him, finally getting to a boulder just above. But the rest had helped the fish, and off he shot, plunging through three more pools before he held again. I knew I was going to lose him, but I went after that brown anyway and unexpectedly reached him once more. He must have sensed my closeness, for he darted under two nestled boulders and stopped.

Now that to do? I couldn't pull him back, nor could I reach far enough under to catch him by the gills. I pondered the possibilities and decided to try scaring him back into the open by getting on the other side of the submerged stones and reaching under. As I did, I felt a strong tail push against my hand, and off he charged to the next pool. Amazingly, the trout was still on.

A few more minutes of wading brought us together again, and this time, whether tired or bored, the big brown let me slide my net around him. I let him rest for a couple of minutes, then released him back to his native currents. An osprey had been watching my adventure, no doubt disdainful of such a ludicrous performance.

My life grew hectic after that October lull—too full of dissertations, gray cities, and a broken heart—and it wasn't until springtime that I reentered the canyon. The rhododendron season was half-finished, sheep laurel past, mountain laurel just beginning, great laurel still a month distant. I followed a deer trail through oaks and beeches to Dated Rock Pool. I've seen pictures of giant browns taken out of this bottomless water, but I've never come up with the correct technique to fish it. A sinking line with a big streamer might do, but that technique seems more suited to Western rivers like the Umpqua or Rogue. It was near here that two fishermen met one afternoon; Ray Bergman going south from Bridgeville, Larry Koller moving north from Oakland Valley. A record of their conversation would have been a remarkable testimony to the Neversink's magic.

By that second summer I had fished every pool in the gorge, working Cat Ledge Pool and Long Eddy, High Falls and Round Eddy. Exploring the deeply shaded tributaries had become my passion. Wolf Lake Brook, the recently named Hewitt Brook, Eden Brook—all had small but fine and feisty trout in them. Larry Koller wrote about one spot on Eden Brook:

> It was a picture pool with the water pouring in from a yard-high fall, churning itself among fat, mossy boulders, then flattening out its glide against a low ledge, then swinging around and around in a whirlpool eddy. The pool was deep, its bed a mass of black boulders; the sunlight barely flickered through the heavy overhead arch of hemlock and beech, leaving most of the hole in deep, mysterious shadow. An ideal spot for trout, I had always thought. . . .

Koller was correct, for a day later a youngster pulled a three-pound brown out of that water. According to Wechsler, much of *Taking Larger Trout* grew out of Koller's experiences in the gorge, and the culminating incident of my second summer would fit in Koller's volume.

A number of people from my hunting and fishing club were staying
over at the Campground Pool as part of their annual Fourth of July celebration. Trout activity all day was nil, the water temperature soaring
into the eighties. Even the late afternoon was dead, though occasionally
one of us would cast a few times with no success. Hope had disappeared
in the early twilight—thoughts turning to the misty coolness of the next
morning—when I spotted a delicate rise about midway through the
pool. That spot is usually reserved for a chub, but on a dull day even a
chub can be fun, so I pulled my waders on.

"Going chubbing?" someone called, laughing.

"Why not?" I answered with a grin.

Nobody paid attention to me as I began casting above the fish letting my big Adams drift down to the chub. But this fish wouldn't touch
the Adams. Picky chub, I thought. After a few more well-placed casts
brought nothing, I tied on a 7X tippet, changed to a No. 20 Adams, and
a dozen times sent it drifting into the ring of the rise. Finally, something
tipped up; I gave a slight pull and knew it was not a chub I had.
Whatever it was simply moved off, steadily, powerfully then anchored
near the bottom. I was astonished that my two-pound tippet had held.
Now what? Gingerly I tensed the line. But whatever it was didn't move;
my rod just bent a little toward it. It can't be a bass—too stationary.
Have I hooked giant catfish? Impossible. This acted like a big brown.

The people onshore began to take notice, none sure of what I had,
but all aware of it. Again I increased the strain on the line, but the fish
remained immobile. Twilight had edged into night, and my audience
began giving advice:

"Put a little more pressure on."

"Get the rod up higher."

I picked the rod up just a bit, anxious that my great fish not be lost,
but no, it was still on, and I was bringing it closer. Suddenly, it came to
the surface, rolled, and we saw a broad, bright trout. It was by far the
biggest brown I had ever hooked, and now I had to see it in my net.

For another ten minutes I kept working it closer, knowing the tiny
hook could pull out at any moment. Then I saw the fish again not five
feet off, struggling near the surface. Exquisite tension, then the net

slipped under it and I was looking at an eighteen-inch brown, its spots red, its flanks silver and orange.

I have since released many fish from that net. Some were larger but none more memorable. For that evening signified the end of a crucial part of my fly-fishing education. After that, the members of the club fully accepted me, and I felt the river and its gorge had accepted me, too. Walking back along the rutted dirt road that evening, I realized that I could now sense where a brown or brookie might be holding, where a Blackburnian warbler might be found, or a black-throated green, where dwarf ginseng or foamflower might bloom. I had become part of the gorge.

Now, whenever I am away from the gorge and feel the cool steel of the world at my throat, I have only to let myself drift back into those fiery October leaves, to remember that Fourth of July trout in my net, to feel very much at home.

The 100-Year Fly

The 100-Year Fly

PHIL CHASE

The feeding lane of the trout offered an easy down and across cast with a drag-free drift. I had just released a fifteen-inch wild brown of the Neversink when I spotted the trout feeding below me.

My fishing companion, Scott Quinn, was fishing above me so I had called him down to take a shot at the trout. Scott, an old hand with the finicky browns of the West Branch Delaware, presented his fly effortlessly. He was using a classic Hendrickson, perfectly tied, that seemed to match the hatch. He changed flies twice and then retreated back upstream without moving the fish.

"You try for him," Scott offered, "Maybe he wants that 100-Year Fly." My fly drifted into the feeding lane with the wood-duck wings set at 45 degrees easily visible as it rode in an upright position as expected of a parachute. The take was a nice gentle rise but the fight was strong and exciting. I couldn't see the trout as he went by me in an uncharacteristic upstream run but then came the typical grinding under boulders expected of a nice Neversink brown. Eventually the 16-inch trout yielded to the seven-foot bamboo, and the exiting commands of Scott were, "Don't write an article on that fly. Keep it under your hat."

The style had evolved in a typical manner that many flies go through. Alex Osowick, my fishing partner of many decades, had put together his "down-wing" of a few classic Catskill patterns. Fishing the Lackawaxen River in northeast Pennsylvania with Cahills and sulphurs, Alex had great success during the 1998 season. "The down-wing was deadly just in the surface as well as under it. I figured the fly was often being taken for an emerger. At the same time I also used the same patterns in the up-wing style without any such action," he explained.

I looked at the "wet-dry" fly and exclaimed, "Alex, I think you have gone back to the old style that was being tied in the early 1900s, but now with quality hackle." Alex had simply tied his dry fly in the normal manner and tied in his wing up-front. The wing extended past the base of the tail at about a 30 to 45–degree angle. This is also similar to some of today's caddis patterns where the hair-wings start behind the hackles.

A light eventually flashed in my head and I told Alex that with some modification it might be possible to put together a dry fly that would ride in the surface, land perfectly on every cast and have a single wing with a profile very close to that of a mayfly, as well as have the entire body from tail to eye exposed to the trout. All this would rotate around a parachute dry fly.

I had learned a lesson the hard way as my fishing companion demonstrated the effectiveness of small parachutes with posts of calf-body hair on the West Branch Delaware in the mid 90s. Since that whitewash I had been converted and fished with Adams, sulphurs, Doratos, and the other small-sized parachutes with excellent results. These probably represent spinners, such as Scott's favorite traditional red quill, with which he nails the Delaware rainbows and browns.

But the mayfly dun patterns? Here the 100-Year Fly finds a niche by mixing the old style with that of the new. The name I gave the fly represents the time span from today's parachutes to when Theodore Gordon's flies in the early 1900s were tied with a single wing tied canted at about a 50 to 70–degree angle. Crossing Gordon's tie with today's deadly parachute hackle with a full body that floats in the surface film produces a fly that constantly floats upright with wings at the proper angle. Last season's results proved the fly is as deadly as it looks and also very effective as an emerger in broken water.

Theodore Gordon is hailed as Americanizing dry fly-fishing in the Catskills in the late nineteenth and early twentieth century. As a student of insect life he changed the style and size of the English dry fly suited for slow chalk streams to those of free stone, and educated fishermen through his writings. After one hundred years he is still a hero to flytiers who relish the history of the dry fly. To double-check that Gordon's flies had the wing tied up front I called Paul Dahlie, director of the Catskill Fly Fishing Center and Museum. "I looked up Gordon's flies. There are two fan wings and five conventional dry flies. The single wing is tied upright in front of the hackles. Check in your copy of Austin McK. Francis' book, *Land of Little Rivers* (page 171). There is an excellent photograph of one of these." A quick check of the photograph proved extremely interesting in displaying how the wing was tied.

I had the privilege of meeting and interviewing two of Gordon's closest friends in the mid 1960s. Herman Christian was known as a great, rugged outdoorsman and professional tyer and Roy Steenrod was known as the only person Gordon taught his tying secrets. Steenrod developed the famous Hendrickson in 1916 and is credited by Harry Darbee, renowned Catskill flytier, as relaying his tying knowledge to hundreds of Boy Scouts and kids attending conservation schools in the Catskills as well as the general public,

Christian and I visited and corresponded until his death in 1973. He was known as a trapper, guide, and a man with wonderful touch, as his flies demonstrated. Harry Darbee labeled him the finest big trout fisherman of the Catskills, Even Ed Hewitt, another Catskill notable, gave Herman great credit after being educated while fishing with him. "Christian is the finest wet fly fisherman I have ever seen." To this Herman confronted Hewitt with, "You know Mr. Hewitt, I also fish a dry fly."

"Whenever I spotted a large trout of a pound or two jumping (rising) I left it alone and brought Mr. Gordon to fish for it. He was a fine fisherman and tied a beautiful fly—especially his salmon flies. We both tied flies with a single wing. Whoever saw a mayfly floating with its wings apart? I changed to split-wings because that's what the fishermen who bought them wanted," claimed Christian.

Christian tied flies in his fingers for speed until he got to the hackles and then he used a vise. Gordon eventually showed Steenrod his fly tying methods but put everything away when he had company according to Christian. Christian informed me that he had improved upon Gordon's flies by "taking the hump out" from the way Gordon tied in his wings. When I mentioned this to Harry Darbee he stated, "Maybe the hump had a purpose." After tying the wings in Gordon's style there is no doubt that the wings are locked in much stronger than as with a wet fly tie (butt forward).

Roy Steenrod's close friendship with Gordon resulted in "thousands of letters" from Gordon. "From 1905 the correspondence was very heavy but I didn't keep the letters until the last few years [Gordon died May 1, 1915]. We used to tie in our fingers when we first started. We tried to copy the flies as they were on the water. Gordon and I always made wings straight up, no split. You never saw a fly coming down the stream with his wings out unless he was dying. Now everyone likes them split."

Tying the 100-Year Fly is not a simple pattern to tie but worth the extra time. The biggest difficulty at first is keeping the hackles from being tied under by the thread and dubbing. Besides the conventional dub bodies, quill bodies of all patterns come out fine. Just use a complimentary dub for the thorax. Wings of all styles of patterns can be tied: kip tail, guard hairs, wood-duck, mallard, body feathers, hackle tips and CDC. It is important to tie the wing sparse and long.

Tying the 100-Year Fly Hendrickson

HOOK: regular dry fly 10-14 but up-turned hooks as Gordon used are ideal for parachutes as claimed by Poul Jorgensen.

THREAD: tan or brown 6/0–8/0

WINGS: wood-duck side feathers

TAIL: hackle or fibetts-dark dun

BODY: fox fur or synthetic dub

HACKLE: blue dun

POST: dark ⅟₁₆" foam cylinder

The single wing with the "hump" that Herman took out is clearly shown in an original Quill Gordon fly in *Land of Little Rivers*. Tie the butt of the wing in behind the eye so the tip of the wing is facing to the right of the eye. When the wing is pulled back it should be long enough to extend about a hook gap past the bend of the hook. When the fly is completed the wing will be tied back—in step 8.

The ⅟₁₆" foam post is now tied in the middle of the shank or slightly forward (the more forward the more upright will be the wing) so the butt is facing back. Do not trim this post—it will be pulled upright by the body.

Tie in tail, wrap thread under to spread fibers, roll the fox fur on your thigh and catch an end with waxed thread at tail.

Twist the fur and thread together and wrap the noodle to the front of the post. One turn should bring the post upright. Cut off the dub thread 6" and hang out of the way with hackle pliers for weight.

Retie bobbin thread. Tie in hackle horizontally shiny side up. Add one more turn of dub against front of post.

Wrap hackle as to preference for amount of sparseness. I like six–eight turns as the foam compresses. Tie down hackle, run thread just short of wing. Wrap dub to wing, tie off dub and let thread hang down.

Cut post off closely.

The wing will now be pulled back in position at about 45 degrees. Tie down the wing about 2mm back with three or four turns, which will form the "hump," bring thread to eye, and tie off.

Gordon was a genius.

TYING TIPS:

Make a bodkin by epoxying into a ¼" dowel a needle small enough to fit into the eye of your hook. This tool will be used in plucking out hackle from the dubbing and the tying of the wings. Another bodkin of .030 inch wire with a square tip is excellent for applying head cement for any fly.

Don't overload the wing material. Too much overloads the head and is not necessary.

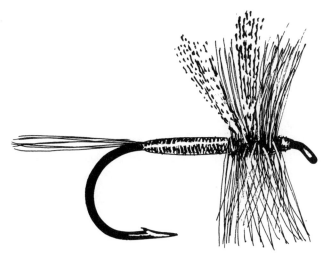

Red Quill

Intimations at Denniston's Flats

JOHN MILLER

It wasn't Denniston's Flats that persuaded me to buy our house at Wolf Lake. Rather it was the closer-by Neversink Gorge with its waters tumbling over rock slabs, pocket water that swirled behind boulders, challenging my cast. I was twenty years younger then, and the Gorge's boisterous, pummeling waters were not all that different from the halls of Martin Luther High School at Amsterdam and 65th Street. In fact, when wading among desks in my classroom, peering over shoulders for promising paragraphs, it was but a small leap to picture myself wading among the Gorge's boulders. The teenager, still in me, shunned boredom, relished excitement, crammed more than could fit into a day. Come June, when school let out, I dropped for several days lower and lower into the

Gorge, making risky crossings, feeling for deepwater footholds, congrat-
ulating myself on remarkable casts.

The Gorge fit me like a glove, so I thought while returning home,
denying that I was pausing more frequently on the climb out or that my
sense of balance was ebbing. But after such raucous excitement, how
could I return to gentler waters? How could I settle for anything less
than those wild fish, which, who knows how, can see through, then bolt
through a watery bulge to nab a bounding dry fly? What could be better
than this—tracking a Humpy, bouncing down rapids, then looking up
to see solid cliff reeling and pitching to the same rhythm?

Rivers are generous. Rivers are accommodating. They do so much
with so little, and the Gorge was that river's pulsing heart. But by the
time I retired, my wife had grown uneasy about my solitary ventures
into such turbulence. Dismissing her worries for a time, I wouldn't give
up. But after taking a few spills off those slimy boulders, I set out to seek
a stretch that might better accommodate my sixty-five years. And so I
scouted thirty miles of the Neversink from Cuddebackville up to the
Reservoir. After having dismissed a two-mile stretch above Bridgeville,
which at first seemed uninteresting, I returned for second look. Here
the river had departed from the road and flowed leisurely, unpinched
by rocky hills, to one side of a wide floodplain planted in corn. This
shallow, flat water appeared unpromising, and for that reason I had first
dismissed it. But I later learned that the farther the river retreated from
the road the more promise it offered. After a hundred-yard-long riffle
the waters ran into ledge on which overhanging hemlocks created a
long, dark and quiet pool. A couple of fish were rising. Farther on, the
water took another descent over more riffles, forming a second pool,
this one quite deep and in open pasture where cows and a menacing
bull gazed from behind barbed wire. Finally, at the bottom of the
valley, a third pool appeared, this one a deep eddy gouged out by water
striking a steep, barricading bluff. The bluff explained the absence of
roads and why only one dwelling, an old farmhouse, could be seen in
the distance. It stood safely above flood line. For eons the bluff contained spring floodwaters, causing them to drop their sand and silt upon
a widening plain.

I stood on one bank, looking up the silent valley, past the grazing cows, past the hemlocks of the first pool, beyond the cornfield where I had parked a mile away. The head of the valley remained at my eye level. Over its course the river had dropped no more than ten feet yet had formed three chattering riffles and three lovely pools, each with a twisting drift line that delivered the sunny valley's menu of insects to waiting trout. A river can make so much of seemingly little.

When the stone-grinding waters of the upper Neversink reach these flats they relax, suggesting to me, each time I return there, to do likewise. The half-mile path to the first pool makes no demanding ascents or descents. Legs find their stride, muscles, after a day's sitting, their release. The walk, the wade, the casting, the catching and netting, the return walk—all equalize, not one dominating, none sacrificed in anticipation of the next. Even during a Hendrickson hatch, my fingers remain steady enough to thread a fly, cinch the knot. Time and attention spread. I lose intention, regain it, then lose it again.

On these calm waters, I can set my internal striker on automatic. While playing a fish my mind keeps wandering from what it had set out to pursue. The river requires no wading staff to keep my balance, no feats of casting to keep me on task. Fishing here, now for many years, is like putting on a shirt made soft from many washings. But not the least boring. To fish here carries me beyond sport to the grandeur of the place, to moments of forgetting why I fish. Yes, I have come to catch fish, and if, after a dozen outings, I were to return empty-handed, I would consider quitting. But, in all honesty, a catch is but an excuse, both to myself and to those I report to on returning.

Fishing, especially at Denniston's Flats, seems to be more akin to poetry than sport. The American poet, the late A. R. Ammons, defined poetry as a "verbal path to a nonverbal source." Would I be stretching it to make the same claim about fly-fishing for trout—the one thing I do in my retirement years with any finesse? That is, I follow a path of rises seeking a place where neither words nor fish are needed. And maybe, if ever reaching that place, I might cease my incessant casting, lay down my rod, and just be there.

In the thirty-five years leading up to the Civil War the Neversink hardly inspired such contemplations. It ran red with tannin, extracted from the bark of native hemlocks for tanning. It was also choked by hair and scrapings of hundreds of thousands of animal hides shipped from Texas, Spain, and Argentina. Some even came from Australia, all the way around the South American continent. Four miles upstream from Denniston's Flats, the town of Fallsburg boomed, profiting from the power the river provided and the abundance of nearby hemlock forests. One of three large tanneries in the area, the Fallsburg tannery employed about 70 men who operated 160 vats holding 25,000 steer hides. Arriving stiff as sheets of plywood, these hides were first steeped in chicken droppings and potash before being scraped of hair and flesh. They were then soaked in increasing concentrations of tannin obtained from the pulverized bark of hemlock trees. For four decades this waste was dumped into the Neversink.

What brought such a rush of tanneries to this sleepy subsistence farm country were virgin hemlock forests that covered most of the inarable upland. The older the trees, the thicker the bark, the more tannin extracted, and tannery owners hired teams of woodsmen to strip these giants, leaving their carcasses behind to rot. Neiderman, in his *History of Fallsburg Township*, estimated, "It took one cord of bark, four by four by eight, to tan ten hides, and it cost from three to ten trees to obtain one cord of bark."

Sullivan County, famed for the quality of its tanned leather, became a leading producer in the nation. Huge profits were made. The leather was bought primarily by the army and prisons, which, at the time, could legally force inmates to work, uncompensated, in shoe factories.

In one generation all but the least accessible hemlock stands were felled, and the dark, wild spirit of the magnificent forests, depicted by the Hudson River School painters, was gone. Hopkins, writing about the loss of "Binsey Poplars" about the same time, might just as well been speaking of hemlocks:

My aspens dear, whose airy cages quelled,
Quelled or quenched in leaves the leaping sun,

All felled, felled, are all felled;
Of a fresh and following folded rank
Not spared, not one . . .
After-comers cannot guess the beauty been.

By the Civil War, when the demand for boot, holster, and harness leather peaked, Sullivan County's hemlocks gave out, and tannery operations moved on to Pennsylvanian and Adirondack forests for still bigger money. Locally, the tree-stripped hills exacerbated flooding, which occurred so frequently and with such torrential power that no one dared build barn or house close to the flood line.

Today, since completion of the Neversink Reservoir in 1950, trees have grown back and floods have been tamed. There has been only one serious flood, in the spring of 2005, to suggest how they once raged every few years. That single event was described to me by Howard Levner, who, standing on Denniston's Bridge, watched water spill over his fields to the west and rise within six feet of the bridge's beam. When it subsided he found it had gouged a trough several box-cars long across his field, spreading the soil in sandy shoals over a cornfield downstream.

The Neversink Reservoir, which funnels much of the Catskill's purest waters to faucets in New York City, is the most recent exploitation of the river. Old-timers might complain that due to the Reservoir the river now is a tame replica of its former self. But a release valve, in the reservoir's depths, sends a flow downstream as icy as any river in the wilds of Labrador. This plume reaches well below a gauging station fifteen miles downstream in Bridgeville; here, by agreement of The Delaware River Basin Commission, it must hold to a summertime mean temperature of 72 degrees, assuring that trout will survive severe heat waves. And an additional stipulation requiring a release of no less than 15 cubic feet per second in times of drought, assures that the river will continue to live up to the name that the Lenni Lenape Indians first gave it: the stream whose waters never sink into the earth.

Stand on the one-lane, trestle bridge at the head of the valley and look below to the riverbed that was once a ford crossed by horse and wagon. A passing car sets off a lovely clatter of wood planks against metal. The driver seems startled, as if suddenly slowed to an earlier epoch. Walk downstream, where the water eases onto the flat along the river's "wind-wandering weed-winding bank." Walk to the bottom of the valley where I have often come upon a scene out of a Constable landscape: Ray Kilvey's herd of ten or so cows drinking, half in pasture, half up to their haunches in water. The river, now healed, exudes tranquillity. Dark patches of hemlocks spread over once mangy hillsides; to the south their young spires again crown the ridgetop.

> And for all this, nature is never spent;
> There lives the dearest freshness deep down things;

The three pools, strung together by shallows and riffles, as familiar as rooms in my house, induce my mind to ramble. I watch myself tying on the same No. 14 Adams at the same pool as I did the time before and the time before that. Am I exploring the familiar, alert to and hopeful for any new surprise? Or is it merely that in aging I now seek the comfort of redundancy? Yes, one outing may retrace another, but all are driven by a common theme: to catch one of the lunker brown trout that sleep out of sight and reach in the depths of the second and third pools. I've heard them feeding when it's too dark to thread a fly—several at a time—jumping for God knows what, their bulks smacking the surface loud as beaver tails.

But when such a fish accepts my offering does that answer the question of why I fish? Does playing one of these leaping beauties, or finally holding it still enough to marvel at its "rose-moles all in stipple" bring me any closer to knowing why I'm here? Or does the single-minded pursuit of quarry usurp those rare glimpses, which come when my attention is less captive? Might such glimpses, beyond rising or caught trout, explain why no outing feels complete without my having walked the full reach of the valley?

Of course this question, no matter how long pondered, has no answer. But what a privilege to be in such a place and in such a quandary! Long live Denniston's Flats! Long live redundancy!

So I walk back, over the cornfield, which this fall has been planted to clover, tuck my fly rod and waders into the car trunk, and, again borrowing from Hopkins, take a parting look:

Rural scene, a rural scene,
Sweet especial rural scene.

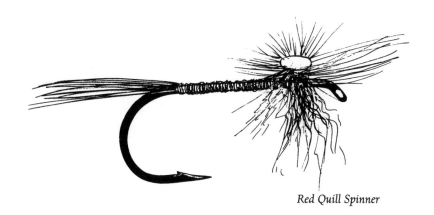

Red Quill Spinner

A Camp on the Neversink

JAY CASSELL

James waded slowly into the fast water below Denton Falls, eyeing the pool carefully. When he found a spot where he could stand without slipping, he pulled line off his flyreel and began his backcast. In less time that it takes to say "Neversink Skater," he had snagged his Adams in a branch right behind him. Muttering, he looked over at me, angrily, "I give up," he said. "I can't stand fly-fishing."

I wasn't surprised at his reaction. For a kid who was brought up fishing plastic worms and spinnerbaits for bass, trying to switch over to flyfishing is tough. The fact that he was a teenager with zero patience didn't help. But he thought it over, changed his mind, and pretty soon was back at it, trying to cast into the trout pools just below the falls.

Up above the white water, we heard James' buddy, Dave, whooping and hollering. "Got another one," he yelled. "This place is amazing." I could see a dark, gloomy cloud beginning to form over James' head. With a shrug, I turned and started hiking downstream. Rounding the bend, I spied a trout rising to caddis flies in the middle of a long pool. I forgot about the boys, and immersed myself in my own fishing.

The boys had worked for their reward of fishing the river. We were at our hunting and fishing camp, "The Over The Hill Gang," located about a mile from the Neversink Gorge, on land owned by Benjamin Wechsler. Wechsler, who has owned a huge chunk of property, including the Neversink Gorge, since 1968, is one of those rare individuals who actually gets it, who knows how to manage private property correctly. His land is just a "small," couple-thousand-acre parcel in the 100,000 acres of Catskill wilderness that sprawls from the Bashakill Wildlife Refuge to the east, to the Mongaup River Valley to the west. Through his good graces, our camp has survived, first on the east side of the Neversink, and now at its current location on a ridgetop to the west, on the Denton Falls Road.

I had brought the boys up for the club's annual summer work weekend. The deal was that they could fish at the end of the day, so long as they pitched in and helped with the work. And they had, sweeping out the cabin, picking up pieces of wood, twigs, and branches from a recent windstorm, stacking firewood . . . anything they could do.

While the boys were hard at it, the rest of us busied ourselves with the chores that must be done to keep a sporting club functioning. Dan Gibson, his twenty-one-year-old son Keith, and I unhitched the splitter from my truck and started splitting the logs we had piled up earlier in the summer. Kevin Kenney, the forty-year-old son of the camp's founder, Jerry, was down the road about a quarter mile, chainsawing a black cherry that had come down in a late-spring windstorm. Last hunting season was an especially cold one, with temperatures consistently below 20 degrees. We came close to running out of wood for our two woodstoves—one in the kitchen, the other in the bunk room—so we were making doubly certain that we had enough for the upcoming season.

While all this was going on, Vin Sparano was out behind the cabin, installing a new floor in the outhouse. Every couple of years, the local porcupine population decides it's time to feast on our outhouse, and then we have to rebuild it. It's an ongoing battle, with us staying about one step ahead of the always-hungry porkies. Rod Cochran, out in front, was replacing rotted planks on the front deck, while Matt had grabbed a bucket of paint and was touching up the cabin's trim.

When Ken Surerus and his son, Raymond, showed up, they pitched in with the firewood, stacking the logs that Dan, Keith, and I had been splitting.

By the end of the day, the old camp—it was built in the 1950s—was in pretty good shape. A new American flag was up on the roof, all of the weeds and brush around the building had been cut back, and the inside had been swept clean. By summer's end, we'd all be back again, sighting in our rifles and doing last-minute chores such as getting the propane tank filled and stocking up the kitchen with food for hunting season. Eventually, the roof will have to be replaced. It leaks like crazy in the bunkroom, and we're getting tired of putting new blue tarps on it every year. And the eclectic mixture of tarpaper and multicolored shingles on the exterior is starting to fall off. But the repairs will be made, because they're important. It's good work.

Author Rick Bass, who wrote *The Deer Pasture*, once said this about his hunting camp: "For a place we visit only one week out of the year, we worry about it far too much."

That's the way the guys in my camp feel. We think about that place a lot. We do go there more than one week a year, of course; there's turkey season in May, trout and smallmouth fishing in the Neversink from mid-April to the end of September, plus deer season in November— but we'd all go there more often if we could. It's tough to explain, but a good sporting camp becomes a part of you. The years go by, and members come and go, but you come to realize that part of you is always in camp, cooking up venison stew in the kitchen, debating guns and loads or flies and leaders with your colleagues, or playing poker until the wee hours of the morning. I don't even see most of the guys during the year except at camp, but that doesn't matter. When I do see them, we just pick up where we left off last time. The camp has a life of its own, with a pulse that keeps beating from year to year, generation to generation. So you bring the youngsters along and teach them about the woods, you take them down to the river and teach them flycasting, and you show them the types of pools and riffles where the brown trout like to lie. (James, by the way, did not catch a thing that day, but he did later in the season!). And when they get old enough, you let them into the camp as full members, sharing in the work, in the fun, in the good times and, when they happen, the tough times, too.

Work weekend—it's the beginning of another cycle of seasons. Before you know it, it'll be opening day of deer season and I'll be in my treestand overlooking the Neversink. Then, in May, I'll be out the woods well before dawn, hoping to find a gobbler. At noon, I'll come back to camp, change out of my hunting clothes and put on my flyvest and waders, and hike down to the river to see if the Hendricksons are hatching in the pools below Denton Falls. And life will be as good as it possibly can be.

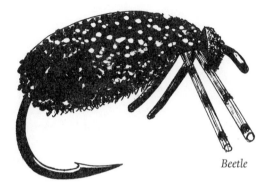

Beetle

Brief Selected Bibliography

Askins, Justin. "A River's Tale." *Home Waters.* Ed. Gary Soucie. New York: Simon & Schuster, 1991

Atherton, John. *The Fly and the Fish.* New York: MacMillan, 1951.

Bergman, Ray. *Trout.* New York: Penn Publishing, 1938.

Darbee, Harry, and Austin Francis. *Catskill Flytier.* Philadelphia: Lippincott, 1977.

Evers, Alf. *The Catskills.* Woodstock, New York: The Overlook Press, 1982.

Flick, Art. *Streamside Guide to Naturals and Their Imitations.* New York: Putnam, 1947.

Francis, Austin. *Catskill Rivers.* New York: Nick Lyons Books/Winchester Press, 1983.

_____. *Land of Little Rivers.* Beaverkill Press,1999.

Gingrich, Arnold. *The Well-Tempered Angler.* New York: Knopf, 1965.

Gold, David M., ed. *The River and the Mountains: Readings in Sullivan County History.* South Fallsburg, New York: Marielle Press, 1994.

Gordon, Theodore. *The Complete Fly Fisherman: The Notes and Letters of Theodore Gordon.* Edited by John McDonald. New York: Scribners, 1947.

Halford, Frederic. *Floating Flies and How to Dress Them.* London: Low, 1886.

_____. *Dry Fly Entomology.* London: Vinton, 1897.

Hewitt, Edward R. *Hewitt's Handbook of Flyfishing.* New York: Marchbanks, 1933.

_____. *A Trout and Salmon Fisherman for Seventy-Five Years.* New York: Scribners, 1948.

Koller, Larry. *Taking Larger Trout.* Boston: Little Brown, 1950.

_____. *The Treasury of Angling.* New York: Golden Press, 1963.

La Branche, George M. L. *The Dry Fly and Fast Water.* New York: Scribners, 1914.

Lyons, Nick. "Last Days Are for Dreamers." *Fly Fisherman.* December 1985.

_____. *My Secret Fishing Life.* New York: Atlantic Monthly Press, 1999.

_____. *The Seasonable Angler.* New York: Funk & Wagnalls, 1970.

McClane, A. J. *Fishing with McClane.* Englewood Cliffs, New Jersey: Prentice-Hall, 1975

McDonald, John. *The Origins of Angling.* New York: Doubleday, 1963.

_____. Quill Gordon. New York: Knopf, 1972.

Miller, Alfred W. ("Sparse Grey Hackle"). *Fishless Days, Angling Nights.* New York: Crown, 1971.

Norris, Thaddeus. *The American Angler's Book.* Philadelphia: Butler, 1864.

Schwiebert, Ernest. *Remembrances of Rivers Past.* New York: MacMillan, 1973.

_____. *Trout.* New York: Dutton, 1978.

Scott, Genio. *Fishing in American Waters.* New York: Harper, 1869.

Skues, G. E. M. *The Way of a Trout with a Fly.* London: Black, 1924.

Walton, Izaak. *The Complete Angler.* Edited by George W. Bethune. New York: Wiley and Putnam, 1847.

Wright, Leonard M., Jr. *Fishing the Dry Fly as a Living Insect.* New York: Dutton, 1972.

_____. *Neversink.* New York: Atlantic Monthly Press, 1991.

_____. *The Ways of Trout.* New York: Nick Lyons Books/Winchester Press, 1985.

Woodchuck

Appendixes: Eyes on the River

The Gorge Controversy
JUSTIN ASKINS

The Neversink Gorge has always been a wild place. Due to its inaccessibility, even as the rest of the Catskills were being clear-cut in the mid-eighteenth century, most of the gorge remained untouched. It was one of the few places where deer survived in the Catskills and virgin hemlocks can still be found. Later, private ownership kept the gorge unsullied. Starting with Ambrose Monell in 1902, then with William Bradford in 1927, and continuing with the Wechsler family in 1939, the gorge has remained "the hidden jewel of the Catskills."

In the early 1970s, the Gorge attracted the attention of the newly formed New York State Department of Environmental Conservation. Officials there concluded that the gorge should be protected under state ownership, and began negotiations with Benjamin Wechsler, the owner of more than four thousand acres of land and rights in the center of the Gorge. Wechsler's property included two major waterfalls and was a spectacular wild trout fishery. DEC knew this and in 1972 drafted a contract to purchase almost all of Wechsler's property for $1,750,000. Unfortunately, the commissioner later changed his mind, and the troubles in the Gorge began.

When DEC applied in 1980 for a million-dollar grant from the National Park Service to purchase the Gorge, the Wechsler rights and property were specified. However, instead of purchasing the 1,800 acres of Wechsler's rights, the DEC inexplicably bought the land underneath the rights—which did not include the ability to hunt, fish, or trap—from Orange and Rockland Power with the million dollars.

After that fiasco, the DEC engaged in numerous attacks on Wechsler, a conservationist who had been a member of the Governor's Reservoir Release Task Force. They also made several offers to him at far below fair market prices.

Things seemed to be taking a turn for the better with the appointment by the DEC of the Neversink River State Nature Preserve Advisory Committee in 1985. After a couple of years of meetings and public input, the committee finally made a series of recommendations for a smaller, more manageable park. Unfortunately, this was not what the DEC wanted to hear and the committee was abruptly dismissed.

Though Wechsler made several offers, including the donation of hundreds of acres of his land, the DEC never treated his proposals seriously, and in the mid-1980s DEC, which had been buying up other properties to the north and south, began to consider condemnation. Despite much local opposition, the DEC in 1988 won the right to condemn Wechsler's 1,800 acres of rights on the east bank and 1,067 of his fee simple acres on the west bank. The court decision stipulated that the DEC had to purchase both the rights and the land, but inexplicably, after waiting five years, the DEC simply took Wechsler's rights, disregarding the court mandate and creating a park with the most important part missing. Since then Wechsler has been selling off his land, and the DEC has done nothing to acquire any of his property.

Catskill Victory Nears
PHIL CHASE
(*Sunday Record,* July 4, 1976)

The greatest environmental victory for Catskill resources is on the threshold of completion. Governor Hugh Carey is expected to sign into law the necessary authority for the Department of Environmental Conservation (DEC) to properly manage New York City reservoirs, resulting in safeguarding over 200 miles of rivers.

Environmentalists who have battled with New York City since the early 1960's have seen the total unwillingness of City engineers to protect below reservoir streams through negotiations. Although initial promises of stream quality improvement were made with completion of the dams, none was carried out.

Negotiations over the years by conservationists, politicians, and the Sullivan County Environmental Management Council did accomplish a nunber of plus factors. Primarily, negotiations proved that there was no possible way to reach any satisfactory agreement with the City. Far too many attempts with the City to negotiate for better releases were pursued but each one educated the general public to the river problems. Had City engineers been less stubborn in their approach of "We own the water and we will manage it for the good of the City only," and used some political ploys with a small amount of cooperation, the City would still hold the reins of the reservoirs.

For this we can thank top City engineer Abraham Groopman who, through both his stubbornness and God-like attitude of water possessor, gave Catskill people the realization that further negotiations with the City were impossible. The downfall of bureaucracies such as the one that runs the City's water supply is that they believe themselves untouchable, and they are right, but not in a democratic society.

Certainly the democratic procedure proved that if citizens are willing to get involved, dig out facts, educate the public, and work through proper channels that even City Hall can be bucked and beaten. One can't find a larger City Hall than that of Mayor Abraham Beame and Beame lobbied his best to prevent passage by the Assembly and Senate for the DEC control.

The many failures by environmentalists in negotiating with the City proved to be beneficial politically. There has been a unique change in the politics of Sullivan County over the last decade. Many of those who would sell out their own county for a buck have departed politically.

Today Sullivan County, led by Chairman of the Supervisors David Kaufman and Supervisor Dennis Greenwald have not only backed the battles but have picked up the torch of environmental leadership.

In the rivers' battle both have pressured Albany right up to the Governor and much of their efforts have been done quietly and behind the scene.

If there was a bouquet to go to any one individual in Sullivan County for major political and environmental reforms I would send it to Benjamin Wechsler. Wechsler, an environmentalist from Forestburg, has made more enemies and more new political friends than one could imagine. His main asset is that he is not only highly competent but 100 percent truthful. Combine this with a hyperactive personality that pulls no punches and usually little concern for diplomacy when he vehemently speaks out and you can easily understand why fence sitters have no love for Ben.

Albany bureaucrats who are competent in their work respect Wechsler. But far too many deadwood bureaucrats have made the mistake of meeting with Wechsler and having to lay out the cards.

If there was ever an individual who should be a deputy commissioner of the DEC representing the Catskills, Wechsler is the person. But will there ever be a politician who appoints under him someone who would clean house of incompetent flunkies? Don't expect it.

Today one doesn't have to look far to find local politicians who strongly supported the rivers' battle. On the congressional scene both Rep. Matthew McHugh and Benjamin Gilman were superb in their actions for state legislation. Both men testified at release hearings and both have been in constant touch with Governor Carey. Their correspondence with Carey should set the stage for signature by Governor of the release bill to make it into law. The Catskills must recognize the excellent job done by both representatives to the State Assembly Maurice Hinchey and Jean Amatucci. Hinchey has been vocal since Catskill Waters (CW), a coalition of environmental groups, asked for his help two years ago. Jean Amatucci showed that she can stay forward, pick up a torch, and deliver the goods. When was this done last on the Albany level?

And what was behind the machinery to move politicians in a complicated cause that could stem the predicted death of Catskill rivers? An organization of sportsmen's groups drawn together by fisherman-author Frank Mele of Woodstock. Mele, an articulate spokesman, stressed the need of saving the rivers and his efforts paid off with groups from as far as Binghamton, Port Jervis, Albany, and New York City, meeting monthly in Roscoe, working closely with the Attorney General's office and the DEC.

President of CW is youthful John Hoeko of Fleishmanns. CW has done something that is extremely rare; it sent Hoeko to Albany to lobby for the rivers. Hoeko has been at Albany about 20 days during the legislative battle.

"This week during a three day period I worked on six hours of sleep," said an exuberant and exhausted Hoeko when the Senate passed the legislation at 6:35 A.M. "We had great help from Jim Biggane (former DEC Commissioner) between 4 and 5 A.M. when Senator Rolison was under tremendous pressure. He looked like he was sitting on a powder keg."

Hoeko and Biggane sat down with the senator and what they had to say turned Rolison for the necessary support.

"Right now we need a flood of letters from everyone who loves these rivers. Write to the Governor and mention that this won't cost the State a cent to save water resources that must be protected."

On the Road in the Catskills: The Lost River of Xanadu
PETER BORELLI
(*Catskill Center News*, November–December 1979)

It seems incredible that there could still be a wild and relatively unexplored area anywhere in New York State. But there exists a river valley in the southern Catskills that boggles the mind with its splendid scenery and isolation. Since my discovery of it more than a year ago, I have come to think of it as the lost river of Xanadu, the kingdom of Kubla Khan. But for the uninitiated and deprived public it is a 3½-mile stretch of the Neversink River known as the Neversink Gorge.

On a road map it can be pinpointed as the large roadless area four miles downstream from Bridgeville and three miles upstream from Oakland Valley in the Sullivan County Town of Forestburgh and Orange County Town of Deer Park. The area totals about 5,000 acres, the core of an even larger area of wild land, including the state's 600-acre Wolf Lake Multiple Use Area on its northern boundary.

There are two falls in this stretch of the river, one approximately six to eight feet above the bed of the stream and known as Denton Falls. The other is High Falls and is approximately sixteen feet above the stream bed and 160 feet wide. The river has large pools which average three to four feet in depth with rock cliffs rising 200 feet straight up from the water's edge. The only man-made structures in the entire area are two small hunting camps, a suspension bridge, and the historical remains of a dam and village once known as Hackeldam.

Expert canoeists who know about the area agree that the river in the Gorge is for experts only. But one does not have to be an expert to sense the exhilaration of cascading through the Gorge. Walter Burmeister, writing in "Appalachian Waters: The Delaware and its Tributaries," describes the water course near Denton Falls as follows:

"An impressive white-water turmoil introduces the Upper Denton Falls, the most severe of the canyon rapids. It is approximately one-half mile long and gradually builds up to a crescendo of awe-inspiring fury. Funneled between boulder-strewn shores and vertical walls of rock, the enormous rapids drop steeply over natural steps around a fomidable promontory. Beyond the bend the downstream vista discloses the final roughly tilted streambed composed of a series of angular ledges. From any given upstream point, assiming adequate stream flow, one does not fully grasp the magnitude of the individual steps; however, one does behold the foaming at the end of a huge natural staircase. The final 200 yards have the most pronounced gradient. While MH and MH-to-H levels fashion a very intricate series of stair case rapids, H and HH levels create an indescrible combination of powerful chutes, cascading side sluices, and tow~ ʾ

standing waves beyond ominous sinkholes. The huge rocks and vertical step-like pattern of the ledges create complex hydraulics."

If the river sounds wild the land around it is in many respects wilder, especially the steep slopes rising up from the river. Although the area has about 16 miles of dirt road, virtually none of it can be negotiated by anything but a four-wheel-drive vehicle. There is an abundant deer population, black bear, bobcat, eagles, beavers, and mink. The forest cover is predominantly a mixture of northern hardwoods and hemlock.

For a number of years now people familiar with the area have recommended that it be acquired by the State of New York and preserved as a primitive recreation area. Following passage of the Environmental Quality Bond Act in 1972 the idea became a possibility as funds were provided for the acquisition of such areas. It was not until 1978, however, that the Department of Environmental Conservation headed by Peter A. A. Berle identified the area as a Unique Area eligible for acquisition with bond monies by the State Nature and Historical Preserve Trust. Since that time the Department has been involved in the time-consuming and sometimes frustrating process of surveying the land and appraising it. Fortunately, the owners of the tract, Orange and Rockland Utilities and Benjamin Wechsler, are receptive to the idea of state acquisition. If an agreement can be reached the Catskills and State of New York will have added another crown jewel to the State's treasury of spectacular open spaces.

There are several other reasons why this unique area should be acquired. They do not exactly fit into the objective acquisition criteria of public administrators, but they have bearing on the spirit and significance of the conservation effort in this state. First, it was only a few years ago that one would have been hard pressed to wax lyrical about the Neversink Gorge. Sewage outflows from upstream municipalities and erratic releases from New York City's Neversink Reservoir had virtually depleted the trout population and made the river a stinkhole. But now most of the sewage is being treated and the city is experimenting with conservation releases. Together these changes have helped bring the river back, enough so that the Neversink and its ten tributaries in this stretch support a good trout fishery. In other words, the Neversink Gorge is an environment success story. We ought not to forget it again as we have in the past. Another consideration in this matter is the private stewardship of the present owners. From the day Ben Wechsler first acquired the land it has been his dream to protect the land and to keep it intact. This kind of dedication should not be ignored or go unrewarded. Even Orange and Rockland which originally acquired its portion of the tract to construct several hydroelectric dams is now persuaded that conserving this area in a natural state may be the best use for the land.

Fishing Prohibited in New York State Park
HAROLD FABER
(*The New York Times*, February 22, 1982)

New York State has just bought 2,865 acres on the east bank of the Neversink River, one of the finest trout streams in the United States, but the purchase will not enable the public to fish the river for years, if ever.

The land, in Sullivan County, was bought for $675,000 from the Clove Development Corporation, a subsidiary of Orange and Rockland Utilities Inc. of Pearl River, N.Y. But the price did not include hunting, fishing, or trapping rights. They are mostly owned by a local resident, Benjamin I. Wechsler, a one-time public relations executive in New York City.

Mr. Wechsler also owns about 1,900 acres on the west bank. Thus he has control of the fishing along three and a half miles of the river at the spectacularly scenic Neversink Gorge, southeast of Monticello and about 85 miles from Manhattan.

Mr. Wechsler inherited the land and the fishing rights from his grandfather, Philip Wechsler, a coffee merchant in New York City, who bought them in 1938. He operates his property as the Turner Brook Reserve, open to members only for hunting and fishing.

Recognized as an ardent conservationist even by his critics, Mr. Wechsler is angry with the state for what he calls its "disorganized, incomprehensible and outrageous" land-acquisition policy. He said that he had had more than ten years of on-again, off-again discussions with state officials about selling his property. The last contact, he said in an interview here, was more than two years ago, when an offer worth less than half the state-appraised value of the property was made.

The difficulties between Mr. Wechsler and the state have caused local conservation organizations to question whether the Neversink Gorge can be preserved for the public. "Paradise Lost?" said a recent headline in *The Catskill Center News*, published by the Catskill Center for Conservation and Development, a private, nonprofit organization. The organization blames the State Department of Environmental Conservation for "the seemingly lost opportunity for public ownership."

Robert L. McManus, director of communications for the department, defended the state's dealings with Mr. Wechsler. "Back in early 1980," he said "we made an offer for the property. He declined. There have been no negotiations since, so you can't say that we failed to negotiate in good faith when there are no negotiations at all."

At his home here, Mr. Wechsler displayed a mass of documents, maps and letters dating back to 1971 about a possible sale of his property to the state. One of the documents showed that in 1972 the state put the cost of acquisition at $1.8 million.

However, Mr. Wechsler said that in a subsequent conversation with one state official $1.2 million was mentioned, and in January 1980 another state official suggested $600,000 as the price.

The last offer was confirmed by Paul Keller, the regional director of the department in New Paltz, who explained that the state was trying to stretch the money it had for acquisitions.

Last month, Mr. Wechsler sold a section of his land to M. Michael Kulukundis, a New York City businessman who has shipping, broadcasting and real-estate interests. He paid $910,000 for 395 acres on the west bank and for fishing rights to 504 acres of the new state property on the east bank.

"I am going to sell more land," Mr. Wechsler said. "My vision of how to preserve the property now is not to invite public participation through the state." Mr. Keller said that the state intended, when more funds were available, to approach Mr. Wechsler about acquiring his fishing rights and his land.

Meanwhile, he said, the newly acquired land would be open to the public for hiking, bird-watching, and enjoying the solitude, but not for fishing.

Local public officials have raised several questions about the state's purchase and the future of the Gorge. Although the new state property could be a major tourist attraction, the local officials said that they were worried about the loss of tax revenue, the cost of added services, such as police, roads, fire protection, and possible rescue operations on the rugged terrain.

The loss in tax revenue has been estimated to be $20,000 annually. "Someone else is going to have to pay for it," said Bryan Ingebar, chairman of the Sullivan County Board of Supervisors. "We can't see any benefits in it," said Paul Rausch, Supervisor of the Town of Forestburgh, where most of the land is. David Kaufman, Supervisor of the Town of Thompson, where the rest of the land is, said he could see the potential of the Gorge area as a tourist attraction, but added, "They don't have a development plan and they don't even have a proper plan to police the area and keep it clean."

State Owns a Prime Fishing Spot but Can't Use It[3]
SAM VERHOVEK
(*The New York Times,* April 4, 1986)

Ever since it bought the land more than four years ago, New York State has wanted to make a park out of 2,865 acres of canyons and forest along the Neversink

River in the southern Catskills. The site would be a trout fisherman's paradise, officials believe.

There is a problem, however: the state cannot fish there.

In most of the area, the only person who can is Benjamin I. Wechsler, a Forestburgh resident, and members of private clubs to whom he leases the fishing rights. Mr. Wechsler also owns the rights to hunt and trap on much of the land, which is on the east bank of the river about 70 miles northwest of Manhattan, in Sullivan County.

Regarded by friend and foe here as a determined conservationist, he opposes the present plan for a park because, he said, it could turn the site into "a garbage pit."

The state's inability to obtain the recreational rights to the land, a tract that it bought for $675,000 from a utility company in December 1981, has effectively prevented the public from using the area at all. Mr. Wechsler maintains that his exercise of the recreational rights precludes anybody from even walking on the property.

"What if I'm out hunting and I accidentally shoot somebody hiking around there?" he said.

The state has a different view. "Our interpretation is that he has the right to hunt and fish, but that we have the right to walk," said Henry G. Williams, the state's Environmental Conservation Commissioner. However, Mr. Williams conceded that plans for a park have been stymied. He termed the situation "embarrassing," and said that if "worse comes to worst," the state will take Mr. Wechsler's rights by eminent domain and go ahead with the park.

The ownership and the recreational rights were originally split in a 1923 deed, which assigned the utility company, now known as Orange and Rockland Utilities Inc., the right to build a hydroelectric dam on the land (it never did), and reserved for another party the hunting and fishing rights that Mr. Wechsler now owns.

Mr. Wechsler said that if officials try to take the rights by condemnation, he will battle them in court. "I could end up owning Albany, and they know this," he said. Mr. Williams acknowledged that the process would be "lengthy, difficult and expensive."

Meanwhile, relations between the Department of Environmental Conservation and Mr. Wechsler have already degenerated into a round of lawsuits.

Last August, Mr. Wechsler found two department officials on the state's land fishing in the Neversink, and he sued to have the action established as a violation of his fishing rights. The department responded with a countersuit that sought more than $1 million in damages against Mr. Wechsler, charging that he had illegally posted "no trespassing" signs, cut down trees, and built a cabin on the state-owned land.

Two weeks later the state withdrew the charges, saying they contained inaccuracies, but filed a new suit seeking to prevent Mr. Wechsler from doing anything on the land except fish, hunt, and trap.

The land in question includes a spectacular gorge, wild forest that is home to deer and black bear and a river bank that twists for more than three miles along the Neversink, considered one of the finest trout streams in America.

Mr. Wechsler said he is intransigent because he wants to protect the land, on which he grew up. Nearly 20 years ago, he inherited the rights once held by his grandfather, a Manhattan coffee merchant, along with ownership of 1,800 acres of land along the west bank of the river that the state has said it would like to buy for the park.

Mr. Wechsler said he might sell both his own land and the rights to the state's land if the state offered a fair price and came up with an acceptable management plan. But he said he believed that department officials had so far shown themselves incapable of protecting the area. "They are inappropriate people to have control of anyone's land in this state," he said. "We have in this county a large number of state-operated parks, and it would be charitable to describe each of them as abandoned."

Local officials, largely out of agreement with Mr. Wechsler's contention that the state might not manage the area properly, leaving a burden on them, appear lukewarm on the idea of the park.

The Environmental Conservation Department is "understaffed and underfunded, and the property they have is not being managed, to the point that certain parks are becoming garbage dumps," said Paul Rausch, Supervisor of the town of Forestburgh, in which most of the proposed park lies.

Criticism of the department's park management is "valid in some respects and not valid in others," Mr. Williams said. "Overall, we do a pretty good job."

In a move that has further strained his relations with the state, Mr. Wechsler recently proposed, before the town of Forestburgh's Planning Board, a subdivision for his own property that would create a private park with cabins, and that would yield to members use of his fishing and hunting rights on the state-owned property.

Mr. Williams last month formed an "advisory committee" of local people to discuss plans for the park. He said "at a minimum" it ought to be open to anyone who wishes to hike in it.

But Mr. Wechsler, citing a state estimate of peak use by 1,500 people a day, said that kind of traffic would ruin the Neversink Gorge.

A question that has endured throughout the dispute is why, in the first place, the state bought land it could not use.

Paul Keller, regional director of the Environmental Conservation Department, said he had recommended the purchase in 1981 because he was "optimistic" then that the state could negotiate ownership of the rights with Mr. Wechsler.

"But," he said, sometimes things don't happen like they should or as you would want."

Two Neversink Tributaries to be Renamed[4]
NELSON BRYANT
(*The New York Times,* September 13, 1987)

Two tributaries to the Neversink, a famous trout stream in the north-central portion of New York State's Sullivan County, will be given new names next Saturday as part of the Forestburgh Township sesquicentennial celebrations and the Catskill Heritage Project's program to honor anglers and conservationists of yesteryear.

Noting that the Catskills are often called the birthplace of American fly fishing, Benjamin Wechsler of Forestburgh, the Heritage Project's founder, says its organization wishes "to replace ugly and repetitive names with meaningful memorializations" of the men and women who have contributed to that tradition and who have also labored to protect the natural beauty of the region. "Practical considerations are also involved," said Wechsler. "For example, if a fellow angler suggested that you meet him at Beaver Pond in Sullivan County, the chances are exactly 12 to 1 that you would be waiting at the wrong pond."

The project began last October when Wechsler, James Gorman, supervisor of the Town of Neversink, Olga Parlow of the Forestburgh sesquicentennial committee and various others including reporters hiked into Mullet Brook (which tumbles into the Neversink Gorge from the east) and its 40-foot waterfall, where it was announced that the stream would henceforth be called Hewitt Brook. Edward Ringwood Hewitt, engineer, inventor, author, designer of trout flies and conservationist, bought 2,700 acres—including four miles of the stream—in the Neversink watershed in 1918, and established a trout laboratory. By the early 1930s, he was this country's leading authority on trout stream improvement techniques. Shortly before his death in 1957, Hewitt said that he wanted his ashes cast upon the Neversink, adding that the ceremony would give the trout a chance to get even.

It is, of course, one thing to say that a stream's name has been changed, and quite another to have that new name appear on the Federal Government's

---

topographic maps of the area. One of the criteria for such a change to be officially recognized is, says Wechsler, acceptance of the new names by the public.
No one in his right mind would, for example, attempt to rename the Hudson
River, or, for that matter, the Neversink. In this, Wechsler and his group have
been sagacious.

It is unlikely that any champions of "Mullet"—which probably refers to the
white sucker, a fish that ascends small streams in spring to spawn—will emerge,
and the other three streams have no names on topographic maps. All four are,
moreover, situated in a wild and highly inaccessible region on land owned, or
controlled in part, by Wechsler.

The other stream that was renamed last fall also flows into the Neversink
from the east, a short distance below Hewitt Brook. Locally, it is sometimes
called Pound Brook. The Heritage project dubbed it Cinberg Clove, after
Bernard Cinberg, a Manhattan obstetrician and gynecologist who was also an
accomplished fly fisherman who did most of his angling on the Neversink.
Cinberg, who died in 1979, was named New York State Conservationist of the
year in 1975, for, among other things, his successful efforts in persuading offi-
cialdom to schedule trout-saving cold water releases from the Neversink
Reservoir during periods of drought. Some might feel that "clove"—in this con-
text it means gap or ravine—is a bit precious, but as one who fished the
Neversink with the good doctor, I have nothing but praise for "Cinberg."

The two streams to be given new names this month enter the Neversink
Gorge from the west, slightly upstream of the others. They will be called
LaBranche Brook and Monell Brook. The former is sometimes called Long
Swamp Brook and the latter, Black Bear Swamp Brook. George LaBranche is
best-known for his two fishing classics, *The Dry Fly and Fast Water* (1914) and
Salmon and the Dry Fly (1924). He was also a tournament-class fly caster. When
LaBranche died in 1961, the late Sparse Grey Hackle (Alfred W. Miller) wrote
that LaBranche "was the prophet of what is still the distinctive and unique
American school of dry fly angling."

Ambrose Monell, sportsman, inventor of Monell metal, and chairman of
the board of International Nickel, bought thousands of acres in the Neversink
Gorge area in 1903, including homes and farms supporting about 230 people
which were situated in the area where the two brooks enter the Neversink. "He
paid fair prices for those holdings, which included a little factory that made
wooden shovels," Wechsler said. "The buildings were razed and the land
returned to wilderness, its condition today."

Hewitt, LaBranche, and Monell were friends and fishing companions, and
together they advanced the sport of dry-fly fishing for trout and salmon. In the
preface to *Salmon and the Dry Fly*, LaBranche gives Monell the credit for being
the first to take an Atlantic salmon on a dry fly in this country.

An island—which bears no name on topographic maps—in the Neversink downstream of Cinberg Clove is scheduled to be named after Larry Koller in 1988. Koller was an author, conservationist, hunter, angler, and editor-in-chief of *Field & Stream* magazine for many years. Koller's hunting and fishing retreat, the Eden Falls Club, still flourishes on the Neversink. Also in 1988, Neversink township will honor Theodore Gordon, who died in 1915 and who spent his later years in a cabin on the Neversink. It has not yet been decided what brook, stream, pond, or island will bear Gordon's name. Gordon is one of the major figures in the history of American fly fishing.

There are some who are put off by Wechsler's intensity, in his fight, thus far successful, to block what he and many others believe is an ill-conceived and poorly executed plan by the state to create a wilderness park in the Neversink watershed, but few would deny that he regards the Neversink with reverence, and there should someday be at least "Wechsler Burn" within that magnificent river's gorge. Wechsler has lived in the area nearly all of his 56 years, and the 2,300 acres he now owns in the Gorge have been in his family for more than 80 years. He also possesses the exclusive hunting, fishing, and trapping rights on another 1,800 acres, also in the Gorge, owned by the state.

New York Plans Action on Neversink Land[5]
NELSON BRYANT
(*The New York Times*, February 21, 1988)

The controversy over New York State's effort to establish a park, the Neversink River Unique Area, in the river's magnificently wild gorge in Sullivan County has entered a new phase. On February 4, Thomas C. Jorling, commissioner of the Department of Environmental Conservation announced that his office would seek to accomplish that end by eminent-domain proceedings. Few would question that the idea of protecting a wild region from the works of man and setting it aside for the public's enjoyment is a laudable goal.

Nonetheless, some of those who cherish the Neversink Gorge and who have labored in its behalf believe that the conservation department's plan is overambitious, that it might very well result in the area's being degraded, and that it also displays a lack of sensitivity to the wishes of many area residents and to Benjamin Wechsler of Forestburg, the private landowner who would be most affected by the proposed takeover.

The Neversink is one of the Catskills' most famous trout streams, and the region embraced by the proposed park includes about five miles of the river, its upstream, or northernmost, limit being about a mile north of the boundary between Thompson and Forestburgh towns.

A tedious series of failed negotiations over the past several years between the conservation department and Wechsler brought the issue to its present stage. In 1981, the conservation department purchased 2,800 acres in the gorge from Orange and Rockland Utilities, but Wechsler continued to hold the hunting, fishing and trapping rights that he inherited from his grandfather on 1,800 of those acres. Earlier, Orange and Rockland had unsuccessfully challenged Wechsler's possession of those rights, which appear to give him the authority to say who shall venture onto the land and waters involved, in court. In 1986, Henry Williams, commissioner of the department, who was replaced by Jorling several months ago, formed an advisory committee of local citizens to come up with suggestions for a way out of the impasse.

In June 1987, the committee said it was opposed to eminent domain, the right of a government to take private property for public use after compensating the owner, and added that the conservation department was ignoring the committee's plan for a relatively small park of 1,600 usable acres, plus 1,000 sanctuary acres, along the river. The committee said that only a park of that size was "within the capabilities of the D.E.C. to manage and maintain."

The committee feared that a strikingly beautiful wild area, presently preserved by private stewardship, would be ravaged by unthinking or deliberately destructive people whom the state wouldn't be able to control. "The state," said Ken Schultz, the committee's chairman, "has consistently purchased land without having either the money or a plan to take care of it."

Jorling ended the committee's role as an advisory group to the conservation department earlier this month, and most committee members have protested their dismissal. The Forestburg Town Board and the Sullivan County Board of Supervisors have both asked the committee to continue its work, and last week a letter from the chairman of the supervisors to Schultz requested that the committee be prepared to testify at a March 23 public hearing on the condemnation proposal in Monticello, N.Y.

Jorling has said that his decision to resort to eminent domain proved necessary after exhaustive efforts to acquire Wechsler's rights on the 1,800 acres had failed. Subject to the same action are an additional 1,067 acres owned by Wechsler. In addition to those 1,800 acres, the state owns 1,653 acres in the Gorge area. Should the conservation department succeed in its present efforts, the park would include 4,500 acres. Three other contiguous parcels totaling about 2,650 acres—privately owned, but not by Wechsler—are also being considered for addition to the park, but are not involved in the current action.

Eugene Carpenter, president of the 10,000-member Federation of Sullivan County Sportsmen's Clubs, says that his organization favors the conservation department's gaining control of the hunting, fishing, and trapping rights on the 1,800 acres it purchased. He also says that, at the moment at least, the federation does not think that the state should own any more of the Gorge, and adds, "Wechsler has taken good care of his land."

Last September 25, Jorling wrote Wechsler's lawyer, Mark Schulman of Monticello, that he knew of the bad feelings that existed between the conservation department and Wechsler, and that he would like to wipe the slate clean and start negotiations anew. He wrote that the state was willing to pay Wechsler $900,000 for the fishing, hunting and trapping rights on the 1,800 acres, and, referring to land actually owned by Wechsler, $823,125 for a "certain specified tract of approximately 300 acres" and "approximately" $525,000 for a conservation easement on some 577 additional acres.

He also suggested that, as part of the fresh start, "the state and Mr. Wechsler each drop all actions pending before the Supreme Court," and that "the Commissioner issue a statement expressing regret over the past impasse and an apology to Mr. Wechsler for the anguish he has experienced as a consequence." In a second letter on December 18, this time to Wechsler, Jorling wrote that he had received no reply to his first communication, that time was running out and that eminent domain action was the next step unless Wechsler "responded positively" to his offer.

On December 23, Schulman wrote Jorling that even though his response should not be considered an "acceptance or counter-offer" to Jorling's proposal, his client "would not entertain acquisition of his property" until "maliciously untrue accusations" made against him by the D.E.C. were either dropped for all time or brought to trial.

In a telephone interview last week, Wechsler said Jorling's offer was ludicrous in that it did not identify the parcels the conservation department wished to buy or obtain easements on, then added that the proposed apology was the first step Jorling should take.

The "accusations" to which Schulman alluded refer to charges alleging violations of environmental law brought against Wechsler by the department in the State Supreme Court. Wechsler leases, and once sold, hunting and fishing rights on some of those 1,800 acres controlled by him to various individuals and clubs. Some of the department charges stemmed from a club's using and maintaining a long-existing cabin on a portion of the 1,800 acres on which it leased the rights to hunt and fish from a third party who had purchased them from Wechsler, who later recovered those rights.

Another charge came from the club's posting such land. The department also challenged Wechsler's allowing lessees to build a cabin on another portion of those "rights" acres. In the same court, Wechsler had earlier charged the department with trespassing on his hunting, fishing, and trapping rights acres.

Debate Over a Proposed Park[6]
JACK HOPE
(*The New York Times,* October 14, 1990)

In principle, anyone who has seen the wilderness in Sullivan County compromised by developers would applaud the increase in the amount of land under control of the New York State Department of Environmental Conservation.

It would seem that such property is invariably safer from plunder than land held by individuals and that pristine places should be protected in parks, preserves and the like.

But the ongoing attempts of the DEC to acquire land for a proposed park—the 8,200-acre Neversink River Nature Preserve, 85 miles northwest of New York City—has given area environmentalists and residents second thoughts on the subject.

At the core of the proposed park is roughly 4,100 acres in and around the scenic Neversink River gorge that is controlled by Benjamin Wechsler, a Forestburgh, N.Y., resident.

Wechsler owns 2,300 acres on the west bank of the river and, by deed, holds "the exclusive rights to hunt, trap and fish" on 1,800 acres on the river's east bank. After nearly 10 years of costly confrontation with the DEC, Wechsler refuses to sell either his rights or his land, because he is convinced the agency will not properly protect the fragile ecosystems of the proposed park.

The department's actions so disturbed local residents that the town of Forestburgh initiated a lawsuit in July 1989 claiming that the DEC, by failing to provide a management plan and an adequate environmental impact statement for the park, had violated provisions of the State Environmental Quality Review Act. The suit is the first of its kind in New York State.

On May 1, 1990, the State Supreme Court, in Monticello, N.Y., ruled in favor of the petitioners. Arguments in an appeal of the case will be heard Wednesday in the State Appellate Court in Albany.

Over the years, the DEC has employed the usual sticks and carrots to soften Wechsler up for sale, including legal efforts to condemn his property and offers to name the once-completed park after him. But it has also used tactics foreign

---

to the land-preservation business: On November 7, 1989, and without a court order, DEC employees from the Region 3 headquarters in New Paltz, accompanied by guards and a dozen inmates from a nearby prison, broke into two of Wechsler's hunting/fishing cabins in the Neversink gorge and removed possessions of his lessees.

The department has also pursued Wechsler in court with nuisance lawsuits—illegal cutting of firewood, for example—forcing him to incur legal costs in defense, and has supplied journalists with the misinformation that Wechsler was about to sell his land in the Neversink gorge to a housing developer.

Early on in the DEC's head-butting with Wechsler, in 1982, Paul Keller, then the director of the department's Region 3 office, argued before the Sullivan County Government that Wechsler's recreational rights to the 1,800 acres within the Neversink gorge—his rights, not his land—should be assessed and taxed, a proposition illegal if not impossible under Anglo-Saxon law.

The department's ongoing conflict with Wechsler in the Neversink matter may be due to an error made a decade ago: in 1981, using most of a $1 million land-purchase grant it received from the United States Department of the Interior, the DEC made its first purchase in the Neversink gorge—a 2,800-acre tract bought from the Orange and Rockland Power Company. But on a crucial two-thirds of that acreage Wechsler held the recreational rights and the department thus owned a vast tract of land on which state residents could not legally hunt or trap or fish. As time passed without a park in place, the agency's embarrassment grew.

Moreover, Wechsler's stewardship of the potential park land in question, over the decades, has been applauded by environmentalists who know the area, including the former DEC commissioners Henry G. Williams and Peter A. A. Berle. And the nine-person Neversink Advisory Committee, a group of local environmental experts specifically appointed by the department to shape the park, pointed out that the large number of hikers, boaters, hunters and fishermen the agency projected for the area (1,500 a day) would quickly and permanently damage its flora and fauna, notably its renowned wild trout population.

The committee strongly urged a smaller and more environmentally protective park, one the DEC could oversee with its admittedly limited funds for management. Wechsler subscribed to this plan and made the unusual offer of a $1 million trust fund (to be matched with public and private funds), which would pay for the park's management, in perpetuity.

But the DEC commissioner, Thomas Johrling, rejected the recommendations contained in the Neversink committee's report and promptly disbanded the group without ever meeting with it. Johrling was unavailable for comment for this column, but Phil Wardwell, an attorney with the DEC's Albany headquarters, said, "The commissioner saw the report and the recommendations of the committee as a final product and considered that their work was done."

In environmental impact hearings in December 1988, the department proceeded with their original Neversink plans despite voluminous public testimony which overwhelmingly opposed the park. The department also made light of the trust fund offer, stating that the $180,000 income it would provide each year was far more money than needed to manage and protect the Neversink wilderness. And in March 1989, the department began its attempts to condemn Wechsler's land and rights in the gorge.

Of the July 1989 suit brought by Forestburgh, along with nine members of the disbanded Neversink Advisory Committee, the Town Attorney, Kenneth C. Klein, said: "Our action is simply asking the DEC to do what any business or developer or private citizen would have to do. That is, to 'identify, analyze, avoid and mitigate' any adverse environmental impact the park may have. And this has to be done upfront, not once the park is in place." But the department fears a victory for the petitioners would set a crippling precedent, further slowing its already slow processes of park creation.

"It would certainly slow and impair our ability to purchase a selection of lands statewide," said Wardwell, the DEC attorney. "Based on our experience and our overall generic analysis, our staff feels confident that these lands could be managed properly."

Historic Neversink River: A Legal Dispute Runs Through It[7]
PETE BODO
(*The New York Times,* October 3, 1993)

It is impossible to imagine that a wild trout stream can have too many friends. But that condition may pose the biggest threat of all to the historic Neversink River and the scenic gorge it flows through in Sullivan County, just 90 minutes from New York City.

This is because many of the river's friends are mutually suspicious of, or downright hostile toward, each other. And their cries of "Save the Neversink" throw back echoes that resound in the Gorge from Eden Falls to Oakland Valley, asking: "Save it from whom?" or "Save it for what?"

The principals in this battle are Ben Wechsler, the New York State Department of Environmental Conservation, various conservation-minded angling groups and the local communities of Forestburgh and Sullivan County.

---

[7]Copyright © 1993 by *The New York Times* Co. Reprinted with permission.

Wechsler owns some 2,300 acres of land in the heart of the Gorge, as well as the exclusive hunting, fishing and trapping rights on an adjacent, 1,800-acre parcel of land that the conservation department purchased some years ago, partly with a $1 million Federal grant, despite Wechsler's clear and legal control of the vital rights. The purchase was part of a long-term department plan to acquire the Gorge for public use, despite Wechsler's unwillingness to part unconditionally with his land and rights on both banks of the Neversink.

In 1988, the courts established the department's right to acquire the land over Wechsler's objections under controversial eminent domain proceedings, giving the department until October 18, 1993, to act. As the date approached, various angler organizations, led by the Manhattan-based Theodore Gordon Flyfishers and supported by the national group Trout Unlimited, lobbied the state to seize Wechsler's rights on the state land, along with some 1,100 acres of land owned by Wechsler, for the preservation of the Gorge and the establishment of a public fishing area.

This campaign outraged many members of the local community, along with some conservationists and outdoor writers, who maintain that the best friend the Gorge has ever had is Wechsler. He has been praised by many organizations, including government agencies, for his efforts as a conservationist. Although Wechsler had hoped to develop some of his land under strict, conservation-minded guidelines, his supporters point out that he did nothing to defile the Gorge during a time when there was no local planning nor through the booming economy of the 1980s, when real estate prices skyrocketed.

Finally, Sullivan is one of the few New York counties in which state land is removed from the local tax rolls. Many local politicians and observers believe the loss of tax revenue combined with the incidental costs that would accrue through the establishment of yet another state park would be devastating for the local economy. They see the DEC's plans and methods as autocratic and see supporters of the agency as remote special-interest groups—armchair environmentalists whose statist policies are unexamined, ill-informed, and insensitive to the communities they will affect.

Langdon Marsh, a senior official of the DEC, said that the department had tried to have good-faith negotiations with Wechsler. "We have made a number of efforts directly and through third parties," Marsh said. "It's fair to say there has always been a large difference of opinions."

The latest skirmish for control of the Neversink Gorge occurred this past Thursday, when the department served Wechsler with notice that it was divesting him of his rights on the 1,800-acre state-owned parcel for a settlement of $230,000, giving Wechsler 26 hours to respond before the department filed papers to seal the seizure at the county courthouse. Wechsler called the offer "deplorable" in terms of the conservation strategy, the financial terms, and the methods used by the department to devise and propose the settlement.

And the department's action was deemed unsatisfying by all the other "friends" of the river, in that it apparently served no purpose other than to rectify a bad deal consummated by the state with Federal funds earmarked for outdoor activities—activities ruled out by Wechsler's control of the land-use rights.

"At the moment, our main concern is that we straighten out the situation in order to satisfy the National Parks Service," said Marsh of the DEC. "The rest of the property remains of interest to us, but right now we have the money to do this."

On Friday, a Sullivan County assemblyman, Jake Gunther 3d of the 98th District, persuaded state officials in Albany to hold off completing the department's seizure of the rights for at least seven days, giving Wechsler time to meet with state officials and to present his case against the department. The meeting is scheduled for tomorrow.

Wechsler, who already has one multimillion-dollar lawsuit against the state in the courts, says that he is willing to sell conservation easements to the state that would subject any development on his land to high environmental standards. He is also willing to negotiate some division of access rights. But he insists on the creation of a sophisticated management plan and that the land remain on the tax rolls for local revenue purposes. Unless the state changes its tax laws, this means that the Neversink Gorge would have to become a private conservancy.

If the department remains adamant about taking Wechsler's rights and his land by eminent domain, the 63-year-old landowner maintains that he will sell lots to finance a continuing guerrilla war waged mostly by lawyers and paid for partly by taxpayers.

"I'm too old to enjoy wine, women and song," Wechsler said. "And as a bachelor, I have no hostages to fate. I feel I've been abused and mistreated, and the one thing I don't want to do is to wake up one morning, look in the mirror and say to myself, 'You fought them for fifteen years, but you just got tired at the end and quit.' If I did that, I couldn't face myself, and I couldn't face my neighbors."

The Neversink War
JERRY KENNEY
(*New York Daily News,* December 30, 1994)

Gov-elect George Pataki's administration, which is rumored to be "environmentally sensible," is expected to make a lot of upstaters happy, but none more than Ben Wechsler, the beleaguered squire of Turner Brook, a private conservancy in the western Catskills.

His 2,300 acres lining the spectacular Neversink River Gorge in Forestburgh have been the target of "acquisition" projects by the Department of Environmental Conservation for more that twelve years.

And all the state has managed to do is mutilate Wechsler's land while creating a vast, misshapen, unmanageable and inaccessible park at a cost of millions to the taxpayers.

It started when the Orange and Rockland Electric Co. sold 1,800 acres on the Neversink River to the DEC. What the DEC didn't know, though, was that Orange and Rockland, under a previous agreement, granted the "exclusive hunting, fishing and trapping rights" to the Wechsler family.

After the embarrassing acquisition from O&R—land the public could not use—the DEC demanded Wechsler sell his rights to them. He refused.

In hopes of finding a way out of the mess, Thomas Jorling, DEC commissioner at the time, appointed a nine-member panel headed by outdoors author Ken Schultz.

To Jorling's surprise, the panel blasted the DEC's land-grabbing tactics. The angry commissioner responded by firing the whole panel.

Still hoping to work out a deal so a manageable park could be created, Wechlser offered to give the state 900 acres of rights and property with two miles of Neversink River frontage. The only stipulations were that the park would remain on the local tax rolls and the smaller projects be locally managed.

The offer got a resounding "thumbs down" in Albany and the parties have been in court ever since.

During that period, the DEC bought 2,100 acres adjacent to Wechsler's property. Then in 1993, exercising the right of eminent domain, the state seized the recreational rights to 1,800 acres of Wechsler's property.

So the DEC has a nice park now. The river has been declared "no kill," vehicular and horseback entry have been banned, campfires outlawed, and overnight use prohibited. And on top of all that, the park is surrounded by Wechsler's property and is three miles on foot from the nearest public road.

Wechsler says he has not been paid a cent for his seized property, and he is suing the state for $9 million. And to keep the state from taking any more of his property, he has started selling expensive lots that, unlike the state's park, have vehicular access to the river.

The war of attrition, as it is described in Sullivan County, has turned many landowners against the DEC. "The state takes what it wants," said conservationist Phil Chase, "and then makes up the science to justify it."

Turner Brook is prime deer, bear and turkey country. The river and its spectacular gorge are known for the wild-trout population and as the cradle of fly fishing in the East.

Such prominent fly-fishing pioneers as Theodore Gordon, Edward Hewitt, George LaBranche, Ray Bergman, and Larry Koller helped make the Neversink famous. More recently, Nick Lyons and Don Bingler have been casting their flies across Denton Falls and to the surprise of the DEC (Wechsler has been keeping the secret for years) have caught not only trout but land locked salmon.

Neversink Gorge Controversy: One View
Rod Cochran
(*Catskill Center News,* Winter 1996)

To the Editor,

"Hostile stand-off ends Neversink Gorge controversies." The lore and legend of fly fishing run deep in the Neversink River. For more than 150 years, trout fishermen have treasured these waters in the southern Catskills where Theodore Gordon and other angling pioneers perfected the tackle and techniques of the sport in America. If "A River Runs Through It" in the East, it is likely the Neversink.

South of Monticello, the Neversink pierces a gorge, producing blue-ribbon trout pools (where state lands are now designated no-kill) and spectacular wilderness scenery. The area known simply as "the Gorge" has been preserved by private owners who recognized its rare value and history, most recently by conservationist Benjamin Wechsler.

But the future of the Gorge has been plagued by controversy and uncertainty for the past 25 years as the State of New York, and its Department of Environmental Conservation have negotiated successfully with local officials upset about removing thousands of acres of state land from local tax rolls. Weschler has refused to sell any of his 1,300 acres in the Gorge's center unless the State would commit to pay local taxes (as it does in the case of the Forest Preserve and in some other areas), and produce a locally approved management plan with assured funding.

In 1981, the DEC began acquisition of parcels for a future unique natural area, including some 1,800 acres on which Wechsler held exclusive hunting, fishing, and trapping rights. Thus the public could not hunt, fish, or trap on 1,800 acres of the state lands in the Gorge. Controversy heated up in 1986 when then Commissioner Thomas Jorling dismissed a state citizen's committee appointed by his predecessor, Henry Williams. This Advisory Committee had been asked to define the boundaries of the proposed park. It recommended a smaller park, locally managed.

The Neversink Gorge tale is but one of a rare national treasure and lost opportunities, but, currently, the battles are winding down:

The 5,400 acres of public lands acquired at an estimated cost of well over $5 million are divided by the 2,300 acres held by Wechsler.

From October 1993, the DEC took by eminent domain the hunting, fishing, and trapping rights owned by Wechsler. The ensuing Court case concerning the amount of payment due Wechsler is still pending and Wechsler has received no payment to date. The State's court-awarded three-year right to condemn Wechsler's primary tract has expired. R. W. Groneman, DEC spokesman, last winter stated that the remainder of the Gorge is no longer on the active acquisition list.

The DEC is holding public meetings in the area to determine public sentiment on future uses of the 5,400 acres in State ownership.

Wechsler is selling expensive wilderness retreat sites on his 2,300-acre tract, which includes 6,000 feet of waterfront where trout no-kill regulations do not apply. Site buyers have vehicular access to the river, while public access to the center of the Unique Area is by way of a three-mile foot trail.

Wechsler has vowed to preserve the riverfront he still owns in its natural stare. "The center of the Gorge is now divided between two hostile parties for the foreseeable future," he says. "There is no chance that the administration of Gov. George Pataki will continue hostile condemnations over local objections, and with no management funding available. The Gorge has been preserved for over 100 years by private owners, and we are not going to end that heritage. This will be a competition to see who can do better," he challenged.

Some Effective Flies on the Neversink

Tied and described by Phil Chase and Skip Rood
Drawn by Barry Glickman

ADAMS—This buggy fly catches trout everywhere. It matches no specific fly—and maybe, from the trout's perspective, it matches them all, both mayfly and caddis.

LIGHT CAHILL—This is another go-anywhere pattern. Port Jervis's Dan Cahill hit a homer on his first try, in 1884, and it has endured for all these years because it fools fish.

BRIDGEVILLE OLIVE—Named by Ray Bergman in his classic *Trout* after a great day of fishing the Green Drake hatch on the Neversink below Bridgeville.

ROYAL COACHMAN (WET)—No less a Catskill luminary than Harry Darbee proclaimed of this pattern, "If I had but one fly to fish with, it would be the Royal Coachman wet." Harry had a way of cutting to the chase and who can argue with his verdict?

QUILL GORDON (CATSKILL SCHOOL)—The great Catskill tyers were all iconoclastic to one degree or other. Their sparse, slim-bodied flies often defied convention until they were tied to a leader and presented to wary trout. Then all doubts were dispelled! Their flies caught fish! Amazing.

100-YEAR FLY—The early tiers, like Gordon, Christian, and Steenrod, tied their flies with one upright wing. Phil Chase asked Herman Christian why he started tying his Quill Gordons and Hendricksons with split wings and Herman replied, "Because that's the way my customers wanted them."

BROWN BIVISIBLE—Edward Ringwood Hewitt developed this oft-overlooked fly that still fools trout, especially when fished in fast water. It is easy to tie and deserves to be represented in every angler's fly box.

NEVERSINK SKATER—Sometime referred to as Hewitt's Skater, this is a teaser pattern that coaxes trout everywhere to rise, often with heart-stopping strikes.

CINBERG—A tough fly to tie, but deadly in pocket water. Dr. Bernard Cinberg championed the reservoir releases for the Catskill trout streams. He was a student of Hewitt, "standing on their tails" with his short line and perfect drift.

RAT-FACED MCDOUGAL—A deadly white-water fly. According to Harry Darbee, a young lass in the Heartwood Club on the renowned Bushkill (a tributary of the Neversink) named this fly.

RED QUILL—This important fly imitates the male (imago) of the Hendrickson. Art Flick deserves credit for the development of the Red Quill and the flies that came off his vise were marvels of the craft.

RED QUILL SPINNER—This fly makes a lot of sense. The imago stage of the mayfly is basically the last stop before eternity for the mayfly. When they have done their life's work and fall spent to the river's surface, the fishing can be superb.

BUMBLE PUPPY—Theodore Gordon originally tried to develop a pattern that would work on trout, bass, and pickerel. Gordon's friend and guide, Herman Christian, is given credit for the final version of the pattern. Christian fooled many large trout using this seductive pattern at night at Old Falls on the Neversink.

DORATO—Developed jointly by Bill Dorato and Del Bedinotti, this pattern, like the Adams, doesn't try to match any specific fly, it just catches fish like crazy. One look at it is enough to understand the reason why.

CATSKILL CLIPPER (HELLGRAMMITE)—First tied by Phil Chase of Port Jervis, N.Y., this variant of the Muddler/Wooly Bugger is a killer pattern. It is especially effective on large trout.

WOODCHUCK—This pocket-water fly has a reputation as a large trout producer on the Neversink when the stoneflies are on the move. Red tying thread is essential.

GREY FOX—This large mayfly usually occurs at about the same time as the March Brown on the Neversink and lasts until late June. Trout love these big insects and fishing during a major emergence of Grey Foxes can be memorable.

FLUTTERING CADDIS—Len Wright developed this cone-shaped caddis pattern on the upper Neversink. The section above the reservoir is a rushing, crystal-clear freestone river and this sturdy, buoyant pattern works wonderfully under such tough conditions.

BEETLE—The beetle is certainly the most overlooked fly in every angler's fly box. We all carry them; too few, wise beyond their years, use them. They produce results that are astonishing, especially late in the season. Fish like beetles and ants.

ISONYCHIA EMERGER—A simple pattern that has proven very effective when the *Isonychia bicolor* mayfly is emerging.

EARLY STONEFLY—In March and early April this fly hatches on the lower Neversink. Its fluttering wings look like a parachute skimming the water and it wakes up the trout for a season of fun.

Credits

Conditions of the Life of Trout. *A Trout and Salmon Fisherman for 75 Years,* Edward R. Hewitt. Used by permission of Sylvia Hewitt Stevenson Adelman. • The Point of View. *The Dry Fly and Fast Water,* George M. L. La Branche. Used by permission of Derrydale Press. • Sunshine and Shadow. *Trout,* Ray Bergman, used by permission of Derrydale Press. • Some Big Fish on the Neversink. *Taking Larger Trout,* Larry Koller. Little, Brown & Co. • With Hewitt on the Neversink. *The Fly and the Fish,* John Atherton. Used by permission of Mary Varchaver. • The Quest for Theodore Gordon. *Fishless Days, Angling Nights,* Sparse Grey Hackle. Used by permission of The Globe Pequot Press. • The Golden Age. *Fishless Days, Angling Nights,* Sparse Grey Hackle. Used by permission of The Globe Pequot Press. • Neversink Fishing. *Remembrances of Rivers Past,* Ernest Schwiebert, used by permission of Erik Schwiebert. • The Woman Flyfishers Club. *Land of Little Rivers,* Austin Francis, used by permission of the author. • Incident on the Bushkill. *Fishing with McClane,* A. J. McClane. Used by permission of Simon & Schuster, Inc. • The Great Days, R. Palmer Baker. Used by permission of the author. • *Salar Sebago. Neversink,* Leonard M. Wright, Jr. Used by permission of the Estate of Leonard M. Wright, Jr. • The Endless Belt. *The Ways of Trout,* Leonard M. Wright, Jr. Used by permission of the Estate of Leonard M. Wright, Jr. • Last Days Are for Dreamers, Nick Lyons. Used by permission of the author. • On the Road in the Catskills: The Lost River of Xanadu, Peter Borrelli, used by permission of the Catskill Center. • The 100-Year Fly, Phil Chase. Used by permission of the author. • A Camp on the Neversink, Jay Cassell. Used by permission of the author. • Intimations at Denniston's Flats, John Miller. Used by permission of the author. • Fishing Prohibited in New York State Park, Harold Faber. Used by permission of *The New York Times.* • State Owns Prime Fishing Spot But Can't Use It, Sam Howe Verhovek. Used by permission of *The New York Times.* • Two Neversink Tributaries to be Renamed, Nelson Bryant. Used by permission of *The New York Times.* • New York Plans Action on Neversink Land, Nelson Bryant. Used by permission of *The New York Times.* • Debate Over a Proposed Park, Jack Hope. Used by permission of Jack Hope. • Historic Neversink River: A Legal Dispute Runs Through It, Pete Bodo. Used by permission of *The New York Times.* • The Neversink War, Jerry Kenney. Used by permission of *New York Daily News, L.P.* • Neversink Controversy, Rod Cochran. Used by permission of the Catskill Center.

THE NEVERSINK RIVER

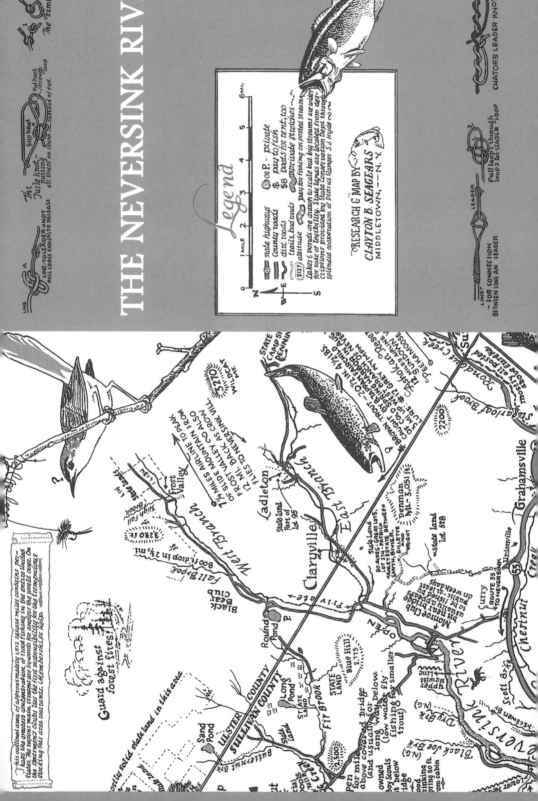

Legend

state highways	⊕ or P. - private
county roads	$ - pay to fish
dirt roads	$B - boats for rent, too
trails, bad roads	private stretches
2131' altitude	pay for fishing on posted streams

Lakes & ponds are drawn to scale but big streams are wider for sake of legibility. Size legends are located from descriptions provided by Conservation Dept. through spirited cooperation of District Ranger S.J. Hyde.

RESEARCH & MAP BY
CLAYTON B. SEAGEARS
MIDDLETOWN — N.Y.

LINE-TO-LEADER KNOT
PULL LOOSE END/AND RELEASE

The Turle Knot, putting all stress on line, instead of eye.

Slip Knot
Put hook through loop instead of eye.

The Simplest

CHATOR'S LEADER KNOT

LEADER

Pull loop 1 through loop 2 for LEADER loop

LINE
— FOR CONNECTION
BETWEEN LINE AN' LEADER

This outlined area of approximately 1,512 square miles contains, perhaps the greatest concentration of trout fishing in the entire United States. The region's main streams are however, so dependent upon tributaries. Most of this area is privately owned. Stocking this area insures, CHENANGO LIB helps.

Guard against forest fires!

Mostly solid state land in this area

ULSTER COUNTY
SULLIVAN COUNTY

Sand Pond

Long Pond
STATE LAND

Fir Brook

STATE LAND

Blue Hill 2,775

Round Pond

Black Bear Club

Fall Brook 800 ft. drop in 2¾ mi.

3280 ft.

High Fall Brook

Frost Valley

7¼ MILES AIRLINE TO PEAK
OF FROST VALLEY & CROW MT.
12 MI. TO DENNING VIL.
FLESTO

3270 WILDCAT MT.

STATE CAMP SITE DENNING

West Branch

East Branch

Claryville

Ladleton

State land Part of Lot 95

Denman Mt. 3,051 ft.

State land Lot. 518

Private

OPEN

Bullennut Brk.

1,500'

Neversink River

Upper Limit

Black Joe Brk. (N.G)

Dry Brk. (N.G)

Scott Brk.

Lower

Grahamsville

Unionville

Curry

Route 55
TO NEVERSINK

Monroe Club usually near bridge to public at least on week days

Chestnut Creek

Rondout Creek

Sugarloaf Brook

mostly posted above Curry